Figuring the

School for Advanced Research
Advanced Seminar Series

James F. Brooks
General Editor

Figuring the Future

Contributors

Anne Allison
Department of Anthropology, Duke University

Ann Anagnost
Department of Anthropology, University of Washington

Jennifer Cole
Committee on Human Development, University of Chicago

Deborah Durham
Department of Anthropology and Archaeology, Sweetbriar College

Paula S. Fass
Department of History, University of California, Berkeley

Constance A. Flanagan
Department of Agricultural and Extension Education, Pennsylvania State University

Tobias Hecht
Independent Scholar

Barrie Thorne
Department of Sociology and Women's Studies, University of California, Berkeley

Brad Weiss
Department of Anthropology, College of William and Mary

Figuring the Future

Globalization and the Temporalities of Children and Youth

Edited by Jennifer Cole and Deborah Durham

School for Advanced Research Press

Santa Fe

School for Advanced Research Press
Post Office Box 2188
Santa Fe, New Mexico 87504-2188
www.sarpress.sarweb.org

Co-Director and Editor: Catherine Cocks
Manuscript Editor: Kate Whelan
Design and Production: Cynthia Dyer
Proofreader: Sarah Soliz
Indexer: Catherine Fox
Printer: Thomson Shore, Inc.

Library of Congress Cataloging-in-Publication Data:

Figuring the future : globalization and the temporalities of children and youth /
edited by Jennifer Cole and Deborah Durham.
    p. cm. — (School for Advanced Research advanced seminar series)
Includes bibliographical references and index.
 ISBN 978-1-934691-05-2 (pa : alk. paper)
1. Children—Social conditions—21st century. 2. Youth—Social conditions—21st century.
3. Globalization—Social aspects. I. Cole, Jennifer, 1966– II. Durham, Deborah Lynn, 1958–
HQ767.9.F54 2008
305.2309'0510112—dc22

                            2008007920

Cover illustration: Leketra's sons, Madagascar, photograph by Jennifer Cole.

Contents

Figures

Acknowledgments

The essays presented in this book are the product of an advanced seminar held at the School of American Research (SAR, now the School for Advanced Research) in April 2004. We wish to express our gratitude to SAR for hosting the event and providing an incomparable context in which to discuss our work and share the ideas presented here. We especially thank Leslie Shipman for taking care of us during our week in Santa Fe, Nancy Owen Lewis for facilitating the arrangements, James F. Brooks for his continued interest in the project, and, above all, Catherine Cocks for shepherding the book through the production process. We also thank Kate Whelan for her copyediting work on the manuscript. Finally, we wish to acknowledge the anonymous reviewers for the press, who gave us fabulous feedback on an earlier version of the manuscript, and all of our contributors for sharing their ideas and making the seminar an inspiring experience.

Figuring the Future

1

Introduction

Globalization and the Temporality of Children and Youth

Jennifer Cole and Deborah Durham

In recent years, a connection between children, youth, and the social, cultural, and economic transformations widely referred to as globalization has become apparent. Child laborers in South Asia, child soldiers in Sierra Leone and Uganda, Chinese youth playing computer games to earn virtual gold, youth involved in sex trafficking in the former Soviet republics and Thailand: these are just some of the young people featured in the news of late. Most scholars have tried to theorize the empirical link between youth and globalization by highlighting how young people promote new social relationships over previously daunting distances. Such analyses recognize that youth rework globally circulating commodities, ideas, and images, emphasizing how children and youth are agents reshaping relationships to and across space. But young people create these new cultural geographies insofar as they also embody locally variable relationships to time, particularly the future.

The idea that young people are more malleable and the truisms that "youth are the future" or "children are our hope for the future" give the news stories and scholarly accounts added meaning. To address how and why youth and children have come to seem so important to globalization, the chapters in this book look not just at the spatial relations of globalization but also the temporal dimensions. Discourses of, and practices by, youth and children bring the new temporal conjunctions of globalization into relationship with people's negotiation of the life course. Such discourses and practices, which reach from the design of children's toys to youth political mobilization, are critical sites through which people everywhere conceive of, produce, contest, and naturalize the new futures.

Much of the scholarship that examines youth and globalization in relation to space builds on the Birmingham school youth-culture studies of an earlier era. These emphasized how youthful subcultures resisted and contested class oppression by playing with and creatively re-presenting cultural codes embodied in specific commodities and styles (Hall and Jefferson 1991[1976]; Hebdige 1979). The studies situated youth creativity in the context of changing geographies of class and labor practices in post-war Britain, including an influx of former colonial subjects to England. Anoop Nayak (2003) uses this type of analysis to show how British youth reconfigure local geographies of race and ethnicity through their cultural practices. The recent volume *Youthscapes: The Popular, the National, the Global* continues to use the geographic image of a "scape" when looking at youth practices,[1] to bring together "questions about popular culture and relations of power in local, national and globalized contexts" (Maira and Soep 2005:xviii). Another edited collection focused on youth in Africa, though not explicitly tied to Birmingham-style analyses, similarly uses the term *youth(e)scapes*, inadvertently emphasizing the spatial dimensions of youth practice (Christiansen, Utas, and Vigh 2006:20).

Birmingham school youth studies are also significant for their emphasis on processes of social reproduction, a temporal phenomenon. Some recent writers have continued to explore how adults' reorganization of processes of social reproduction takes place in the lives of children and youth. States and corporations deploy images of children and youth to enact specific globalized agendas, some of which are detrimental to children. Sue Ruddick argues that the constitutive elements of globalization include "a celebration of risk, reduction in state funding for social reproduction in developed nations and pressures to modernize in underdeveloped ones" and that these "are being 'smuggled in' in the guise of new discourses about youth and childhood" (Ruddick 2003:334).[2] And Cindi Katz (2004) demonstrates the differential effects of global capitalism on processes of social reproduction in a rural village in the Sudan and in New York City, highlighting how global capitalism creates common problems for youth in different places and circumstances.

Temporality is critical to the processes of global capitalism with which Ruddick and Katz are concerned. Many images discussed by Ruddick have powerful temporal references associated with the ideologies of modernity, in which historical backwardness is encapsulated in the body of the feral or stunted child. Similarly, Katz (2004), though focused primarily on remaking local geographies, is interested in how global economic changes shift the grounds of the future when many children learn skills that will not help them later on because of rapidly changing environmental and labor conditions. Brad Weiss (2004:8) has observed that as people negotiate the emerging and shifting possibilities of inclusion or exclusion in new forms of community, an important question for them is not only how to join but also "what will the [criteria for participation] be tomorrow?"

These examples suggest that temporality is an important dimension of globalization and that youth and children help negotiate new futures. Nevertheless, existing work persists in foregrounding children and youth's role in reworking the emergent cultural geographies associated with new spatial relations. The result is that it analytically privileges space over time. The analytical focus on space emerges in ideas about scapes, mobility, and geographically expansive imaginations. It also appears in the recurrent use of a language of marginality and in the debates that envision global flows more in terms of moving through space than carving out new temporal dimensions. The role of youth and children in the remaking of place is surely important, but most current analyses fail to take sufficient account of the temporal nature of youth and childhood.

We begin our project of making temporality more central by examining more closely the key categories at the heart of our inquiry: childhood and youth, on the one hand, and globalization, on the other.

SHIFTING DEFINITIONS OF CHILDHOOD AND YOUTH

Childhood and youth are notoriously difficult categories to define. Euro-American common sense suggests that the life course unfolds according to a developmental teleology in which human beings move naturally from infancy and early childhood through adolescence, adulthood, and old age (Erikson 1950; Schlegel and Barry 1991; Steedman 1995). This assumption of naturally unfolding, age-prescribed stages underpins psychological studies of human development, as well as research in psychological anthropology. Even Margaret Mead, who famously contested G. Stanley Hall's (1904) description of adolescence through her research in Samoa, never questioned the existence of the stage per se, just its content.

Contrary to this perspective, many studies have pointed out that social processes determine who can claim to be in a category called childhood or youth and who can describe others as being in this category. Studies of

African societies make this point most sharply by highlighting the disjuncture between chronological age and generational age. Meyer Fortes (1984) described how very young people can be senior to elderly people through the generational logic of lineal descent groups. Similarly, Marc Schloss (1988) explained how a four-year-old who has undergone an initiation ceremony that Senegalese Ehing hold every twenty-five years may be given all the privileges and rights to exercise knowledge of a forty-year-old whereas thirty-year-olds who have missed the ceremony are treated, in many respects, as children. Jennifer Johnson-Hanks (2002) goes even further, using her Cameroonian material to argue for abolishing a life-stage approach altogether. Instead, she suggests that analysis focus on how individual aspirations intersect with institutions in what she terms "vital conjunctures," allowing for a more fluid model of how individuals move through time. In conjunction with scholarship on the life course drawn from many contexts, this work makes clear that age categories vary by historical period (Ariès 1962[1960]; Hanawalt 1993; Kett 1977; Levi and Schmitt 1997); across cultures (Herdt and Leavitt 1998; Mead 1964[1928]; Raum 1996[1940]); among classes (Kett 1977; Liechty 2003); and between genders (Cole 2004).

In the mid-twentieth century, this common sense model of age categories and the unfolding of the life course was enshrined in laws and public institutions and held up as a natural progression to which all should aspire. Consequently, Euro-American ideas about the life course provide an implicit foil against which the chapters in this volume are written. It is important, then, to sketch out some key elements and background.

During the late nineteenth and twentieth centuries, new ideas about childhood and adolescence were shaped by a complicated network of changes: transformations in the organization of production and consumption, shifts in women's political and professional voices, the rise of new disciplines in the academy, and the growing impact of consumerism. Taken together, these created an increasing gap between the possibilities of physical reproduction and social reproduction, a gap we have come to refer to as adolescence. Experts in child development and social welfare justified these changes by arguing that this age was uniquely fragile, requiring adult supervision and protection (Kett 1977).[3] Around the same time, labor laws were created that prevented younger people from working. Sometimes, these laws supported the desires of older people to keep younger competitors out of the labor market (Hareven 1995). At other times, new laws attempted to enact broadly a class- and culture-specific vision of childhood, as Paula Fass discusses in chapter 2 of this volume. Transformations of a labor-centered life course were not confined to childhood and youth. At the other end, particular interest groups lobbied for the creation of retirement benefits and a retirement age, contributing to ideas of an old age in which one does not have to, or cannot competently, work (Chudacoff 1989).

Two broad shifts relating to this model are particularly relevant, although the periodicity and timing are different for each. First, during the twentieth century, with increased travel and communications and in the context of colonial and neocolonial encounters, different constructions of the life course increasingly came into contact with one another. When new chronologies of the life cycle are introduced, the temporality of growing up often becomes a source of tension, with different age groups claiming the privileges of a new social space (Durham 2004). Recent examples are the programs for youth based on UN guidelines (such as the UN convention on the rights of the child) and the international child-saving projects, which may or may not match local conceptions of the life course. The introduction of new life courses may have deep historical roots, but this process has accelerated in recent years.

At the same time, the naturalized life course has not remained static. The modernist model of a linear life course has undergone its own transformations. Scholars even refer to a "post-modern" life course in which "age" and "youth" are detached from their biological referents (Moody 1993). In some cases, changing social and economic conditions extend the social markers of youth further and further up the chronological life course, with varying implications, depending on the socioeconomic context. In the United States, rising affluence, changing demographics, and better health combine with consumer culture to enable people in their thirties, forties, and fifties to enjoy aspects of physical fitness and leisure associated with youthfulness. Ages forty, forty-five, and even fifty become "the new 30" (Jefferson and Hey 2003; see also Arnett 2004). The same phenomenon, which indicates relative wealth in the United States, is connected with poverty in Africa. There, the economic crisis of the 1980s and 1990s meant that the ability to grow up (to pass through and beyond the social dependence associated with youth) is increasingly difficult to achieve (Cole 2004, 2005; Durham 2004; Masquelier 2005). Many young people are "stuck in the compound," as Karen Hansen's (2005) informants describe their predicament in a Zambian neighborhood: they cannot acquire the resources to move out of their natal homes to create new households of their own. As a result, they are unable to achieve social adulthood.

In other places, evidence now suggests that changing social, cultural, and economic conditions push the responsibilities and stresses formerly associated with social adulthood down the life cycle onto people who, in fairly recent times or in other social classes, would have been conceived of as children meriting protection. In the United States, developmental psychologists and newspapers report that puberty (the physical marker of adulthood) comes earlier because of better nutrition associated with rising affluence. In France, as in the United States, the age of childhood has been creeping downward in the courts. Younger and younger people are being held morally responsible for criminal actions and intent (Terrio in press). Perhaps not surprisingly, young immigrants and descendants of immigrants are more often judged as capable of criminal intent and morally culpable than are young native Frenchmen. In Japan, young people shut themselves in their rooms for months, even years, rejecting the stresses of a highly competitive schooling system (Allison, chapter 8, this volume; Lock 1988). One author (Field 1995) even referred to this intense exam preparation as the "loss of childhood."

We make these points to alert readers to the slippery nature of the categories and also to remind them that such categories are profoundly entangled in social processes. What is also important to understand is that shifts in the chronology of life stages are significant not only because of the changing content of the age categories—these shifts are part of how the changes associated with globalization come to be naturalized. Before addressing how this happens, we need to look more closely at the equally slippery set of processes referred to as globalization.

MODERNITY AND GLOBALIZATION: REWORKING SPACE AND TIME

Two aspects of recent social and economic changes are relevant to our concerns here. First, since the late 1970s, there has been an increased and more rapid movement of goods, people, and ideas around the world. These movements are uneven in reach and direction, with new landscapes of wealth and opportunity, or their lack, connecting and disconnecting different parts of the globe in highly differentiated ways (Ferguson 2006; Hoogvelt 1997; Neilson 2003). The movements of people, capital, goods, and ideas do not necessarily happen in tandem, creating what Arjun Appadurai (1996) has called disjunctures in the experience of globalization. One widespread effect of these movements is that people increasingly imagine themselves as part of a global landscape with potential horizons now much more far-flung and varied. In scope and content, this imagination differs considerably from place to place. Urban middle-class Americans may be more convinced of growing global horizons than, say, young people in rural Sudan, whose only choices are local farm tenancies (tied, nonetheless, to global capital), higher education in Khartoum, and the Sudanese military as potential sources of income (Katz 2004).

Second, transformations have taken place in the organization of social reproduction. In places such as the United States and parts of Europe, the state has ceded aspects of social reproduction to other agencies or parts of society, including families and individuals. Some of these agencies are transnational, including corporations, nongovernmental organizations, criminal networks, and religious groups. New social legislation on marriage, medicine, taxation, and immigration tightens the state's hold on citizenship and social reproduction in still other ways. Because the welfare state was never universal, its contemporary decline and reorganization can be grasped only comparatively. Americans and French citizens may complain about cuts in welfare benefits, but elderly nonresident South Asians find state benefits in the United States abundant compared with those available in India (Lamb 2007).

We do not make a causal argument here, but we do know that these facets of globalization are linked. The rapid and increased movements of people, images, and commodities foster global imaginations. In turn, widening horizons feed increased movements. The weakening of the welfare state is part and parcel of the increasingly flexible mobility of capital. Rising membership in non-state-based communities (ethno-national, religious, and of other social character, such as women, gays, and Pokémon masters) is partly symptomatic of the failure of the social contract that bound, or aimed to bind, people to their states in order to guarantee well-being. These new kinds of communities are also a product of the explosion of new forms of communication and movement of consumer goods through which some identities are made. Increased movement of commodities and people and the decreasing role of states in assuring the social reproduction of a people are but two sides of the same coin.

Whether one focuses on the movement of capital and ideas or on new arrangements to ensure social reproduction, both entail the reconfiguration of space and time as they characterized mid-century modernity. In *The Consequences of Modernity*, Anthony Giddens (1990) emphasizes the transformation of temporality that occurs as the reorganization of capital, combined with new technologies, alters the relation of time to space. He argues that, in pre-modern contexts, time and space were intertwined because one could not tell what time of day it was without reference to particular spatial markers (such as the sun setting in the west). In modern contexts, new technologies (including the clock) and modes of transport have created what he calls "space time distanciation." People experience events in remote places as if these were close at hand. The "extreme dynamism and globalizing scope" of modernity are closely connected to the separation of time and space (Giddens 1990:16). The result is the linking of vast distances into a single temporal structure encompassing both simultaneity and difference. Johannes Fabian's (1983) argument—that persistent evolutionary narratives, when mapped onto space, imply that our past is still being lived by distant others—makes this phenomenon especially apparent.

In Reinhart Koselleck's 1985 study of the semantics of historical time, he argues that the idea of the future being different from the past is a temporal structure that emerged in the context of Western modernity. There is a reciprocal interaction between the speed of technological inventions and people's perception of the future. An increased orientation toward the future characterizes the emergence of modernity as a particular historical epoch. Koselleck observes, "If the contemporary in question detects in his subjective experiential balance an increase in the weight of the future, this is certain to be an effect of the technical-industrial modification of a world that forces upon its inhabitants ever-briefer intervals of time in which to gather new experiences and adapt to changes induced at an accelerating pace" (Koselleck 1985:xxiv). This changing ratio of expectation to experience is what shapes a sense of progress—the idea that the future will be better than the past.

Analyses of more recent patterns (those often seen as iconic of globalization) highlight the intensification and reconfiguration of modern structurings of time and space. David Harvey (1989) has argued that the hallmark of the current moment is the development of new, flexible kinds of labor and production practices that shrink time and space. Whereas previously it took a few days for a telegram to deliver information across vast distances, now people located in very different parts of the world can simultaneously watch the same event unfold on TV. The reorganization of capital and the new technologies, in turn, accelerate social and cultural life as people make business decisions and transmit information faster than ever before.

Manuel Castells (1996) similarly highlights the reworking of space and time in what he refers to as the "network society," his term for the set of processes that others call globalization. New technologies and kinds of organization such as cottage industries, in which people can work from home and telecommute, entail the reorganization of space. Castells also describes the emergence of what he calls a "timeless time," especially in the domain of capital. Timeless time includes even the "capture of future time in present transactions" (Castells 1996:436), as in the market for futures, options, and derivatives. Against this timeless time, disjunctive times proliferate. Flexible labor and production arrangements that foster the use of different temporal zones disrupt the neat chronologies of the modernist life cycle organized around an adulthood of regularly scheduled, paid labor. The exclusion of many locales and social groups from the new "network society" produces further temporal disjunctures. Against the universal clock of modernity, Castells (1996:445) observes a new "social arrhythmia," a disruption of the social clocks of work, reproduction, aging, and especially death. As provocative as his proposals are, he gives little attention to childhood or youth. He does draw upon classic modernist developmental metaphors, however, in expressions such as "embryos of a new relationship between our social and biological condition" (Castells 1996:450).

These different lines of inquiry into contemporary social and economic changes suggest that in recent years there has been a profound reworking of how space and time are experienced in everyday life. To date, anthropologists have focused primarily on the reworkings of space in the form of "global imaginations." When exploring time, anthropologists have focused more on the past and its relationship to the present. Munn (1992:115) notes that "futurity is poorly attended to as a specifically temporal problem" in anthropology. By examining children and youth and the practices they engage in, we can begin to discern the temporal disjunctures and potential futures that are central to processes of globalization.

FIGURING THE FUTURE IN THE CONTEXT OF GLOBALIZATION

In examining the role of children or youth around the world in creating the future, the volume's authors write from the perspective of various disciplines, including history, sociology, and social psychology, but mainly anthropology. Some focus primarily on children or youth's engagement with commodities, work, and the restructuring of class relations. Others focus on youth in relation to conceptions of agency and political action. The authors touch on topics such as clothing, religion, toys, music, and the creation of children and youth as historical categories.

We conceive of the "future" as comprising three dimensions: (1) how the future is imagined through specific representations of temporality, (2) how one orients oneself and others to it through sentiments like hope or anxiety and their relationship to risk, and (3) how one substantively creates it by designing and normalizing new kinds of practices. A common theme in all the chapters is the sense that youth practices—by which we mean the actions undertaken both by young people and by people and institutions concerning youth—are fraught with risk and uncertainty and are, in the phrase often invoked during the seminar, on the cusp of success and failure.[4] Rather than summarize the chapters here, we draw upon various aspects of them to illustrate these three points.

Embodying Temporality, Making Subjects

At first glance, one might think that the way children and youth embody temporality in the context of globalization differs little from what took place during the early-to-middle part of the twentieth century. During that historical period, youth worldwide often mobilized diverse interests around a rupture with the past in order to move toward a new and better future (Anderson 1972; Chow 1967; Neyzi 2001). Such a vision dovetailed well with modernization theory, a widely used scholarly and popular paradigm for interpreting historical change. Given that some theories of globalization share this sense of futurism with earlier theories of modernization (Cooper 2001; Walley 2004), one might expect that youth continue to figure the future in this way. But if one looks at the current ways children or youth embody temporality, the picture becomes considerably more complex.

Two chapters demonstrate how practices associated with children and youth conceal and also reveal the disjunctures of globalization, through a process we call "temporal folding": the bringing together of different chronotopes and temporalities. Anne Allison's chapter 8 examines the cultural politics of Pokémon production and consumption, mainly in Japan but also in the United States. Pokémon becomes a medium that combines anxieties about an almost inhumanly asocial future with various relationships to the past. The inventor of Pokémon drew on his experiences as a child collecting insects to create a game that would address fears about the isolation and alienation of people caught up in the demands of school, work, and long commutes. In the playscape of Pokémon, the creators brought together traditions and myths of an ancient Japan, relations to nature that are key symbols of Japanese national identity, notions of measured and disciplined growth, and, paradoxically, the increasingly frenetic tempo associated with late capitalism and globalization. As Japan faced the economic downturn in the 1990s that followed its dramatic earlier success, Pokémon became a way to reinvent the basis of economic recovery and resurgence. Far from the universalist conception of space/time compression advanced by David Harvey, the commodified cultural specificity of Pokémon enables the persistence of particular ideas about the past and future in the context of intense time/space compression.

By contrast, the youth practices featured in Brad Weiss's chapter 9, on apocalyptic hip-hop in Tanzania, offer a very different vision of temporal folding. Set in the context of post-socialist market reform in Tanzania, Weiss's chapter examines how unemployed and underemployed male youth eagerly perform and listen to African American–inspired hip-hop music with religious themes. The songs warn listeners of the coming apocalypse, urging them to "keep it real" in the face of worldly temptations. In Allison's chapter 8, children appear to embody new forms of temporality closely linked with social and economic reorganization. But the male youth discussed in Weiss's chapter, though equally affected by recent changes associated with economic liberalization, embrace an alternative, oppositional vision. In their lyrics, they reject the sped-up, disjunctive life in which money, women, and friends are gained and lost at dizzying speeds and rapid shifts in fortune undercut the possibilities of a new, adult future. Instead, they advocate a radical break with the past and a reorientation of the present that comes to terms with the approaching apocalypse, the known future.

The institutional settings through which different age groups move also shape the subjective experience of temporality. Certain disciplines of temporality regiment how subjects move through time. In US society, a well-known example is the careful measurement of childhood, its institutionalized precision and slow progress. Early months are momentous, years in school carefully monitored, and advancement measured, even regulated, yearly. In a related vein, upper-middle-class Americans monitor their children's math and science test scores as carefully as they monitor export and import figures, constantly comparing their children's progress with that of children in other nations. These practices constitute a particular temporality of childhood and a particular way of conceiving of, and investing in, the future. Two chapters address disciplines of temporality and how such temporal disciplines relate to particular conceptions of the subject, which imply a particular relation to the future.

Ann Anagnost's chapter 3 examines childrearing in market-reform China. She illustrates how such disciplines of temporality in childhood play out as Chinese parents anxiously scan their children's bodies for the appropriate signs of physical and cognitive growth and compare these with growth of children in other nations. Chinese parents fear that their children will be unprepared for the new kind of future created by the demise of state socialism and the integration of China into global markets. Before, the state had an active role in shaping a future that departs from the past, but now individuals increasingly bear the burden of economic success or failure. As a result, adults are anxious about how to prepare children for the future. Parents, particularly mothers, invest a huge amount of labor in training children to embody the right kind of value and therefore future. Children become sites of value creation, accumulating their mother and father's anxious investments.

Anagnost implies that the increased liberalization of China's economy makes parents invest in their children in ways that echo practices familiar from upper-middle-class European and American contexts. By contrast, Deborah Durham's chapter 7, which offers a critical analysis of the concept of youth agency popular in much contemporary writing on youth, stands as a sharp reminder that strikingly different ways of conceiving of subjects and their relation to temporality persist. The idea that youth have a special agency that is different from adults' lies at the heart of Western liberal conceptions of youth. By contrast, Herero imagine the life cycle as organized around stages that are sequential, instead of a progressive developmental unfolding. In Botswana, the life course is not perceived according to the romantic narrative in which life's unfolding necessarily leads to liberal, individuated persons who forge a new identity in tension with that of their elders, creating a rupture with the past. Rather, Herero youth are supposed to make new connections and links and to root those links within their relationally imagined home society. The vision of temporality embodied by Herero youth contrasts with the dominant romantic narrative underlying Western ideas of youth.

Orientations to the Future: Hope and Risk

The intense anxiety enveloping Chinese parents' efforts to make their children into the right kind of subjects is a poignant reminder that the future is not created only in relation to symbolic representations of time, or its structuring and regimentation in daily practice. It is also constructed through sentiments like hope and anxiety, which orient people to particular kinds of expectations. Closely intertwined with hope is risk—the dangers one might face in attempting to achieve one's hopes.

Risk taking, whether calculated, intentional, or rebelliously reckless, has been assumed to be part of everyday life by the practice-oriented anthropology of the past twenty-five years. Risk was at the heart of the temporal gap through which Bourdieu (1977) broke down the legalistic, static notion of gift reciprocity. Each gift, before it is returned, entails a risk to the parties involved, to the web of social relations, and to the expected logic of social life. Given how central risk has been to earlier anthropological work, it is curious that most past work focused explicitly on risk has looked at how people try to conserve what they have against the dangers posed by the natural environment or society: risk as something to be minimized. As a result, Zaloom (2004:366) notes, "[e]xplorations of active, intentional engagements of risk are particularly underdeveloped."

Youth, in particular, are known for taking risks (Jackson and Scott 1999), and risk is presented in a negative light. No surprise, then, that in the context of efforts to minimize risk, there is a large literature in public health and public policy trying to understand the "risky" behavior of youth and discussing "youth at risk" (for one example, see Dryfoos 1990). Rather than pathologize youth, however, as earlier studies of youth and risk are often accused of doing, we argue that aspects of youth practice previously represented as "risky" accrue new value in changed social and economic circumstances. Several chapters argue that, in the rapid shifts of late capitalism that quickly make certain kinds of knowledge obsolete, youth are increasingly central to more general, social processes of hope, risk taking, and the production of new knowledge.

Hope is an idea debated in philosophy and economic theory more than in anthropology; both disciplines speak more in terms of human universals than in relation to cultural variation and social motivations. There have been a few recent attempts to create an anthropology of hope, notably a speculative essay by Crapanzano (2003) and ethnographic studies in Fiji and Japan by Miyazaki (2004, 2006). Crapanzano (2003:6) states that hope is linked to temporality—hope implies a futurity, albeit in culturally distinct ways—and to the more familiar anthropological and psychological concepts of desire and agency. He focuses on cargo cults and on the South African Whites who "waited" for a resolution to the contradictions of apartheid (Crapanzano 1985). These examples lead him to suggest that hope "is the passive counterpart of desire," that "one acts on desire" whereas "hope depends on some other agency" (Crapanzano 2003:6). He also acknowledges the uneasy relationship between the two orientations.

By contrast, members of our seminar came to see hope as an active and even agentive modality specific to particular times and places. When interpreted as an agentive orientation toward the future, hope fits into the anthropology of sentiment and emotion, which recent literature suggests are culturally and historically specific phenomena (Farquhar 2002; Geurts 2002; Lutz 1988; Seremetakis 1994; Stoller 1989). Emotion and sentiment are "formations of everyday life (temporal, dispersed, shifting) and everyday life [is] thoroughly suffused with discourses (collective, concrete, historical)" (Farquhar 2002:8). Emotion and sentiment are also specific forms of human action on self, other, and the wider world. Because globalization is associated with disjunctive sets of "flows" of people, goods, images, and ideas, it seems possible that hope can increase in the contemporary context. After all, each new flow carries different forms of knowledge and the potential for new orientations and new hopes. Looking at hope and its enactments in everyday life allows us to examine not just the spatial dimensions of these flows but also the ways they enter into the temporalities of people's lives and relationships.

Conceived in this way, hope is political, a sentiment that diversely situated actors deploy to link, challenge, or reconfigure domestic, national, and transnational relationships (Durham n.d.; Lutz and Abu-Lughod 1990). Particular institutions embody hope. Particular actors seek to fulfill their own hopes by engaging with those institutions. Such institutions stretch across the domains of family and state: the Red Cross and Green Crescent, the transnational projects of Habitat for Humanity, the anti-globalization movements that prompt consumer buying and boycotts for Fair Trade. In this sense, hope is a form of social action that is deeply engaged in human connections.

Because hope is oriented toward the future, it draws our attention to the temporality of sentiment. The specific ways that hope, as an aspect of future making, is intertwined with social relationships and institutions are particularly visible in Paula Fass's chapter 2. In offering a historical account of children, youth, and globalization from the perspective of the United States, Fass provides a snapshot of how hope was embodied in institutions related to children in the early and mid-twentieth century, against which more recent changes can be read. In the United States, the institutions of childhood, including schools and child labor laws, were first created in the expectation that childhood could be protected from the market. Ironically, the institutionalization of romantic cultural ideals designed to protect children's innocence actually helped constitute "the market" as a separate realm of activity (Zelizer 1985). Ideally, these changes were to create the agents of a better society characterized by greater equality and social progress. Of course, this romantic vision of childhood never applied to immigrant lower classes. Fass notes that as global inequalities increase, any continuation of childhood as it was conceived in the late nineteenth and early twentieth centuries in America will require a renewed commitment to the libratory and progressive hopes enshrined in institutions and laws created in the name of childhood at that time.

Fass urges that we heed the history of US efforts to protect children from the market. Many of the chapters suggest that the current climate of economic liberalization has plunged children into the center of the market in ways that previous laws sought to prevent. The processes associated with globalization—be they socially progressive or neoliberal—challenge older ways of constructing childhood.

These links between hope, access to knowledge, and risk are discussed in several chapters. Constance Flanagan's contribution, chapter 6, directly addresses the issues raised by Fass by showing how youth struggle with the new social contract, which has eroded the institutions created one hundred years ago explicitly to protect them from the vagaries of the market. US youth understand that the new conditions of flexible capital mean that they must work harder and regularly retool in order to meet the needs of the market. These youth are involved in new forms of political activism, such as United Students Against Sweatshops (USAS), that offer more collective solutions to these problems. Hope is inscribed in their attitudes toward education and the political field; it is neither passive nor dependent on outside agencies. Among disadvantaged young people in America, hope is embodied in their determined belief that hard work and personal moral choices produce one's future. Much as Anagnost describes for China, hope is also paired with anxiety, self-doubt, and enormous risk because young people can see, all around them in America, those who have failed—the unemployed, the homeless, the eternally dependent.

Although hope is knit together with desire for material or social betterment, it is neither the same thing as desire nor merely the passive aspect of desire that Crapanzano suggests. This point becomes clear in the attitudes of the more privileged youth with whom Flanagan worked. They are more cynical than their disadvantaged counterparts about the ability of schooling and the power of their individual will to fulfill their desires. These more privileged youth pursue societal betterment through the rapidly changing new technologies that enable new forms of political action: conscientious shopping, blogging, participating in evanescent political groups. It is too soon to tell, however, whether this new style of politics—which encourages autonomy, creativity, and entrepreneurship, the very traits that flexible capitalism also celebrates—will endure.

The links between hope and risk are also visible in Jennifer Cole's chapter 5, on youth fashion practice and sex-for-money relationships in contemporary Madagascar. During the post-independence and state-socialist period, most urban Malagasy sought upward mobility through schooling, believing that they would gain the skills necessary to ensure their futures. Since economic liberalization in the early 1990s, however, the future opened up by schooling has become more uncertain. An increasing number of young women use fashion as a way to attract European men, with whom they want to forge relationships. The ability to perform fashion correctly relies on particular kinds of knowledge about which fashions make women desirable to European men, as well as on the transient quality of a youthful body. The girls hope that, by marrying a European, they can move up social hierarchies within Madagascar or jump tracks by moving out of Madagascar to become part of a global middle class. If successful, they can convert youthful physical beauty into more enduring cultural capital. However, these young women put themselves at considerable risk because of their brief window of time in which to succeed and because of their vulnerability to AIDS, other sexually transmitted diseases, and pregnancy.

Tobias Hecht's chapter 10, about a Brazilian street youth who imagines herself in global society, offers another example of how hope, knowledge, and risk intertwine. Hecht's chapter focuses on his interactions with Bruna Veríssimo, a transgendered, homeless youth who works as a prostitute in northeast Brazil. Bruna is well aware that images of street children have been transmitted abroad, even commodified, by global humanitarians and that, as a result, her story is also a potentially valuable commodity. Indeed, the primary way Bruna imagines herself in global society is as a commodity, that is, "photographed and written about, in whose name money is raised and social movements galvanized." While Bruna struggles to realize her life as a desirable prostitute and to defend her independence and femininity on the streets, she also traffics in images of herself with the anthropologist. Her self-representation is a form of commerce and also a form of self-making through which she attempts to realize her hopes. But she must constantly place herself at risk. The only future Bruna can imagine is one in which she moves spatially but remains a street child—as if the future she hopes for is always elsewhere.

Transforming Practices: Commodities, Attachment, and Emergent Sociality

Children and youth create the future in a third way, as others have also noted: children and youth's practices, sometimes inadvertently, generate new ways of thinking, feeling, and being that carry into the future. Flanagan observes in chapter 6 that "the lens of youth is a good vantage point" for framing what society will look like in the future. It would be easy to argue that youth practices rarely outlast the context of their production—essentially, the vision of youth enshrined in the Eriksonian notion of a moratorium. There is good evidence, however, that some of the practices created by youth do become routinized, so these provide an important site for illuminating patterns of social change.

Children and youth often create new practices by drawing on available resources and transforming them. During the 1950s, young men in Britain wore certain clothes (as in the case of the teddy boys' use of Edwardian fashions) to forge a particular class-based identity for themselves, drawing on older items to refashion new kinds of identity and cultural practices (Hebdige 1979). It was this aspect of youth on which Karl Mannheim (1993) focused when he wrote about the process of "fresh contact." Through fresh contact, each new generation reshapes existing social and cultural practices into new forms. For example, college students in the 1920s pioneered practices such as fads associated with mass culture (Fass 1977), and young participants in the countercultural movements of the 1960s changed the ways in which they parented their children (Weisner and Bernheimer 1998). This aspect of how youth create the future could cover an infinite number of topics; the chapters in this volume focus particularly on young people's use of commodities in relation to affective attachments.

In highlighting the relationship between commodities and attachment, the chapters build on earlier studies from within the tradition of psychological anthropology that emphasized how culturally specific socialization practices molded children's psychological development. Attachment—the profound emotional bonds that a child develops with its primary caretakers—mediated this process. Early psychological anthropologists were inspired by the imperatives of Boasian anthropology to understand cultural specificity, yet equally engaged in probing Freudian claims about universal patterns of human development. They sought to illuminate patterns of attachment and how these contributed to personality formation in other societies. The desire to explain broad patterns of culture and personality has given way to more nuanced approaches emphasizing how individuals make sense of, and deploy, wider cultural meanings (Briggs 1998). Patterns of affective identification, however, continue to provide important clues as to how this happens. Unlike earlier work, which situated such processes within a private domain conceived of as separate from the market, this volume demonstrates both the mutual constitution of home and market and the role of children in these processes (Stephens 1995; Zelizer 1985). The chapters are in step with a broader movement within the social sciences to conceptualize affect in ways that stretch beyond the individual (Clough 2007; Massumi 2002).

During our seminar discussions, it became obvious that commodities purchased for or used by children are part of historically unprecedented patterns of attachment and/or parental investment associated with recent social and economic changes. As Allison argues in chapter 8, for example, the makers of the game Pokémon created it partly to assuage Japanese adults' worries that children are becoming "amenbo kids" (Hakuhōdō Seikatsu Sōgō Kenkyūjo 1997). The concern is that children, "like water spiders, attach easily, but superficially, to multiple things" (Allison, chapter 8). Ironically, Pokémon "promises an alternative world of connectiveness." The logic of this connectiveness, however, works to socialize children into a worldview of accumulation, competition, and consumption associated with the very patterns of behavior parents fear. Likewise, Anagnost's chapter 3 highlights the new commodity practices to cultivate "quality" children in China and the new kinds of mother/child relationships these entail.

Other chapters make clear that such micro-level commodity practices help shape new macro-level social connections and cleavages. By engaging with commodities in everyday practices, children and youth transform the categories and the processes that constitute broader patterns of globalization, linking intimate domains to larger social formations (Cole and Durham 2007).

The links between more micro-level, child-centric practices and wider patterns of social inequality are particularly well illustrated by Barrie Thorne's analysis, based on research in Oakland, California. Her chapter 4 probes how children's use of commodities like Pokémon in the Oakland public schools shapes new global lines of class. Accelerated rates of immigration combined with state cutbacks for social services have made California's class structure increasingly polarized. Class-privileged children live in wealthy enclaves in the hills, protected from the cultural and racialized differences that are part of day-to-day life for children who attend the public schools in the flats. Young African Americans can coax their parents into buying expensive shoes and clothing for them; Asian immigrant children cannot. Thorne shows how, in the context of widening class differences, the Pokémon cards and Hello Kitty items that circulate in exchanges, barters, and sales enable kids to interact as peers in ways that obscure class differences. The children develop a complex reading of material culture, based on an affective strategy that Thorne calls "shame work." Payless shoes, out-of-date Disney characters, and lunchtime swaps translate into a language of race, ethnicity, and age grading, overwriting the profound class inequalities in Oakland childrearing. In the vision of the future that emerges from Thorne's chapter 4, similar to the one presented by Flanagan in chapter 6, wealthy people pull their children out of the public sphere, and middle- and lower-income children are left to do the work of democracy by making sense of difference and commonalities through their use of mass-produced commodities.

CONCLUSION: FIGURING THE FUTURE

All the authors suggest different ways that youth and children contribute to how the future is figured—how it is symbolized, hoped for, and made—in the context of globalization. We are building on the well-known truism that "children are the future," which has been used in so many times and places. Rather than take the association of youth and the future for granted, however, we seek to unravel some of the mechanisms driving this powerfully naturalized association. We parse the vague (and very ideologically useful) idea of "the future" into three dimensions: temporality; the relationship of hope and risk; and the substantive practices through which children, youth, and adults forge new futures. In combination, these suggest some of the ways that children and youth provide the symbolic and practical material through which any group *projects*—a word that, of course, also means "to throw forward," as well as a "project" in the sense of a life plan—the future.

To conclude, we point out our argument's implications for the studies of children, youth, and globalization with which we began. As mentioned, most of the existing literature that specifically addresses youth and globalization focuses on how children or youth mediate the transformation of space currently taking place. By contrast, all the chapters in this volume highlight how children and youth naturalize new relations to time, especially the future, whether it is one filled with risky and uncertain opportunities, increasing poverty and alienation, or hopes of plenty. This emphasis on children and youth's connection to temporality enables us to make a more general point about contemporary studies of children and youth.

Much recent work has argued that it is important to study young people not as adults in the making, like the anthropology of children and youth beholden to Euro-American models of human development, but as active agents who create cultural forms in the here and now that are worthy of scholarly attention (Amit-Talai and Wulff 1995; Scheper-Hughes and Sargent 1998; Sharp 2002). In many ways, this argument was a valuable analytical move because it freed scholars to consider aspects of children and youth's lives apart from adult concerns. The irony is that it champions the perspectives of children and youth but increases the likelihood that we will ignore the more general kinds of insights gained from taking children and youth as a site for social and cultural inquiry. And part of our ability to generalize is that all of us do have some kind of childhood and most of us do age.

In fact, the only two books on the subject that have made it into the mainstream of anthropology did so because they used features of youth to illuminate widely shared dilemmas or aspects of the human condition.

Margaret Mead's (1964[1928]) *Coming of Age in Samoa* used the experience of adolescence in Samoa to establish the primacy of culture, refuting European-derived developmental models and making policy recommendations for the United States in the process. Paul Willis's (1977) *Learning to Labor: How Working Class Kids Get Working Class Jobs* turned the predicament of working-class youth in England into an illustration of how any group, not just young people, can participate in the reproduction of a system that is ultimately harmful to the group's own interests.

The chapters in this volume provide plenty of empirical detail about children and youth, because children and youth want and use the products of multinational corporations; because they actively produce new popular culture and new kinds of hierarchies and social configurations; because they are the objects of intervention for transnational NGOs; and because some of them use technologies such as the Internet to engage in new kinds of politics. We have not chosen to highlight these points in our introduction, as those who hold the perspective that youth are interesting in their "own right" might expect. Rather, we have argued that certain aspects of children and youth make them a particularly sharp lens through which to understand the figuring of the future for all age groups in the contemporary moment. And we have shown how broad social science claims about space/time compression become imagined, routinized, and sometimes contested for people of all ages because of the actions of, and practices around, youth. For these reasons, the youth and children of the world and the processes they reveal should be taken very seriously.

Acknowledgments

We gratefully acknowledge Jessica Cattelino, Judy Farquhar, Danilyn Rutherford, and two anonymous reviewers for their comments on earlier drafts.

Notes

1. *Scape* is borrowed from Arjun Appadurai (1996), who coined terms like *ethnoscape* and *financescape*.

2. Ruddick's thesis builds on Sharon Stephens' (1995) earlier essay "Children and the Politics of Culture in 'Late Capitalism.'" Stephens argued that the image of the innocent child in need of nurture (as well as its inverse, the working-class child in need of control) was produced by social divisions that emerged in the late nineteenth century. This particular image of the child underwrote divisions—between public and

private, male and female, old and young—that were central to the reorganization of Western industrial society. Stephens argued that the sense of children in crisis emerged, in part, because older arrangements of labor, gender, the domestic realm, and class relations were being reworked.

3. These changes took place in schools, family and new juvenile law, the organization of play, and commodity culture.

4. The expression "on the cusp of hope and failure" first arose in Ann Anagnost's chapter 3, on childrearing in a liberalizing China.

2

Childhood and Youth as an American/Global Experience in the Context of the Past

Paula S. Fass

The United States invented neither the faith in the expanding market that underwrites what we usually mean by "globalization" nor the image of childhood that haunts it (Fass 2007). But the United States has made powerful contributions to the momentum of both, and it practically invented modern adolescence and youth culture. Therefore, understanding something of America's historical experience is important as we think about children, youth, and globalization. A clearer grasp of the history can dispel mistaken notions that sometimes vex discussions of globalization, such as the idea that globalization necessarily means the exploitation of children, or that it will lead inevitably to the re-creation of childhood in the rest of the world along the lines of the West. The valorization of childhood and an expanding market were part of nineteenth-century American development, and though their parallel evolutions were not completely fortuitous, neither were they fatefully interdependent. And their history can alert us to the difficulties in a view of globalization as unalterable, foreordained, and coherent.

I argue that, in the United States in the nineteenth century, childhood came to represent a reprieve from the market and that the preservation of that perspective today will require a commitment to the hopes that the concept of childhood once enshrined. Childhood as we know it in the United States will not arrive in other parts of the world with a world-encircling market. Youth as a modern Western experience, however, may well be carried along with that market because it is deeply embedded in the market's commercial energies. I suggest that, despite its US roots, where it originated as an extension and amplification of childhood, modern youth culture now has a life of its own and is exportable. We need to understand the historical dimensions of these phenomena as we wrestle with their implications in today's world.

THE EARLY AMERICAN ECONOMY

Historians contemplating our origins in the British empire may still be unable to decide whether the United States in the nineteenth century was a post-colonial or post-imperial society (Chaplin 2003). But few question that the United States after the American Revolution was a special kind of European cultural outpost in which capitalism flourished in a rapidly expanding geographic terrain. Born late in the eighteenth century, American development was little hindered by pre-capitalist beliefs such as mercantilism as it looked toward its inland agricultural realm to the west while exploiting its Atlantic seacoast connections to Europe and the rest of the world. Heir to John Locke and Adam Smith, America's almost unimpeded laissez-faire approach to economic development nevertheless provided a particular twist to early capitalism because its vast continent was both labor-poor and resource-rich.

This unusual combination is not often available today in most places experiencing capitalist development, but many other elements we have come to associate with globalization nevertheless define American growth by the middle of the nineteenth century. These include a reliance on rapid transportation and communications as Americans built by far the largest railroad network in the world (with the aid of British capital) and invented, and pioneered the uses of, the telegraph and later the telephone. These inventions turned America's huge size into a massive market that encouraged American adventurers and investors, transforming the Constitution's hopeful possibilities into reality when it created the largest free trade zone in the world.

Labor was trickier. The need for labor was an American problem well before capitalism took root. In the colonial period, the British and other imperial powers brought slavery to the western hemisphere as part of the developing Atlantic trading system. In British North America, the first known transport arrived early in the seventeenth century, though the laws that differentiated these Africans from other kinds of servants did not appear until the 1640s (Morgan 1975). Indeed, well after Americans had left colonial dependency behind, they found it difficult to give up slavery as the continent expanded with the immense Louisiana Purchase lands that Jefferson acquired from Napoleon in 1803. These huge territories became an internal empire where already established American habits of westward migration could be often repeated. These territories also provided the site for continuing devotion to slavery as the society sought to define itself by inscribing its identity in the western regions in the nineteenth century.

The subsequent battle against slavery left an indelible mark on American culture and identity and would eventually lead to its bloodiest and most traumatic conflict. Indeed, the growing antagonism to slavery in New England and the upper Midwest, the use of negative images of Southern slaveholders to promote visions of humane and proper childrearing (Cleves 2005), and the identification of American ideals of self-ownership in contrast to slave dependency would strongly mark attitudes toward childhood and children during the nineteenth century and beyond.[1]

Starting in the early nineteenth century, the dominant economic commitment to free, not forced, labor encouraged unlimited European immigration for the rest of the century (Eltis 2002; Higham 1955). Indeed, the importation of slaves was prohibited by the Constitution after 1808. Only the immigration of Asians, seen as truly threatening on the West Coast, was restricted in public policy, but even that limitation did not come until late in the century and was often resisted (Higham 1955; Ueda 1994). Immigration came steadily and regularly as Americans set about cutting trees; digging mines; laying track; making steel, locomotives, electrical equipment, and cloth; and processing the grain of its abundant harvests and the carcasses of domestic animals thriving on its pasturelands. Initially, in the eighteenth and early nineteenth centuries, immigrants came from the British Isles and Germany and then, at first gradually and later rapidly and profusely, from Ireland, the Scandinavian countries, Switzerland, Russia, the Austro-Hungarian Empire, the Balkans, Armenia, Poland, Italy, Greece, Portugal, Syria, and many other places. These immigrants included people of many religions, a matter of considerable disturbance to a Protestant-proud culture. But this extraordinary heterogeneity was also claimed as the substance of America's uniqueness. Herman Melville observed, "We are the heirs of all time, and with all nations we divide our inheritance. On this Western Hemisphere all tribes and peoples are forming into one federated whole; and there is a future which shall see the estranged children of Adam restored as to the old hearthstone in Eden" (Higham 1955:21).[2]

By the end of the nineteenth century, few regions of Europe and the Middle East had not contributed to the extraordinary dynamism of the American economy. In the twentieth century, the United States eclipsed its European parent to become the major driver of world economic growth. It also transcended European nationalisms to become the site of a newly hybridized white population whose multiple origins had created a genuinely new social and cultural phenomenon. None of this took place without social conflict and cultural tension, especially over the future of children, but all of it contributed to the substance of the American economy and the texture of American social life. It also anticipated (and some believe actually surpassed) the dependence on migratory labor associated today with "globalization."

America's development as a nation—its vast free market, economic differentiation, dependence on communications technology, and diverse migrating population—presaged, in many ways, current developments in a world opened up to investments, the recruitment of cheap labor, and a new global culture negotiated through media and migrations across national and ethnic boundaries.

CHILDREN IN THE HISTORY OF AMERICAN DEVELOPMENT

The logic of economics, some would have us believe, knows no bounds, and, in the American context, economic logic recognized no children. Much of the labor in the seventeenth and eighteenth centuries, outside of New England (which was peopled in family groups), arrived in the form of un-free or semi-free labor, as African slaves or indentured servants (Eltis 2002; Fass and Mason 2000; Hofstadter 1971). These men and women were useful and worth their investment price only if they were young and strong. From the beginning, youth has been an asset in America. As early as 1619 (a dozen years after its founding), the Virginia colony noted in a letter to the mayor of London that it "had been very grateful" for "those children to be apprentices" sent to the colony that year and requested, "Furnish us again with one hundred more for our next spring" (Fass and Mason 2000:241). The letter specified that they should start at around twelve years of age. Some children came very young, but almost all came before what we would consider full maturity, to work in the fields, the workshops, and the homes of pre-capitalist colonial America.

A century and a half later, when Alexander Hamilton turned his brilliant gaze on the future of the newly formed republic, he looked beyond the still largely rural economy toward a producer population composed of the young and the available, mainly children and women. "It is worthy of particular remark that, in general, women and children are rendered more useful, and the latter more early useful, by manufacturing establishments, than they would otherwise be" (Fass and Mason 2000:248). Noting that the English employed women and children in their "cotton manufactures," where they made up four-sevenths of the workforce, he observed that "the greatest proportion are children, and many of them of a tender age" (Fass and Mason 2000:248). Hamilton wanted to use, to the fullest extent possible, the available resources of the American population. In drawing a picture of the country's future, he also introduced new economic possibilities that would require more labor than was available. It was this impulse to future prospects that opened wide the gates of immigration. Hamilton's planning coincided nicely with the needs of the four million people already here and the many millions yet to come, whose drive for survival and desire for improvement meant that work was the governing fact of life for young and old.

The factory work that Hamilton intuited as he looked out at the not yet bustling countryside of the late eighteenth century grew into reality by the middle of the nineteenth, and, with it, one could find the child and youth workers of America everywhere. Useful for America's growing industries, these young workers were also valuable to their families' survival and prosperity. Most child workers did not disappear until well into the twentieth century. One need only look at the textile workers of the American South in the 1930s and 1940s to observe the descendents of these earlier workers in the "lint-heads" (children literally raised in the work routine of factories in North Carolina and elsewhere) as Southern families replaced the families and girls of New England because labor was so much cheaper in the American South in the twentieth century (Dublin 1979; Hall et al. 1987; Jones 1992). Those textile plants are largely closed today, replaced by factories in Bangladesh, China, and Honduras, where children continue to work.

There was nothing particularly liberating about this work, but neither was it very much worse than the conditions these children had known before. The work of children, like the work of women, is one of the great, unheralded features of our history (Cunningham 1995; Hall et al. 1987; Levine 2004). It is remembered today largely because of the campaign against child factory labor that was mounted in the late nineteenth and early twentieth centuries. Before that time, it was not much commented upon because children were expected to work unless they were especially favored by birth to aristocratic or unusually wealthy parents. The majority of children, and certainly the overwhelming majority of those over the age of twelve or thirteen, worked in the United States as they did in Europe and elsewhere in the world (De Coninck-Smith, Sandin, and Schrumpf 1997). In the nineteenth century, even school attendance did not significantly alter the routines of young rural workers, and school terms were established around the planting and harvest calendars (Tyack 1974). Well into the twentieth century, urban children worked after school (Nasaw 1985).

In the late nineteenth century, progressive reformers in the United States began to attack child labor as part of the general attempt to save the children of the poor from degradation and exploitation. Thus, Felix Adler noted in the *Annals of the American Academy* in 1905:

> At the beginning of 1903 it was estimated that there were in the factories of the South—chiefly cotton factories—about 20,000 children under the age of twelve. Twelve is a very early age at which to begin work; under the age of twelve, and 20,000?... Where are our instincts of mercy, where is the motherliness of the women of this country, whither is the chivalry of our men that should seek a glory in protecting the defenseless and the weak?

> The lack of adequate statistical inquiries makes it impossible to express in figures the extent of the evil of child labor. But wherever investigation is undertaken, wherever the surface is even scratched, we are shocked to find to what an extent the disease is eating its way underneath, even in those States in which legislation on the subject is almost ideal.... I find that in New Jersey, in one of the woolen mills, 200 children under the legal age are at work. In the glass industry of Ohio, Pennsylvania, and West Virginia, the evils of premature work and of night work are combined.... In one of the glass houses of Wheeling, W. Va., forty boys were seen by the agent, apparently from ten to twelve years of age; one child looked not over nine years old, "but too busy to be interviewed." In this place 3,000 children of the school age were found to be out of school.[3] [Adler 1915(1905):417–418]

By the early twentieth century, such observations—and the sensibility behind them, that children needed to be protected by the "motherliness of women" and the "chivalry of men"—could be found endlessly repeated by those who worked hard to expose the "evil" of child labor. In so doing, child labor became an oxymoron, a self-negating idea. It was viewed as destructive of the child's health, morals, mental development, and future. As such, it was destructive of the child (Zelizer 1985).

FINDING CHILDHOOD IN THE HISTORY OF CHILDREN

In this outline of history, we can find children but very little childhood, at least not in the sense to which we have become accustomed to imagining it—a childhood of leisured, protected development, free from care and toil, a childhood nurtured through learning and play. Felix Adler was measuring the reality of the working children's lives in 1905 against this vision of childhood. Already, by the early twentieth century, this childhood image had a long history of its own. Since 1960, with the publication of the French edition of Philippe Ariès's *Centuries of Childhood* (1962), we have become accustomed to seeing childhood as emerging from a specific place and time, and we now understand how deeply embedded in Western developments it has been. Ariès placed its origins in France in the late sixteenth and early seventeenth centuries. At the same time, too many have misread Ariès to conclude that childhood was only a modern Western institution.

In fact, all societies have a conception of childhood and its specific intracultural requirements. Whether in ancient Greece and Rome, in early Christianity in Asia Minor and Europe, in Islamic societies, in Africa, or in China, every society has beliefs, practices, and often texts and rituals that enshrine some idea of childhood and what is required for its protection and development.[4] The early Christians were eager to proscribe the exposure of children, common to the Romans, thereby distinguishing their own "Christian" habits from earlier pagan civilizations. Sharia law has elaborate property protections and rules about appropriate treatment that define Islamic childhood. No society leaves its progeny entirely to the hazards of nature and the whims of its parents. All societies, more or less, tightly swaddle young children in a set of social norms appropriate to what they call childhood. Many also have ceremonies that chart the child's progress into adulthood. For this miscue about childhood, Ariès is, at least in part, to blame because he has often been read to imply that childhood, *tout court*, is a modern invention.

Ariès was actually pointing to a more specific phenomenon. A careful reading of Ariès suggests that he was looking to find the early European origins of our own particular modern view of childhood as a wholly separate estate—a period of sequestration in which children are set apart and protected in an elaborate circle of institutions and cultural forms. It was this specific childhood (and its subsequent extension into adolescence in the twentieth century) that Ariès believed began to emerge in the late sixteenth century and developed over the next four hundred years. He emphasized especially the role of schools created by church moralists who were newly conscious of the potentials of the inner life as first realized in children and were devoted to protecting the physical virtue of the young. Children, according to Ariès, had earlier been raised promiscuously in and through the community, participating in various rituals, games, and other expressions of the common life. By the seventeenth century, however, the family became more private, and schools designated for instruction divested the community as a whole of its earlier, much more informal means of supervising the young. Closely related to these developments, Ariès noticed a growing awareness of age. The very boundaries of childhood were increasingly charted and patrolled as age became an important form of cultural information. To that newly separated and age-embedded childhood, Europeans began to attach ideas of children's innocence as the very essence of the age category.

Some historians have questioned Ariès's ideas as a whole (Pollack 1984) or in significant part (Hanawalt 1993), but most have accepted at least the historicization of childhood he proposed. And most historians who have subsequently developed his ideas agree that the elaboration of childhood as a full-fledged social commitment in the Euro-American world did not take place until later, certainly much later, in regard to the child population as a whole. In art (a medium of the privileged few), it becomes apparent in portraiture of the early eighteenth century (Brown 2004); in philosophy in the mid-eighteenth century, with Rousseau especially; and in literature by the early nineteenth century. The heightened consciousness of age-appropriate behavior as something necessary to all children, as well as its subsequent extension to adolescents, almost certainly did not appear until the mid-to-late nineteenth century (Gillis 1996; Kett 1977; Zelizer 1985; for a contrary view, Greven 1977). The extension of the vision of childhood to all children hardly appeared as a serious undertaking until the twentieth (Cunningham 1995; Hendrick 1997).

In fact, childhood was born as an idea well before it informed popular views of children. The most persuasive argument I have seen inscribes the growth of the consciousness of childhood deep in the Enlightenment sensibility. In Larry Wolff's (1998) close and brilliant reading of the Abbé de Condillac's *Essay on the Origin of Human Knowledge*, he shows how necessary childhood was to the elaboration of Enlightenment views about the nature of human memory. Others, of course, have observed the centrality of childhood to Rousseau's philosophical texts and to his very popular novel, *Émile* (Fliegelman 1982). Rousseau's vision of the child's natural vitality and innocence helped to define political discourse in advanced circles in Europe and America.

Rousseau's ideas, together with the essential Locke, were especially attractive in literate circles in the American colonies by the mid-eighteenth century (Fliegelman 1982), when the revolutionary implications of an autonomy enshrined in a protected childhood and the possibilities of more democratic relations between the generations were played out in a revolution against the patriarchal authority of the king. Americans very much identified their nation as the more innocent child to Europe's decadent parent and were naturally drawn to the ideals of the child as innately good, closer to nature, and charting an independent and better future. The equality enshrined in the American Declaration of Independence was far from a description of all members of the society but became increasingly appropriate to a context in which sons could and did set out to find their own way in a nation of broad spaces and ample land. They increasingly felt justified in doing so with or without their parents' approval. Alexis de Tocqueville was much taken with this unusual generational relationship when he traveled in the United States in the early 1830s. Fathers and sons, he argued, were much more naturally comrades because the young were empowered to look to themselves and their own resources rather than submit obediently to the dictates of age, authority, and inheritance (de Tocqueville 1990[1832]).

Although the Enlightenment possibilities rooted firmly in American soil and the American Revolution established ideals of youth and autonomy, this did not automatically translate into a gentle path for children. The tenacious heritage of American Calvinism was at least as vigorous as the Enlightenment imports, and Protestant views of children could be harsh and unforgiving (Greven 1977). Also, as I have suggested, the American need for labor and the facts of immigration made the work of children a pragmatic fact of life for most. It was not simply enlightenment ideas that stimulated the American commitment to childhood by the mid-nineteenth century. Rather, it was a confluence of factors native to the land. Indeed, the very conflict between these ideals and the facts on the ground often allowed childhood to flourish as a value to which a profound sentiment attached itself. Whatever the ideals of equal treatment for all and of enlightened commitments to individual self-realization, the new United States was still a society of brutal realities. Slavery provided the most profound challenge to those ideals. Its wretched presence became a sore on the Protestant conscience, as well as a manifest denial of a rational Enlightenment ideology of free self-ownership (Foner 1970). By the 1840s, public awareness of the contradictions between the American belief system and American practices became widespread, and, with it, a new commitment to a future made better through directed human action.

The heightened sensibility about the need for social change to fulfill an ideal created the context in which the special solicitude for children became a nineteenth-century American specialty, though never exclusively American. Those seeking to mold the American future realized that two parallel courses of action were required: the reform of adult habits such as drink, crime, and slavery (Rothman 1971; Walters 1978) and the careful formation of child life. Tutored by Locke and Rousseau, Americans understood the vital importance of a carefully formed child life, and in the nineteenth century they set about creating the institutional network that would make it possible. Above all, they created the school as a necessary component of American civic beliefs (Kaestle 1983; Katz 1987). The public school was probably more widely available and commonly used in America than almost anywhere else in the Western world, and American literacy rates, for both boys and girls, were very high as a result. Schooling became a necessary extension of childrearing.

By the end of the century, reformers had also created a brace of other institutions that served, with the schools, to project a vision of childhood as a necessary component of a more progressive future. In many ways, childhood itself became an altar to democratic possibilities—a childhood properly created and, where this was lacking, effectively reformed. Toward that end, America created a series of institutions such as camps, kindergartens, playgrounds, orphanages, and juvenile courts. It is arguable that even the topmost invention of the American Victorian imagination—the ideal woman devoted to home, chastity, fidelity, and selflessness—was, in good part, a byproduct of the need to create a perfected childhood, because the child required just such a mother to care for and nurture it (Kerber 1980).

Along the way, Americans created such monuments to the child and to its special qualities as *Uncle Tom's Cabin*, *The Adventures of Huckleberry Finn*, and *Little Women*. The nineteenth century was the century during which the child's special qualities became a national obsession, although this child was by no means exclusively American. British literature of the nineteenth century (Dickens especially) makes this clear. But a protected and sheltered childhood was probably most fully effective in the United States, where it was used as a cudgel first against slavery and then against the many immigrants who came, starting in the mid-nineteenth century, with childhood ideas and practices of their own (Fass 2003). In trying to effect their ideas, Americans brought these children into schools, social settlements, and kindergartens (Beatty 1995; Berg 2004) to learn English and American ways and took these children from the homes that were perceived as inadequate and placed them on western farms or in reform schools and foster care. The sentimental image of childhood was a powerful cultural creation and probably the single most important means by which assimilation took place in America. I think that the final product of assimilation was a hybrid product but that the oversight of its production was certainly under the terms created by the mid-Victorian ideology of the sentimental child (Fass 1989; Fass and Mason 2000).

THE CHILDREN OF IMMIGRANTS AND THE IDEALS OF CHILDHOOD

The struggle to define a proper childhood and to create its conditions was thus central to the formation of American cultural identity. This was the context within which the campaign against child labor took place.[5] By the early twentieth century, various efforts aimed at addressing the mistreatment and neglect of children of the poor were the means by which the broader cultural definition of childhood was accomplished, bringing all children under the umbrella of a proper childhood. The sacralization of childhood and its separation from the taint of the market represented the final implementation of a growing commitment to a particular social idealization in which Anglo-Americans invested their sense of themselves as a civilization.[6]

The struggles that took place around this idealization were least visible, but most potent, in schools. For a long time, historians saw the expansion of schooling as an unqualified good of democracy, but as Stephen Lassonde (1996, 1998, 2005) has shown, the very idea of what a child was and the governing American commitment to a finely graded metric of age were sharply contested by immigrant parents. The definition of a child to an Italian immigrant often differed significantly from the growing consensus among educators and childsavers who saw extended childhood dependency as a force for the creation of citizenship (Fass 2007). Whereas an Italian father might look at a young person and see a person fully capable of making a significant contribution to the family's welfare, school reformers saw a child of twelve as needing protection, advanced training in English, and close supervision. Whether this child was a girl or a boy mattered little to school officials accustomed to the equal treatment of American coeducation. But these issues mattered enormously to the many new immigrants who treated their children differently according to gender and understood protection in very different terms. For them, group ideals of social honor, community authority, and family obligation often carried a price tag in the work of children.[7] Americans had committed their schooling to an individualizing destiny, and Americans viewed immigrant parent–child interdependence as a form of exploitation. Jane Addams, who was generally sympathetic and understanding toward immigrants, often observed that immigrant women were puzzled when the settlements and kindergartens would not punish and discipline children severely. Their view was clarified when one of them remarked to Addams (1907:45), "If you did not keep control over them from the time they were little, you would never get their wages when they are grown up."

The American idealization of childhood was specifically embodied in a series of laws and regulations (child labor regulations, required school attendance, truancy laws) that gave American visions of childhood and its proper requirements precedence over foreign ones. In addition, American childsavers supported mothers' pensions, juvenile courts, and foster care placements. Some of the most fruitful historical work on childhood has made clear just how central this struggle over childhood was to the definition of late-nineteenth-century American social life. Linda Gordon, most prominently, has shown how welfare workers struggled with families over the proper treatment of children by imposing new visions of neglect and child endangerment. More recently, Gordon (1988, 1999) has demonstrated that the dynamics of fosterage even in remote places like Arizona mining towns used children to define a broad range of social relationships, including gender, class, and race.

Certainly, the implementation of these regulations was subject to negotiation among American enforcers and immigrants, as Gordon also shows and as Mary Odem (1995) has demonstrated through a careful reading of juvenile court records. Moreover, David Nasaw (1985) has shown that children actively took part in this evolving story when they worked and played, often illegally, on the very city streets that were patrolled to protect them from harm. This negotiation, however, was always framed by a now taken-for-granted view of the preciousness of childhood. The negotiation was largely at the boundaries of this dominant perspective in which children were to be protected from commerce and market-centered criteria.

In this historical process, the evolving laws of childhood trumped the laws of economics. Although economic laws may know no natural bounds, the evocation of childhood as a sentimental commitment was a potent force for the creation of just such boundaries. As I have suggested, American sentiments about childhood overwhelmed immigrant approaches to parent–child relations and immigrant economic calculations where these were most vulnerable. Regulations for and about the child (and the mother who was its caretaker) became the entering wedge of all kinds of legislation that began to hedge the market in the late nineteenth and early twentieth centuries. In Germany and Britain, the worker and his need for security underwrote the growing power of the state and its regulations. In the United States, the mother and the child she protected provided the critical opening (Rodgers 1998; Skocpol 1992).

By the end of the nineteenth century, reformers and various kinds of progressives envisaged childhood as a sacred trust to be protected from the market. This does not mean, however, that children had no market connections. By the late nineteenth century, middle-class parents sent children to school to improve their chances in the labor market (for a view of how intensely this can be market driven, see Ann Anagnost, chapter 3, this volume); labor unions supported anti–child labor laws to increase the wages of adult workers and to encourage a commitment to a family wage (Glickman 1997); women developed institutions such as settlements to expand their own public role (Gordon 1988; Rothman 1978); and Catholic immigrants built and marketed their own schools to compete for control over their children's future (Fass 1989). But these were responses to a cultural development whose impulses lay outside the marketplace and whose consequences were to put issues concerning children beyond market calculations, as Viviana Zelizer (1985), most importantly, has shown. At a time in the late nineteenth century when Americans could be found estimating the dollar value of each incoming immigrant, the child was removed from this form of calculation (Higham 1955:17). The creation of the "priceless" child was an extraordinary product of earlier cultural and intellectual developments and of the particular forces that created nineteenth-century American social life.

ENTER THE ADOLESCENT

Together, the sentimental ideal of childhood and its growing power over children's lives, the potent American economy and its commitment to education, and the social expression of an ideal of womanly virtue would lay the foundations for the creation of twentieth-century American adolescence. There was nothing natural about the extension of beliefs about childhood into older ages. American adolescence is strongly tied to the extension of schooling, and in the late nineteenth century only a very small proportion of American children (no more than 8 percent) went to high school. Thirty years later, 50 percent did. This veritable explosion of the attendance of young people past fourteen years of age at institutions defined by age was the foundation for twentieth-century youth development. The activity of reformers in the late nineteenth century made this development possible. Young people would eventually stay in school into their adolescent years in ways that did not identify them with or necessarily even prepare them for work and adult roles. Unlike European forms of schooling, the American comprehensive high school was dominated by academic and neo-academic curricula that had no clear vocational connections, although industrial and commercial subjects did begin to develop in high schools during this time as well (Hanson 1997).

In fact, American adolescence would later veer off from childhood, but its initial impetus lay in a confluence of many of the same factors we have been observing in regard to the development of a particular image of childhood, and among the same coalition of reformers. Foremost was the extension of the age of school leaving in the context of the enormous size of the new immigration. By the twentieth century, schooling had become essential to the assimilation of the second generation, and keeping children in school longer became the primary means to curtail fears about disorder and crime (Fass 1989). The continuing availability of immigrant labor at a time of new labor union aggressiveness made labor spokesmen eager to find some controls over the tendency of the labor market to erode wage levels. They now looked to advanced schooling to stop competition from new and younger participants in the job market (Glickman 1997).

In addition, the self-identification of women as caretakers of the nation (which they emphasized in the push for the vote) made the protection of children and adolescents, which women saw as their special domain, a pointed extension of their growing public presence (Rothman 1978). That urge toward protection was embodied in a variety of movements to which women made conspicuous contributions, including the anti–child labor campaign, campaigns to enforce school attendance laws, and the social settlement movement; many of these culminated in the successful establishment of the United States Children's Bureau (Lindenmeyer 1997). Together, these various elements resulted in an emphasis on the high school as an adolescent domain opened up to a much larger clientele, a reshaping of the curriculum, the creation of junior high schools, and the increasing pressure toward higher school-leaving age (Fass 1989).

By the 1920s, public high schools became the symbol of American democracy and community pride. Often the most imposing and modern structures in the city, school buildings became the site of the massive elaboration of the high school curriculum and of the extracurriculum that was a uniquely American product. Athletics, student government, orchestras, dances, and dramatic productions almost overpowered the classroom offerings as schools aimed to keep their older and older "children" (increasingly denominated adolescents) occupied in school and these "children" found ways to direct their own activities within the bounds of the high schools. The high school was the most obvious means by which supervision over young people could be assured, whatever the nature of their education. Just as innocence and play in the nineteenth century became defining characteristics of childhood, so, too, these became guiding values for those supervising the lives of adolescents. As a result, the concept of childhood was gradually extended to those who would have been seen in earlier times as young adults or, at least, on the verge of adulthood and ready to be trained to adult economic roles. The ambiguous status of American adolescents today is still connected to this initial extension.

This supervision and the extension of the organizing ideals of childhood did not stop at the school door. The development of the school was accompanied by a set of other institutions that aimed to control and protect youth. Two of these, the juvenile court and age of consent laws, were particularly revealing and potent. Both drew their inspiration from the protective tendencies inscribed in schooling, child labor reform, and the powerful role of women in all these arenas. In the very late nineteenth and early twentieth centuries, female reformers came together to guard the virtue of adolescent girls by protecting them from too early sexual exposure and male deception. They changed the laws to raise the age of consent, once as young as nine or ten, to anywhere from sixteen to eighteen throughout the United States (Odem 1995). These women were fully cognizant that, in so doing, they absorbed into the sphere of childhood innocence an age group whose sexuality became problematic in wholly new ways. The taming of an exuberant adolescent sexuality was now leashed to a sentimental image that guided the protective ideology. Similarly, by creating courts in which the young were protected from full responsibility for their own behaviors and by placing these behaviors in the hands of family-like judicial monitors rather than before a jury, Jane Addams and the other women who helped to found the juvenile court (beginning in 1899) protected youth fourteen to eighteen years of age from full adult legal responsibility while making many of the marginal behaviors of youth more open to adult scrutiny.

All of this took place under the aegis of a new psychological dispensation in which adolescence was viewed as a time of continuing vulnerability but also as a powerful realm of energy and hope. The psychologist who made this concept of adolescence a Western commonplace, G. Stanley Hall, endowed youth with a spiritual, almost religious, quality and looked to adolescence to provide a new hopefulness that earlier Enlightenment thinkers had seen in childhood (Hulbert 2003; Ross 1969). Similarly, in bemoaning the abuse of youth in work and the distortion of their sexual energies in commercial recreations, Jane Addams attributed to adolescents that natural vitality and insight with which Rousseau had endowed children, and she looked to youth's restless possibilities for the future in just the ways that romantic kindergarten proponents sought enlighten ment in the spirit of children (Addams 1972[1909]; Berg 2004; Hall 1904). Adolescents were surely more difficult to control and to guide. Precisely because they were more dangerous, the image of an extended childhood seemed to make them more available to positive social purposes.

There was always a problem inherent in remaking these young people in the image of childhood. The problem was clear in the workings of the juvenile court, for example, when fifteen-year-old girls were forcibly subjected to intact-hymen examinations when they were caught experimenting with their boyfriends (and those boyfriends could be sent to jail). By supervising these youth as if they were children, the transgressing of childhood boundaries became a sign of social crisis, and its testing became a tempting target for youth. In some ways, this made adolescence an evermore problematic and dangerous arena in twentieth-century life. Partly in response to this problematic sexuality, Margaret Mead proposed Samoa as a romantic adolescent alternative (Fass and Mason 2000; Mead 1964 [1928]). By absorbing into childhood the vitality of youth, Americans also made adolescent rebellion much more likely.

Adolescence, as a marker of childhood's end physically and socially, has a robust place in many societies as a channel toward adulthood. But twentieth-century Americans (and somewhat later, Europeans) made adolescence not only into a turning point but also into the basis for an extended phase of life (Fass 1977), enshrined in a set of increasingly elaborated institutions. These institutions for the adolescent became a terrain for the creation of modern youth culture, protected from work and responsibility and increasingly oriented toward play and leisure. Youth in America—or at least those who were privileged enough for this period of life to take on critical aspects of what Erik Erikson would call a moratorium (Erikson 1963)—became a kind of temporary status that assumed more and more aspects of a leisured class, instead of a way station directed toward adulthood. The institutions developed for adolescent use took on a life of their own, a life determined not just by their founders but also by those who were to be their clients and their hostages (Fass 1977, 1989).

All of this was vastly complicated by the popular culture, which responded to the needs of the young to identify with one another as age peers in music, fashion, language, and other domains. Having been defined in high school largely by age rather than by goals, the young invested age with meaning. Set apart from adults in institutions defined by finer and finer divisions of age (junior and senior high schools, colleges and universities), young Americans seized upon cultural forms that would provide some substance to the new identity created for them. In so doing, they utilized and attached themselves to the commercial possibilities that were also increasingly defined, like age itself, as temporal. By the early twentieth century, movies, music, advertising, and other media were growing with the expanding national consumer economy (Cross 2000); peer cultures, most with local roots, became national phenomena as the young turned to their own use the information provided by these media. In turn, the fads of youth were used as a means by which the consumer economy could grow. Youth, with its vitality and promise, became a selling point as advertisers used and extended youthfulness to the culture more generally. In so vigorously reattaching to the market, now as consumers, young people reversed the logic of their reforming elders.

The general cultural obsession with youth was first noticeable in the American 1920s and then became a regular fixture of twentieth-century culture (Fass 1977; Palladino 1996; Schrum 2004). The question of who was using whom has recently become a lively issue in historiography (Schrum 2004). It is less important, from our perspective, than the fact that both were clearly intertwined by the mid-twentieth century. Youth and commerce fed off each other as the new age group of adolescents, which expanded in both directions (toward preteens and toward the early twenties), soon became a basis for a distinct, national subculture. The appetite for this American culture spread as a privileged, American, leisured youth became the subject of desire both in the United States and elsewhere. Over the course of the twentieth century, America became identified with just those products that were most full of youthful vitality—music, fashion, style (see chapters 9 and 5 by Weiss and Cole, respectively, this volume). This culture of youth, I would argue, much more than the childhood in which it was historically rooted and under whose protective ideas it grew, is an exportable product and one that is very much in demand around the world.

The development in the modern world of youth as a social status is not exclusively American or Western, as many of the chapters in this volume demonstrate. Youth and youth cultures flourish in many parts of the world and are embedded in specific places and societies. Whatever globalization is or is not, it has not simply created youth culture. Nevertheless, I would contend that the international dimensions of modern media have increased the salience of youth cultures and the tendency for youth cultures to connect with one another, as young people eye one another's music, clothes, and fads and import and reinvent these as their own. Global media today, like US national media early in the twentieth century, underlie this tendency while they also democratize desires to participate in taste and age subcommunities. In the United States during the twentieth century, youth culture strongly encouraged conformity that transcended geography. This influence is never unidirectional. Among the young during the twentieth century, jazz, blues, rock, country, and salsa at various times crisscrossed the United States, with sounds whose sources lie in the East, South, North, and West.

There is every reason to expect that, in a worldwide context, youth culture can also have multidirectional outcomes, because youth cultures spread through modern forms of communications. These channels of information encourage rebellion against the local and familiar as the young seek new sources of expression. When I write about the spread of youth culture, I am not suggesting the necessary dominance of Western forms and certainly not that Western youth culture will prevail in some unmodified way. Because American youth are so obviously privileged and are so symbolic of freedom from want and restraint, however, they do provide models that are desired by youth elsewhere. American youth culture is not the only source of influence, but it is a strong force in the modern world.

CHILDREN, YOUTH, AND GLOBALIZATION IN THE TWENTY-FIRST CENTURY

The explosion of global capital in the late twentieth century, together with the post-1980s telecommunications revolution, may or may not be an altogether unprecedented phenomenon. Theorists differ widely on this subject, but historians are likely to notice a number of family resemblances to earlier periods and events (Cooper 2001). In particular, American historians will connect it to special factors in the nineteenth century, when North America was developing a powerful capitalist economy (Fass 2003, 2007). The United States, as I have tried to suggest, witnessed the confluence of several factors that are again today ingredients in contemporary world events, including mass migration and new modes of communication, both vital to its economic development. Just as we are today, Americans and other Westerners were then besieged by images of children (visual and literary) that pricked the public's conscience. These included the poorhouses of Dickens, the slave plantations of Harriet Beecher Stowe, the photos of working and slum children of Lewis Hines and Jacob Riis, the ragged children of David Bernardo (in Britain), and (in Paris) tales of child prostitution (Tardieu 1858). Conscience-stricken British readers of the *Pall Mall Gazette* in the nineteenth century were invited to read about young girls "snared, trapped, and outraged, either when under the influence of drugs or after a prolonged struggle in a locked room" (Walkowitz 1992:81), a description we find echoed today in similar stories in the *New York Times*. Just as today, the reader in the nineteenth century was upset by news of child slavery, child prostitution, and child labor, matters that are often captured in the term *traffic in children* today. Does this mean that what we call globalization will also bring with it calls for improvements in the lives of children, much as the appeal to reform did in the nineteenth century in the United States and Europe?

In part, of course, this has already happened, as is evident in the growth of human rights organizations and the activities of nongovernmental organizations throughout the developing world. Most of these appeal to the Western conscience and are funded in the West. In that sense, Western ideals of childhood are already deeply implicated in global projects. In chapter 10 of this volume, Tobias Hecht brings some of the complex and ironic results of their work to our attention, as he has done in previous work (Hecht 1998, 2002). It is well for us to recognize that images of child exploitation can be put to multiple uses. Since the nineteenth century, as art historian Anne Higonnet (1998) reminds us, portraits of child innocence have had the potential to become pictures of innocence undone. Much of this operates in today's world. Western outrage against child exploitation feeds our continuing sense of superiority. Tales of mistreated children provide lascivious enjoyment, just as the abuse depicted in Dickens at once entertained Victorian Americans and goaded them to seek a solution. In the nineteenth century, a frisson of superiority motivated those who judged other cultures (whether these were immigrants or peoples far away). Today, we observe the misfortune of other people's children with similar mixed emotions.

Just as important, as this brief historical account of the United States suggests, solutions do not come automatically from economics or from outrage, nor do they come free of cost. The source of American commitment to child protection was located in intellectual and cultural developments—in Enlightenment ideas and in beliefs about the necessity for reform—with specific European and New World origins. These made sense to some and were imposed on others. When extended to immigrants, these ideas were often met with sturdy resistance. Today, we may not be able to export our beliefs about children when we export our capital. Moreover, the particular childhood we have adopted in the West and have expressed in terms of schooling and child labor prohibitions is expensive. Thus far, our capital has not brought either of these to the majority of children elsewhere. Where our ideals have struck home, as in the modern-day China depicted by Ann Anagnost in chapter 3, they have come at the cost of other aspects of our ideals, such as a playful, leisured development.

The history I have sketched suggests that it is far more likely we will export commercially loaded youth culture than our vision of a childhood spent outside the market. The world of commerce has attached itself to youth and youth culture in thoroughgoing ways not quite so evident with younger children, although as Barrie Thorne and Anne Allison demonstrate (chapters 4 and 8, respectively, this volume), children too are becoming part of the consumer market. (For a contrary view that sees children's consumption as having a long history, see Jacobson 2005.) As young people in the rest of the world absorb and contribute to an international youth culture that is breaking down national borders, they become an active ingredient of what we call globalization. The rest of the world may or may not completely shield itself from the visions of childhood that the West has adopted and that are implicit in the actions of many international agencies. I am certain, however, that the rest of the world cannot shield itself from youth culture. Jennifer Cole's depiction of Tamatave in chapter 5, this volume, makes this clear. Alternative youth cultures continue to exist, as Deborah Durham demonstrates in chapter 7, but the commercial push underlying Western youth culture makes it a strong and alluring force.

Further, Cole's chapter 5 indicates that the one potential brake on this process—the expense and leisure time necessary, in the modern world, for expressions of youth culture to flourish (at least, as it has developed in the United States)—may not be sufficient. The "cool" youth of Madagascar are willing to engage in a variety of extra-legal and illegal activities in order to obtain it. Indeed, because of youth's ability to view and influence one another over the Internet, on television, in posters and ads, it is developing a universal cultural grammar. In this sense, youth culture is not just an aspect of globalization. It is helping to create it.

Childhood as we have constructed it in the West is less exportable, a product of a particular time and of a particular set of sentimental and emotional valences that stood opposed to commerce and market forces. At this point at least, we seem not to have extended to others the values of child protection it instantiated. Probably, the ways in which children are viewed in other societies, their labor, their sexuality, and their illiteracy, will continue to arouse our consciences far more than images associated with youth (troubled, sexualized, and toughened up, even in the Western world).

At the same time, we should not automatically assume that there is no place for our ideals of childhood or that children have to be left to the uncertain fates that are often worsened today by pressures of global economics. International children's rights organizations, whatever their many drawbacks, are an obvious beginning. Americans in the nineteenth century refused to accept the exploitation of children, even in face of the precarious economics of poor people and their different cultural preconceptions. Through their vision of childhood, Americans created a real alternative to the exclusive sway of market calculation. Whatever its many faults, that vision has given American children unusual opportunities for personal growth and development. These are opportunities we would not like to lose as we become part of a new global marketplace where we compete for jobs, skills, and cheap labor. If we are not to lose the childhood we value, we must be prepared to defend it in a twenty-first-century world.

Belief systems are both tenacious and ephemeral; they outlive the circumstances of their birth but eventually die out. As we look around us today, we can observe the growing emphasis in the United States court system on adult sentences for young children from which the juvenile court was supposed to protect them; a new insistence on schooling as a form of competitive skills preparation instead of individual moral development and playful creativity; the hypersexualization of children in advertising; the inundation in the news of young children portrayed as bloodthirsty murderers. All of these do not bode well for the continuation of our classic views of vulnerable childhood as a period of innocent playfulness and of respite from the market and whose payoff is a better future for the human race.

Americans have always spoken out of two sides of the mouth about children. Even in the nineteenth century, some children were seen as largely irredeemable and were sent to institutions that were hardly better than prison breeding grounds. Much of today's discussion about the preciousness of children and outrage at their exploitation has a similar tendency to separate out the valuable (middle-class) child from the threatening (lowerclass or nonwhite) child. Nevertheless, reformers once employed the rhetoric of a universalized childhood and set themselves the goal of making it a real possibility. It is not necessary to trot out the old chestnut about the United States being the only country in the world (other than Somalia) not to sign the United Nations Charter of the Rights of the Child in order to make the point about the limits of our commitment (Fass and Mason 2000). The issue is much more complicated. I wonder, also, whether the particular sentimental Western version of childhood may not have outgrown its usefulness, becoming so stretched and cliché-ridden that it can no longer cover the needs of our own children, let alone the many children of the world and their different childhoods. Literary critic James Kincaid (1998) has argued that this distended vision leads necessarily to the subversion of innocence.

As the United States enters an increasingly competitive world marketplace, we may need to rethink our conception of a proper childhood, jettisoning some parts while holding fast to those that reflect a truly caring set of values that we hold for our children and should extend to others. Can we do this by valuing the special needs of children (and children do have special needs) while recognizing the exigencies of the many evolving economies and cultures in which child labor, including child prostitution, are necessary (Zelizer 2000)?[8] This not only is complex but also may involve us in apparent contradictions as we become better aware of the particulars of our own historical experience and more sensitive to the many cultures that global media are rapidly connecting. In this process, history can help because history is always a good witness to contradictions, sustaining our understanding of the ironic realities underlying them. Maybe history can also give us two kinds of particular knowledge: the awareness that certain values, however acquired, are worth retaining and an understanding that economics does not always rule.

Notes

1. For an interesting interpretation of the consequences of Western childrearing, see "Reflections on an American Identity" in Erikson 1963.

2. Herman Melville, *Redburn: His First Voyage*, quoted in Higham 1955:21.

3. It should be noted that this article had made its way into a debater's handbook in the late Progressive period, a sure sign of how important the issue had become and how knowledge about it was becoming widespread.

4. For a sense of the diverse treatments of children around the world at various historical times, see Ancient Greece and Rome, Islam, and Early Christianity in the

Encyclopedia of Children and Childhood in History and Society, edited by Paula S. Fass (2004).

5. For excellent documents on the anti–child labor campaign, see especially Robert Bremner and others 1971:601–755.

6. For the fascination with life in a disreputable city, see Judith R. Walkowitz 1992; see also my discussion of kidnapping as a means by which we reinforce our commitments to children in *Kidnapped: Child Abduction in America* (1997).

7. For an insightful discussion of how intimacy and market calculations can be part of the same calculus, see Zelizer 2000:817–848.

8. See the articles in Hecht 2002 and also Ehrenreich and Hochschild 2003 for a sense of the many issues involved.

3

Imagining Global Futures in China

The Child as a Sign of Value

Ann Anagnost

In 1992, a group of Chinese teens left their homes in the city for an international camping expedition to Mongolia. There they met up with a group of young people from Japan with whom they would march to a remote location and set up a campsite. The Chinese youth, according to published accounts of the trip, lacked the physical and psychological stamina to meet the challenge of survival in the wild. Even their backpacks and other gear began to come apart at the seams, as if the inferior quality of Chinese mass-produced consumer goods somehow indexed the lower quality not just of Chinese youth but also of the Chinese people as a whole. This event became something of a cause célèbre, arousing national alarm that Chinese children lacked the qualities that would enable them to compete successfully on a global stage. A newspaper editorial queried, "Are our children a match for Japanese children?"[1]

This incident triggered the incorporation of outdoor survival skills into the school curriculum, as shown by a news documentary on Shanghai television that I viewed in the fall of 1999. Children from an urban middle school were seen happily shouldering their backpacks and hiking to a public park where they set up camp and prepared a meal for themselves over an open fire. The scene might have recalled the mass mobilizations of their parents' generation for the project of socialist development during the

1960s.[2] However, the scene was closer in spirit to the international scouting movement in its focus on building individual character. The erasure of the preceding generation's historical experience was not accidental. Rather, the subject that this outdoor pedagogy was supposed to produce was quite different. What was now desired was the rugged individualist who can survive a struggle for competitive advantage, not the selfless socialist citizen willing to sacrifice his or her youth for the nation.

In this shift, we see an anxiety about national futures in relation to children. This relationship is not new but is one that has figured importantly in national modernity projects in East Asia, as well as elsewhere. The child represents an opening to the future, through which national culture can be remade. However, the specific ways in which this idea has taken form in the context of China's economic reforms must also be understood in a global frame. The shift to a market economy has transformed the stakes in the game of life, in which the individual, increasingly responsible for his or her own profits and losses, is more and more conscious of the cusp between success and failure. This anxiety is translated by parents into the project of ensuring that their only child will be prepared to deal with the heightened competition of a future in which economic opportunity and peril loom equally large. In this chapter, I explore the ways in which adult anxieties about children are central to the larger issue of how globalization is affecting national and personal futures.

THE CHILD AS A SIGN OF VALUE

Since the 1980s, the Chinese state has implemented a stringent policy of population reduction through the one-child family policy. This population policy is intimately linked with the changing value of bodies in a marketizing economy. However, the goal of one child per family has been more successfully achieved in urban areas because of the more effective application of sanctions for over-quota births. Alongside a concern with reducing population size, the state has also encouraged parents to improve the "quality" (*suzhi*) of their child through scientific methods of "superior nurture" (*yousheng youyu*). The Chinese phrase, often mistranslated as "eugenics," does not refer to a politics of racial purity but rather to a set of practices directed toward extracting to the fullest the "latent potential" of the child. Even if the child's "natural endowment" is quite ordinary, a "surplus value" can be produced through optimizing what nature has provided.

One form of potentiality is represented by early childhood. Parents begin their educational efforts during their child's infancy—in some cases, even prior to birth—to ensure that the child will have a competitive edge in exam success. Educational toys, nutritional supplements, private tutors, extracurricular classes, and after-school enrichment activities are new forms of investment in the child. The development of the child through an intensification of maternal labor and the multiplication of educational inputs promises to ensure family futures while also contributing to the transcendence of the nation from a state of backwardness to one of global mastery. These forms of consumption do not just produce social distinctions. They also participate in the logic of the market as a mechanism for sorting out categories of embodied value in a global labor arbitrage (Anagnost in press; Ong 2006; Ross 2006; Weiss, chapter 9, this volume).

The movement from a socialist planning to a market economy has formed this linkage between private domestic consumption and national development. The dismantling of the socialist state has meant massive layoffs of state sector workers, resulting in the loss of long-term job security, old-age pensions, health care, subsidized housing, and schooling for large sectors of China's urban populations. Peasant agriculture has also been devastated by disadvantageous pricing policies, unleashing a flow of peasant laborers from the poorer provinces to the more economically advanced areas. Both of these changes have opened up a widening chasm between wealth and poverty in China's new economy. Educated urban subjects are now taking up the state's notion of population quality to define their position within the new social order, using a language that refuses all references to "class" and the classic categories of Marxism.

Among the rising urban middle class, the poorer "quality" of the rural migrant becomes the "other" against which the "superior" quality of one's child can be measured. At the same time, the desired future for one's child is increasingly imagined on a global scale in which education abroad figures importantly. This has led to an intensified emphasis on academic success, the ultimate goal of which is to pass the college entrance examination and, ideally, go for graduate study abroad.

The Chinese government reinstated the nationwide college admissions exam in 1978, following a ten-year hiatus during the Cultural Revolution (1966–1976). Many of the urban youth who came of age during this earlier period were among the sent-down youth (*zhiqing*), who went to the countryside to "learn from the peasants" and help build socialism in rural areas.[3] Some went enthusiastically, caught up in the Maoist vision of rapid modernization through mass collective endeavor; others were less willing. Repatriated to the cities in the 1980s, the zhiqing generation found that the experience gained in the countryside had no value in the competitive new world of a market economy. Perhaps the most valuable quality acquired through this experience was what they refer to as "tempering" (*duanlian*), an ability to endure hardship and to "eat bitterness" (*chi ku*) through hard physical labor.

Deprived of opportunities for a university education, sent-down-generation parents were determined to make up for lost time through their children. This play of temporality resembles the strategies of the ill-fated Great Leap Forward in 1958, when the entire society was regimented around massive mobilizations for socialist development, resulting in three years of widespread famine. This desire to "speed up" time in a global race for development appears, in the 1990s, to have imploded into the private domain of the family. In both movements, we see the drive to develop intensively the material at hand (uphill terracing for grain cultivation during the Great Leap and early childhood education in the reform-era present), but with increasingly marginal returns. As we shall see, this intensification of childhood education also produces narratives of catastrophic failure.

As the pressure for preparing children for the university entrance exams increased, parents and others began to worry that the dependence on rote learning designed to produce exam success would limit their children's ability to apply what they have learned in practice. Training a child to be capable of standing up to the physical challenge of survival, as dramatized by the expedition in Mongolia, speaks to larger anxieties about what post-Maoist educational practices have wrought: a child who has been groomed for exam success but does not know how to take care of itself, how to respond with flexibility and creativity to new situations, or how to act independently. These anxieties about the child must, therefore, be located in a transnational network of gazes at the children of other nations. Moreover, these anxieties must also be seen in the context of the history of the modernity project in East Asia.

THE FIGURE OF THE CHILD IN EAST ASIAN MODERNITY PROJECTS

In the early twentieth century, the emergence of "the child" as a category of universal history became tied to the temporality of modern nationhood.[4] The child, as a category distinct from the adult, is a characteristic figure of modernity (along with Nation, Class, and History) that allows new possibilities to be thinkable. In the early twentieth century, the neologism *ertong* (children) entered the Chinese language, probably brought back by intellectuals who had gone to Japan for "modern" schooling. Ertong defined a new discursive object in the context of debates about educational reform, the emergence of a children's literature, and the definition of childhood psychology as an academic field in which the child, as a form of being distinct from that of the adult, became a primary site for scientific knowledge and cultural reform.[5]

Kojin Karatani suggests that the "discovery of the child" in Japan (and, I would argue, in China as well) was part of a complex process "whereby something which had never existed before came to be seen as self-evident....It is an allegorical representation of the material apparatuses of modernity" (Karatani 1993:193).[6] For Karatani, the figure of the child was closely connected to the simultaneous "discovery" of psychological interiority in the struggle to establish a modern self. This self was not opposed to the power of the modern state, as is sometimes presumed, but thoroughly implicated in it. "The modern nation state itself is an educational apparatus that produces 'the human being'" (Karatani 1993:132). Notions of modern citizenship were premised on a concept of individuality tied to the notion of psychological interiority, which, itself, is deeply tied to ideas about childhood as the origin of adult subjectivity. The child represented the possibility of a fresh beginning for adult subjectivity. The "overwhelming dominance of the West" is what made the establishment of the modern state and the production of psychological interiority "ineluctable" (Karatani 1993:95). Western norms of subjectivity had the power to define modern subjectivity for people in East Asia.

In East Asian modernities, the child also became closely tied to ideas of time and temporality central to definitions of the modern as the telos of history.[7] Stefan Tanaka, in exploring the temporality of the child in Japanese modernity, suggests:

> Childhood has become a symbol for...that idealized past or orig-
> inary state that must be guided and transformed....It is a site
> where the ambiguities and contradictions of modernity are ame-
> liorated into a coherent whole personified through the child.
> That is, the human body serves as an object that makes the
> abstractions of modernity seem natural. [Tanaka 1997:21–22]

The child, like the national past, represents a place of origin for the adult subject and, by extension, for the modern nation-state. In this sense, the child gives the nation a place of new beginning in the overcoming of the national past. The developmental time of the nation, stretching from "deep" antiquity into the future, becomes condensed in the developmental time of the child in the project to produce new citizens through the education of the young. If the "folk" become emblematic of the past, then the child becomes the paradigmatic figure of national futures.

The child enabled the formation of new forms of discursive practice and knowledge, becoming visible in a new way as "abstracted and isolated from a traditional *lebenswelt* [lifeworld]" (Karatani 1993:127). The making of the child as a domain of knowledge is exemplified by the new science of child psychology and explorations of children's subjective worlds through literature. These endeavors do not reveal the "true child" to us so much as they constitute the child as an object to be known (Karatani 1993:127–128). This process of abstracting and separating becomes implicit in the institutions of power of the modern nation-state. As Stefan Tanaka notes, "modern societies are organized around categorical hierarchies of learning, growth, development, and civility (self-control), a corollary of which is the notion of maturation" (Tanaka 1997:23). Karatani sees the institution of compulsory education in Meiji Japan as effectively uprooting children "as abstract and homogeneous entities" from the "productive relations, social classes, and communities that had previously been their concrete contexts" (Karatani 1993:130). Hugh Cunningham has noted:

> The period from 1870 to 1914 is seen by many historians of different countries as one in which the state began to take a markedly more prominent role in the regulation of family life and in which a definition of childhood as properly a period of dependence became dominant....The main intervention was the introduction of compulsory schooling: this not only had its effects on the management of the family economy but also gave the state the opportunity to try to impose middle-class standards of speech, dress, deportment, and "civilization." [Cunningham 1998:1201]

In 1920, Zhou Zuoren, one of the most prominent Chinese intellectuals among those educated in Japan, wrote of China's "discovery" of the child:

> Formerly, men did not properly understand children, if not treating them as miniature adults to be nurtured by the classics, then ignoring them as ignorant and incomplete small people. Only recently have we known that, although children are somewhat biologically and psychologically different from adults, they are still complete individuals with their own inner and outer life. [Zhou 1920:1][8]

The reform of education in China, influenced by the ideas of John

Dewey, who came to China in 1919 to give a series of lectures in Beijing, was a project to impress upon educators and parents the importance of designing educational practices suited to the child's inherent nature. This idea of child-centered education (*ertong zhongxinlun*) was not limited to schooling. Rather, it implied a radical reorganization of the "modern" family around the function of child nurture. In China, debates about family reform held up the Western nuclear family (*xiao jiating*, literally "small family") as the model for reforming the extended patrilineal family (*da jiating*, literally "large household"). This reorientation of family life around the child was seen as the necessary condition for creating a new kind of national subject, not just in terms of the adult the child would someday become but also in the revisioning of citizenship through elaboration of the role of parenthood.

In the literature of the 1920s cultural reform movement, early childhood emerged as a phase of development distinctively different from adolescence and adulthood.[9] The child was understood to possess a playful creative power and a connection to the material world that should be nurtured, rather than destroyed by the deadly regimentation of traditional schooling (Anderson 1990). The emergence of children's literature alongside "folklore studies" (Zhou Zuoren was instrumental in establishing both) also tied the child metaphorically to the orality of a primordial Chinese culture as a point of origin for the national essence that effectively bypassed the corruption of the Confucian literary culture.[10] By the end of the 1920s, however, for reasons complexly related to the onset of civil war, the figure of a revolutionary peasantry became the site of revolutionary transformation for many cultural reformers.[11]

In the socialist era (1949–1978), the child's potential as the uncertain site of cultural reform became anchored by its refiguration as a "blank slate" upon which Maoist political pedagogy could work its rupture with the past and inscribe a new socialist subject subsumed within the collectivity. The mobilization of a generation of "revolutionary successors" climaxed in the violent excesses of the Cultural Revolution (1966–1976) that demonstrated all the more forcibly the indeterminacy of these kinds of political investments in children and youth. It is ironic that members of the Red Guard generation, who have grown up to become "modern" parents and avid consumers of new modes of childrearing expertise, now view the era of their youth as the time of the historic regression of the Chinese nation. Their practices of parenting have become the medium through which they can "catch up" and regain what they have lost, through active intervention to ensure the mental and material quality of their only child.

The present focus on population quality is reminiscent of concerns first expressed early in this century about the need to "refashion" the Chinese people into a modern citizenry. Both Chinese children and "the masses" (*qunzhong*) are viewed as possessing a potentiality of untapped national vitality that needs to be freed from weaknesses in the national character. Together, they form the ground for any discussion of a national pedagogy. Yet they also share an indeterminacy that inspires fear as much as hope, a performativity that may prove difficult to rein in, threatening the authoritarian structures of the state and domestic orders.

HUMAN CAPITAL FORMATION IN A GLOBAL FRAME

This earlier history of how children have figured in national modernity projects is important because of the ways in which the concerns of the 1920s seem to resonate so powerfully with those of the late twentieth century. Both moments saw the valorization of the "modern family" as a privatized space for the production of value in the child at a time when China was becoming integrated into a global economy, although on vastly different terms. China is no longer a semicolony. It possesses a strong government that can strategically engage with global forces in its own plans to develop the national economy.

The current era of economic reform has also seen a similar cultural obsession with the contradictory potentialities of the child, which juxtaposes the notion of unleashing the child's "natural" creativity and the specter of indiscipline and chaos. Anxieties about the failures of parenting haunt the social realm, not just in terms of the children who fail to make the grade (what Nickola Pazderic [2004:197] has called "success's requisite failures," writing in the context of Taiwan) but also in terms of a generation of "little emperors" (*xiao huangdi*) whose self-centeredness may not be easy to harness for collective social goals. However, another figure that haunts parental hopes is the child who cannot "face society" (*mianbudui shehui*) because of the exhaustive regimentation between school and family, leading to tragic stories of incapacitating mental distress and even suicide (for parallels in Japan, see Lock 1991 and Field 1995). Hence, the child's capacity to yield a latent potential presents to the parents (and the nation) a limit point in this strategy of human capital formation.

Although many parents express ambitions for their child to become a member of a global superclass, such as those who strive for college admissions at prestigious "brand-name universities" (*mingpai daxue*) abroad, the desire for many others is much more modest. If one were to ask, as I did innumerable times, what parents most hope for their child, the most common answer would be, "I hope that my child will be a person who can be useful to society." At first, I thought that they were referring to socialist models of citizenship, but I discovered that they were saying something quite different. Given the uncertainties of a global economic system, they wanted to prepare their children to meet the challenge of the constantly changing demands of the market. A father who must be included in my sample of "disappointed parents" (his son seemed more interested in becoming a rock musician than a scholar—a very different route to achieving globality) confided to me that not everyone aspires for his or her child to be admitted to Harvard. "What parents want is very simple," he said. "It is merely to make sure that their child will be deemed employable for the extent of their working lives." However, even this modest goal seems daunting enough at a time when no sector of employment is without a sense of risk and expendability in a global labor regime.

Therefore, in this desire to be "useful to society," we see a displacement of the social by the economic, in which the national body itself—what embodies the very life and vitality of the nation—is translated from an organic conception of the "people-nation" to a more abstract totality of "the national economy."[12] In this context, a very different calculus of one's life chances emerges, in which some bodies have more value than others and in which some must be sacrificed.[13] The cusp of success and failure divides those who can win a measure of job security and those whose livelihood will always be in a state of peril. The project then becomes one of building as much quality as one can into the child to ensure its competitiveness in a radically transformed horizon of opportunities and risks. The rapid rise of a conspicuously wealthy entrepreneurial class plays against the massive layoffs of state sector workers and the devaluation of rural life. The task for parents is to do everything they can to ensure that their child does not fall into the category of "redundant labor."

THE AGENCY OF THE MOTHER

In this new logic of value creation, the family becomes a space for the production of affective value that nonetheless lies *outside* the logic of market relations insofar as it rests on the unpaid labor of mothering. New notions of women's role as parents are necessary to the creation of certain kinds of value, even as they lie in tension with competing notions of self-development and personal freedom that circulate powerfully as modern "techniques of the self."[14] This tension marks what Lisa Rofel (1999) calls "the fissuring" of China's modernity project: the nation's natural progression to modernity is seen as blocked by the problem of unequal development. This is true not just in economic terms but also in the production of modern, civilized citizen-subjects that issue from certain family arrangements. In this respect, we see how ideologies of motherhood in China are highly aware of the history of other modernities, such as the one detailed by Paula Fass for the United States (chapter 2, this volume). The history of Chinese feminism is complexly related to new rhetorical practices of women's self-development (*ziwo fazhan*) that were also defining new forms of neoliberal subjectivity in the 1990s.[15] The emergence of the female professional has outpaced what is construed as a historical lag in the evolution of the family. In 1990s China, some intellectuals cautioned that feminism had come too soon to China. Women's labor as mothers must be harnessed for developing modern citizens for the nation and its task of meeting the challenge of globalization. Then and only then can China become truly modern and women be free to pursue their own career goals.

As a result, the mother has become a figure that must be "(re)discovered" (*faxian muqin*) in the reorganization of gendered subjectivities.[16] Maternal labor is a necessary supplement to overcome the delays of history. This recent prescription for such a role for women is not the first time it has been articulated by intellectuals as a societal concern. More than a hundred years ago, social reformer Liang Qichao advocated female education so that women would become superior mothers and thereby raise the condition of the race as a whole.

Why then is it that the mother has now become a figure that must be "discovered" anew? This question can be understood only by retracing the history of how "maternal love" (*mu ai*) came under attack during the Cultural Revolution as a concept of bourgeois educational philosophy. Mother love was seen as a form of selfish love antagonistic to the cultivation of love for the proletariat. This critique also took place in the arena of education. The image of the teacher as a "gardener" who nurtures the natural development of the child through love was supplanted by the image of the teacher as an "engineer of the soul" (*linghun de gongchengshi*), whose task was to develop and strengthen the child's political thought and class viewpoint.[17] This position was in line with the class politics of the time, in which children were expected to draw a firm class line between themselves and class enemies, even if their own parents were among the latter. If the critique of mother love under Maoism was an indictment of the private intimacy of the family, then its resurrection in the 1990s was a move to revalorize this domain of family life.

This shift is also tied to the emergence of a new middle class in 1990s China. The state project to "grow the economy" by unleashing market forces is also linked to "growing a middle class" as a goal of government. The expansion of a middle class, which is statistically still small (somewhere between 2 and 15 percent of the total population, depending on how this status is defined), is the desire not just of those who aspire to middle-class status but also of state planners. Chinese sociologists describe Chinese society as possessing a pyramidal structure (*jinzi ta*), a dangerously unstable configuration when compared with the desired "olive-shape" society (*ganlanxing*), which is fat in the middle and pointed at the two extremes (Qin 1999:15). The formation of a large middle class would add ballast to a society undergoing increasing economic polarization between the haves and have-nots.[18] However, this divide is masked to some extent by a discursive shift from Maoist categories of "class" (*jieji*) to a new language of "social strata" (*shehui jieceng*), in which individuals aspire to clamber up the social ladder through their personal investment in their own embodied human capital. The realm of private life was an important arena in 1990s China for the creation of new forms of body capital (for example, consumer taste and class distinction). Therefore, it should not be surprising that, alongside this strategy of capital accumulation, we find also a reorganization of the affective life of the family.

In 1990s China, the officially sanctioned household was the "three-mouth family" (*sankou jiating*) of two parents, one child. Current discourses on the family should, therefore, be understood as a radical revisioning of family life as a place where value is created. This reformulation is suggested by the title of a textbook, *Jiajiao de geming* (A Revolution in Family Education), written for use in parenting school (*jiazhang xuexiao*), an institution that links the discipline of the school with that of the family. The idea of "revolution" (*geming*)—which dominated the Maoist years as a program of radical social change that, in some senses, devalued the family—is now imploded inward into familial space. In much of the childrearing literature that proliferated throughout the 1990s, the idea of "family education" (*jiating jiaoyu*) is produced in a closely articulated division of labor with the school (*xuexiao jiaoyu*) and with society (*shehui jiaoyu*). The family becomes the primary "stage" (*wutai*) for educating the child.

But the target of this pedagogy is not the child alone. Through the discourse and practice of "family education," the family becomes open to the penetration of a new organization of governmentality intent on the project of producing private life. In the midst of this new economy of power, the subject position of "parent" (*fumu*) or "family head" (*jiazhang*) becomes central to the transformation of political reason in reform-era China. These changes are particularly visible in the gendering of parental roles.

The mother is charged with the responsibility for early childhood education to give her child a head start in schooling. Time spent with her child becomes a time that can realize the potentiality for value in the child. The mother's daily interactions with the child address the child's cognitive development. Salons (*shalong*) in urban areas, in which women gather (in coffee houses or private homes) to discuss the challenges they face in raising their only child, set up new models for maternal citizenship. The mother is expected to spend time with her child, engaging in activities that will promote the child's cognitive development in the form of educative play. She should also seek out resources increasingly available for purchase: parenting magazines and other forms of expert knowledge.

Whereas the mother is in charge of the child's domestic education, the father must take charge of the child's introduction to the larger social world and encourage its independence. Yet parents with whom I talked insisted repeatedly that this distinction between the formulaic "stern father, loving mother" (*yanfu cimu*) constantly broke down. Often, the mother would take on the disciplinary role, especially in reference to schooling, because of the father's absence due to the demands of career and the male-centric, after-hours sociality that is becoming increasingly demanded of white-collar workers. The father is charged with the responsibility of exercising the law so that the child learns the behavior necessary for a smooth insertion into the disciplinary structures of a wider social world. It is the father who sets high expectations for the child and guides the child's behavior with praise and supportive criticism, in contrast to the mother's unconditional love.

The father's role is to wean the child away from overdependence on the mother. Nonetheless, this concern about the child's ability to take care of itself recurs in discussions about the putative deficiencies of the Chinese child. This concern on the part of parents is added to another anxiety that stems from the apparent inability of Chinese children to apply in practice what they have learned in school. According to my informants, as well as much of the popular educational literature, this failure is due to the overvaluing of test scores in competition for college admissions, resulting in a dearth of practical knowledge. All these concerns became expressed through a discourse of educational reform known as *suzhi jiaoyu* (quality education), defined in opposition to an education that is primarily focused on test results. The discursive deployment of *suzhi* (quality) is important to note here, although the oft preferred translation as "all-round education" is meant to suggest a more balanced curriculum that values hands-on experiential learning over rote memorization of facts.

A parallel anxiety over the child's apparent inability to "face society" (*miandui shehui*) also suggests a site of crisis. The child, incarcerated by the heightened demands for exam success, becomes a figure of stunted social development, severely incapacitated in developing social relations and fearful (*danzi xiao*, literally "small of kidney") of having to go out into the world. I heard numerous examples of how this social phobia has led to nervous breakdowns and even suicide. Concern for the child's fragility has expanded the discourse on the child's quality to the realm of "psychological quality" (*xinli suzhi*). This image of the damaged psyche calls forth the emergence of what Donzelot calls the "psy"—forces that encircle the middle-class family threatened by the scent of catastrophic failure. As Donzelot (1997[1979]:225) suggested for the history of childhood in Europe, the rising Chinese middle class also can no longer afford the luxury of allowing its children to fail. I was struck by the example of one young man I interviewed. He had set himself up as an adolescent psychologist, his consulting room a little islet of civility in a neighborhood he refers to as the *pinminku* (this is how Chinese translations of Marx's *Das Kapital* rendered "ghettoes of the poor" in a spectral return to the Maoist past). There he awaits a middle class that has not yet quite emerged to pay his 40 yuan (about $5) per hour fee![19]

THE COMMODIFICATION OF CHILDHOOD

The emphasis on the child's latent potential was echoed widely in the rapidly expanding consumer economy of the early 1990s, which began to offer an ever-expanding variety of goods and services devoted to the project of developing the bodily quality and intellectual capacities of the very young.[20] These new patterns of consumption were part of the expansion of "technologies of the self" that proliferated in the new economy of the 1990s. Although consumption is certainly tied to the production of new forms of social distinction, it is also very much connected to ideas of "self-development" (ziwo fazhan), as well as to models of "self care" in an era of shrinking healthcare benefits. These health concerns become folded into the proliferation of new products designed especially for children. Concerns about environmental pollution, exacerbated by the degradation of air and water quality in the freewheeling entrepreneurial culture, also play into consumer desire for healthful tonics and organically produced foods (*lüse shipin*). Concerns about the environment, which have a potential for wider political mobilizations, are thus privatized in the production of new forms of commodities for those who can afford them.

In this context, the bodily quality of the child becomes expressed through very material concerns about height and the development of cognitive functioning. Sometimes these concerns take on a fetish quality. Before his death in 1989, Hu Yaobang, a member of the central party leadership, was an advocate for chocolate and dairy products as contributing to the physical quality of children's bodies. In the early 1990s, I remember seeing potato chip packaging claiming that its contents can "open up" (*kai zhili*) childhood intelligence.[21] One must note the preponderance of highly processed cereals and snack foods in this category of "children's food" (*ertong shipin*). All these foods are associated with Western consumption practices, so a metonymic logic seems at work here, a form of contagious magic in which consuming the food of the other can effect a transubstantiation. My son's Chinese caretaker, a retired children's nurse, became convinced that the oatmeal I served my children every morning was an important causal factor in their "superior" bodily quality, converting her into an avid propagandist for the virtues of this humble commodity, which was being newly repackaged as a "children's food" (*ertong liangshi*).

In this new regime of childrearing, the parent becomes the manager of the child's development, and the child becomes a site of both capital and emotional investment. The malleability of the child's body and its responsiveness to capital inputs enhance its quality. In the face of this consumer demand, educational commodities proliferate in the form of privatized schooling and educational toys that promise to promote the child's development.[22] An example of the latter are toys that require manual dexterity and cognitive awareness in the assembly of complex tiny parts (*pincha wanju*), such as Lego-like building systems and jigsaw puzzles. Special shops catering to the needs of the very young have become a highly visible presence in most city centers and even in neighborhood markets.

This commercial opportunism links the official project of the Chinese party-state to improve the bodily and mental "quality" (suzhi) of the population with family strategies to ensure that their child's blocked reproductive potential results in a single "high-quality" child. The child's singularity intensifies this investment as a site where anxieties about an uncertain future can be allayed through an active intervention. The subjectivity of the "modern parent" is solicited on all sides by the market, the media, and the proliferation of expert knowledge about childhood development. Parents are incited to be actively involved in their child's education even before birth. This interest in educating the child in utero explains, perhaps, a modern reworking of the older practice of "fetal education" (*taijiao*), in which the fetus is imagined as already receptive to commodified inputs scientifically applied.[23] Here we see how this project is invested with a temporal urgency.

Obsession with early childhood education is by no means limited to China. It is a newly intensified concern in North America, where interest in the latent potentiality of early childhood cognitive development articulates with the withdrawal of the state from its responsibilities for public education. Early education becomes a central focus in this context as addressing a time in the child's development that will yield the most profit. If a window of opportunity in early childhood is passed, then later educational interventions might no longer be considered "cost-effective." Educational spending can target just those moments when it can produce the most bang for the buck—an interesting refraction of the "just-in-time" production logics of flexible accumulation.

The loss of time signifies a loss in the full development of the child's potentiality, threatening to put the child at a disadvantage. The implication is that "normal" developmental progression can be sped up by early intervention. Many parents hope that commodities promising to produce developmental precocity will give their child an edge in the competition to get into preschool. The managerialization of childhood entails an obsessive commodity fetishism that makes the child's education an investment (*jiaoyu touzi*). It also requires the intensification of time as a continuously productive time. Time itself is an investment of value in the child's body as a time "completed" (Foucault 1979:156).[24] The accumulation of completed time is measured in the child's embodied capacities. Colorfully illustrated workbooks offering IQ tests (as a kind of "play") to measure the child's intellectual development, according to age, are very revealing of the high expectations against which the child's accomplishment is being measured, not against a "norm" but in terms of how effective the parents have been in extracting a "surplus" from the fund of latent potential.[25] Again, I cannot help but ironically draw attention to this Great Leap Forward mentality that, like its earlier counterpart, insists on exploiting a logic of increasingly marginal utility through additional inputs of (here maternal) labor. What is new is perhaps a capitalization on the temporality of youth itself (see chapters 5 and 7 by Cole and Durham, respectively, this volume) in a society in which older cohorts of workers are becoming increasingly disvalued as redundant labor through massive layoffs.

For parents who grew up during the Cultural Revolution, the emphasis on early childhood education signifies an opportunity to regain the time lost from their own educational histories. Much could be said about the experience of temporality under socialism and its reform. The Cultural Revolution is remembered by some as a time "lost," and the Maoist era more generally as a time of developmental stasis. The present becomes invested as a time for "catching up." The expanded responsibility of parents thereby becomes a way to fill in a gap they locate as indelibly a part of themselves. Parents of that age, however, are often nostalgic about the "tempering" acquired from their experience in Maoist mobilizations, which they feel continues to mark their bodies and their character with strengths and virtues they find themselves unable to replicate in their children. The quality of "tempering" suggests a ghostly presence of a different kind of collective national project, but one that has, in a sense, become privatized as an element of biography through which the subject narrates a *bildung* of survival in the political chaos of the past.

In the demolition of the socialist project, that which once had value has now been evacuated of it. The tempering this generation of parents acquired through a tumultuous and now negated past also has a value in the present. Moreover, it is a value that a new generation of urban youth growing up in the relative economic ease and political stability of the 1980s and 1990s does not have. Tempering is what the generation of sent-down youth of the Maoist period received in place of schooling. It marks a place of lack (of proper educational credentials) and of supplementation (enabling them to confront the new harsh realities of unemployment and economic uncertainty).[26] For their only child, education becomes the supplement for what they lack, but at the cost of a certain psychological fragility, an inability to face the challenges of a new competitive terrain. For a slightly younger cohort of parents, who were young children during the Cultural Revolution, this period offers yet another object of nostalgia, of a carefree childhood on a permanent holiday from school. This image of a "happy childhood" (*tongkuai de tongnian*) often crops up in their desires for their children. The return to childhood as a utopic space of innocence and play is suggestive in relation to Paula Fass's query (chapter 2, this volume) about what we might want to retain from modernist constructions of the child. In this context, the idea of happy childhood represents an imaginary space outside the demands of neoliberal subjecthood and the competitive struggle for survival.

THE CHILD IN CRISIS

The child is therefore to be pitied. Childhood is in danger of becoming a time of ceaseless labor and struggle in a way that fails to respect children's inherent nature and their need for movement and play. Hence, something "of value" is perceived to be lost. This "something" is not always easy to define, yet it, too, is not immune from being folded into a calculus of the child's embodied "capital." It is something that registers as missing from the dispirited body of the child forced to labor too long, a loss of a certain inquisitiveness, of an ability to interact creatively with the opportunities at hand, to face the world bravely, to be in command of the situation. In other words, the regimentation of childhood ultimately fails to produce a fully modern subject, one who is independent, self-confident, and fearless in confronting new situations (see Flanagan, chapter 6, this volume, for a discussion of the psychological costs that global capital has normalized).

One working-class mother expressed these concerns in terms of her daughter's timidity and her attempts to address it by seeking out a prominent elocution teacher. This educational input was one she could barely afford, but she felt that it was essential to her child's psychological well-being. The mother was bitter about the pressure put on her daughter by the educational system, but she also attributed her daughter's lack of confidence to the child's being somewhat overweight and subject to teasing. Elocution classes (*langsong*) are offered by after-school enrichment programs and are tuition based. The goal of these classes is to teach the child to speak well. (In the particularly egregious cases of the overly regimented child, I had noted a tendency in some to speak in a plaintive tone that interferes with clear speech.) But these classes teach more than just proper enunciation of the national dialect (*putong hua*); they also invest the body with a stage presence. They pose the body and teach the child a language of bodily gestures borrowed from Chinese theatrical traditions. Children who excel in these skills enter into local competitions and may even compete at the provincial and national levels.

The content of the langsong presentation is also of interest in that it exemplifies a technique of "values education" (*deyu*). Topics may range from the somewhat worn themes of party ideology to more contemporary themes. One young friend performed for me a eulogy to Zhou Enlai's threadbare and tattered blanket, evoking his travails before the party came to power and exemplifying the values of frugality, endurance, and political rectitude.[27] A langsong teacher in her mid-sixties who is quite celebrated in Nanjing performed for me a declamation of her own composition on the perils of eating too much chocolate, taking on the embodied persona of a young girl.

This latter performance presented to the viewer a somewhat startling substitution of bodies in the sense of scripting what the adult imagines that the child should be. The child receives the lesson from the recitation of the langsong teacher and then learns to internalize it in her own recitation, in which she occupies the subjective position of the "I" as one who must learn to resist the temptations of the tantalizing and ubiquitous presence of the edible commodity. The topic engages with the problem of overconsumption, presumably leading to overweight children, a growing problem among a new generation of urban kids who have never known hunger pangs due to food being in short supply. Hence, my friend's conviction that this sort of training would help her daughter seemed to be working at more than one level. However, my observation of another langsong class, in which the teacher ran from child to child, physically adjusting their posture and moving them through their gestures, muttering denigrating comments all the while about their eating too much candy, caused me to question how effective the experience could be in boosting the children's confidence in their presentation of self.

This concern for overweight children is one that is often expressed. The immobilization of the child employed in the sedentary labor of schoolwork; the lack of sibling playmates; the increasing isolation in the new urban apartment blocks, where access to outside play spaces is impeded by time (too busy); security concerns (a fear of child-napping); and distance (high-rise dwellings) are often blamed for children's inactivity, not to mention the substitute sociality of television viewing and IM,[28] as well as the ready availability of snack and franchise foods. The overweight child marks the failure of intensified child nurture in producing the trim bodies required by neoliberal subjecthood. This condition therefore leads to more consumption of weight-loss products, weight reduction programs in summer camps, exercise classes, and all the rest.

The problems of timidity, the inability to present oneself with confidence, the tendency to weight gain, all threaten a transubstantiation of the body that is counter to the new ideal. In the new bodily aesthetic, height is valued just as much as slimness, evidenced by the commercial promotion of calcium supplements on television. Exceptionally tall children are shown next to considerably shorter parents to demonstrate the efficacy of these supplements to overcome heredity or, perhaps more accurately, a past family history of inadequate nutrition. A number of urban parents I interviewed originally came from the countryside and described childhoods of poverty and famine, the death of siblings from malnutrition and disease, especially during the three-year period following the disastrous production policies of the Great Leap Forward in 1958. Short stature is often attributed to a peasant diet and inadequate nutrition. Therefore, greater height demonstrates the bodily register of a flight from rurality, a body that has been radically reshaped by modern regimes of nurture. Through the magic of televisuality, the viewer is surreally carried into the organic processes of cell biology in a graphic demonstration of the calcium supplement's superior capability to be absorbed by the body.[29] And if the window of opportunity is missed for lengthening the bones during the child's growth and development, bone-lengthening surgery is available for those aspiring to greater height.

COMPETITIVE CHILDHOODS

In *Precious Children*, a 1999 television documentary (channel KCTS, http://www.pbs.org/kcts/preciouschildren/, accessed December 2007) that follows a group of early childhood educators from the Seattle area on a tour of China's new elite schools, we view scene after scene of very young children performing for foreign guests: exhibitions of musical virtuosity, competitive ballroom dancing, demonstrations of calligraphy and Chinese painting skills. While the American teachers applaud what they see as evidence that the arts are better supported in Chinese schools, they are not unaware that the educational skills displayed to them are available to only a very small proportion of Chinese children in primarily urban areas.[30] Nonetheless, this high level of achievement demonstrated by very small children puts Western educators into a quandary. On the one hand, it challenges what they consider to be age-appropriate for the developmental stage of early childhood. Throughout the film, they keep asking, "How do you get children at such a young age to stay on task?" The answer that persistently comes back is "Culture!" Here we see them caught up in the mirror image of the contradiction that Chinese parents and teachers face, between their desire for producing in their children the qualities of creativity and independence that they envision as necessary for "getting on track with the world" (*yu shijie jiugui*) and their desire for cultural reproduction through obedience and respect for elders (Anagnost 1997; Fong 2007:90).[31] Although the American teachers decry what they see as the over-regimentation of childhood for this elite strata of Chinese students, they manifest a sense of growing insecurity about whether their own teaching practices set high enough expectations for their students.

In this articulation of doubt, we also see mirrored an anxiety about larger concerns: the continuing competitiveness of the United States in a globalizing world. Globalization, in this context, registers an expansion of how life futures are imagined as taking place upon a global stage as the preeminent place for self-development (Appadurai 1991). In this respect, the child becomes a site of speculative investment in global *futures* (in the market-inflected meaning of this word).[32] However, also embedded in this anxiety is a concern over the changing boundary between public and private, in which education is becoming increasingly commodified, creating new inequalities of access to resources that can guarantee success in the new world order. If arts in the schools are increasingly seen as an expendable frill, if a return to basics means stripping the schools down to producing a basic standard measured by way of test scores, if test scores become a measure of "accountability" that restructures schooling according to market models of efficiency, then that which exceeds the logic of this calculation becomes transformed into commodified access to "quality" education, a commodification, moreover, that is proceeding as rapidly, if not more, in China as it is in the United States.[33]

Acknowledgments

My interest in this topic was first inspired by discussions with Sharon Stephens, and I dedicate this chapter to her memory. I would like to acknowledge the School for Advanced Research's advanced seminar program for its support of this project. I thank Jennifer Cole and Deborah Durham for organizing the conference and for their indefatigable editorial rigor and also the other conference participants for a week of rich discussion. Research support for this study was kindly provided by the American Council of Learned Societies (through the Committee for Scholarly Communication with China), the National Endowment for the Humanities, and the University of Washington Royalty Research Fund.

Notes

1. The author of *Huangjin jiajiao* (Lin 1999:319) refers to this essay, "Woman de haizi shi Riben ren de duishou ma?" (Are Our Children a Match for Japanese?), which appeared in a Guangzhou periodical, *Huangjin shidai* (The Golden Age). The word for match (*duishou*) is noteworthy here. See also Sun 1999[1993]. The Chinese word encompasses the sense of being both a matching counterpart (a mirror image of the other) and an adversary (literally "the opposing hand") in a competition. See Fong 2007 for another interpretation of the significance of this event.

2. See Selzer 1992 for an account of how scouting fits into nationalist models of human engineering in liberal democracies. The organization of youth in socialist regimes has a parallel history in which similar sorts of goals were pursued (character building, physical development, citizenship training, and patriotic feeling), but in a socialist frame.

3. *Zhiqing* is an abbreviation of *zhishi qingnian* (intellectual youth), referring to those youth, mostly from urban areas, who had received secondary education and

above. The rustication policy relocated urban youth to the rural areas because of the lack of jobs for them in the city. In the countryside, they took up positions as teachers in rural schools and participated in agricultural work as a way of reducing the burden of their upkeep on peasant communities. Presumably, their education there was one of grappling with brute necessity, endurance, and hard physical labor—the antithesis of the intellectual labor of formal schooling that had once conferred class privilege.

4. For a stunning example of such an approach, see Lydia Liu's 1993 exploration of "individualism" as a category of a "translated modernity" among cultural reformers in the 1920s.

5. Before this time, the characters *er* or *tong* might refer to children within the network of kin relations, but never, taken together, to children as a generic category. In the *Cihai* (Sea of Words), the authoritative Chinese dictionary, *ertong* does not appear by itself but is always tied to another binomial, such as *ertong xinli* (child psychology) and *ertong wenxue* (children's literature). These categories are exemplary of how the child figures as a new kind of object for scientific knowledge production and as a subject who can be addressed through a literature that speaks to the special nature of the child. Here Foucault's concept of discourse as a regime of institutions and practices that constitute the object of knowledge is critical. For education, see Bailey 1990; for children's literature, see Farquhar 1999; and for psychology, see Jones 2002.

6. Fredric Jameson, in his foreword to Karatani's (1993) book, describes this notion of inversion as a moment when the historical turns into the natural and "generates an illusion of temporal depth and continuity—a past! The illusion of a past!—where there was none before" (Jameson 1993:x–xi). Brett de Bary, in her introduction to the book, describes it as that which appears to be "timeless nature" but "has a point of origin, a historicity that has been repressed" (de Bary 1993:5).

7. See Duara 1995 for a discussion of the temporality of the modern nation state.

8. One cannot help but note how this passage would seem to anticipate Philippe Ariès's 1962[1960] argument about the modernity of the idea that the child has an essential nature different from that of adults.

9. For a classic historical work on how "youth" (*qingnian*) became thematized at this time as a revolutionary force in its rebellious overthrow of an oppressive traditional culture, see Chow 1967. Bing Xin's *Letters to Young Readers* (*Ji xiao duzhe*) (1949[1923–1926]) offers a look at the relative positions occupied by children and youth (or adolescence) in the thinking of the cultural reformers of the 1920s. She addresses her young readers from a position that has already fallen away from an uncorrupted purity, although she herself was barely out of her teens when she wrote this.

10. For a study of the emergence of folklore studies in China, see Hung 1985. See Chow 1995 for a discussion of how the figure of the child as the place of new

beginning becomes reprised in the intellectual debates of the 1980s.

11. Marston Anderson's (1990) thoughtful discussion of Ye Shengtao's (1958[1929]) novel *Schoolmaster Ni Huanzhi* explores this shift in the politics of the failed revolution of 1927 that led to the split between the Kuomintang and the Communist parties.

12. See Mitchell 2002 for a discussion of "the national economy" as an enframing device for a new logic of governance emerging after World War II and how this has not disappeared but become increasingly salient with globalization.

13. In 1990s China, this sacrifice took the form of massive layoffs of state sector workers in the cities and increasing impoverishment of agriculture in the rural areas. Both result from the transfer of collectively owned assets into entrepreneurial capital for a few. Industrial accidents mostly borne by the bodies of migrant laborers are another form of sacrifice in a system that views them as a disposable resource in the calculus of capital accumulation and in which access to affordable health care is shrinking.

14. The project of self-development is perhaps not unrelated to Jennifer Cole's discussion (chapter 5, this volume) of *fivoarana* as a form of technology of the self. The mother's project of self-development may be understood as having been transferred to the project of developing the embodied value of her only child. However, this does not necessarily mean that she abandons work on herself. Rather, she is incited to be a "modern parent" as the necessary precondition for her to rear a child who can be successful in a globalized future.

15. See Barlow 1994 for a discussion of the twisting course of feminist politics in modern China.

16. *Faxian muqin* (Discovering Mother) is, in fact, the title of an excessively long-winded, two-volume rumination on the necessity of reinvesting motherhood with value for China's modernity project. Donghua Wang, the author of this work (1999), has toured China's major cities since its publication, giving workshops on "maternal education" (*mujiao*). He has become somewhat of an entrepreneur, demonstrating the commodity value of this discourse. See Barlow 2001 on how this argument plays out among China's feminist scholars.

17. See Jin 2000:306–310 and Si 1999:199–201 for recent arguments on the necessity for retrieving what was lost in teaching practice under Maoism. In 1963, Si Xia was a teacher in the primary lab school attached to Nanjing Normal College. Her pedagogy specifically came under attack during the Cultural Revolution, only to be resurrected in the educational discourses of the 1990s. The binomial *yuanding* is translated only as "gardener" in the 1981 edition of the *Han Ying cidian*, but in the 1997 revision, "schoolteacher" was added back in as its secondary meaning.

18. "Class polarization" (*liangji fenhua*) was a specter frequently invoked as a call

to reinvigorate class struggle in the political movements of the Maoist period. Although China appears to have put to rest a Maoist class politics, they retain a ghostly presence that haunts the present.

19. This young man's qualifications were based on a master's degree in philosophy and a degree of self-education available through a popular psychological literature now circulating in translation from English and other languages. This textual production speaks to a whole new area of "self-care" that has grown in the wake of the neoliberal restructuring of self and society. Nonetheless, despite the present "coldness" of the market for this new professional, there is real psychological pain being produced. However, when I advised a friend of mine, a self-described rebel against the educational system, to seek help from this professional, he refused, stating that he was as well read in the popular literature on psychology as this "expert" would be.

20. Bin Zhao (1997:49) reports that, according to surveys done in 1988 and 1993, the proportion of income spent on the only child in urban households increased from one-third to nearly one-half. Jun Jing (2000:6) cites a survey of 1,496 households in Beijing that concludes that children determine nearly 70 percent of family expenditures. See chapters 4 and 5 by Barrie Thorne and Jennifer Cole, respectively, this volume, for parallels in other places.

21. The 1990s has also brought the increased presence of American franchised fast food. See the essays on China in Watson 1997.

22. For an early account of the emergence of private schooling for China's "new aristocrats," see *Zhengming* 1993:38–39. In 1999 and 2000, I had opportunities to visit some of the newly established private and semi-private schools (*minban xuexiao*) in the vicinity of Nanjing (many of them are built in peri-urban locations where land is cheaper).

23. See, for instance, a *Wall Street Journal* (1994) report on the use of English language tapes applied in utero to give the fetus a head start on second language acquisition! The late Qing reformer, Liang Qichao, was also an advocate of "fetal education," believing that this is the period when the forces of education and heredity are working together to produce effects that can be passed down to improve the race (Pusey 1983:102–103).

24. See Tanaka 1997 and Steedman 1998 for the relation of conceptions of "developmental time" with societal progression and child development.

25. In 1991, I bought some of these materials for my three-year-old daughter, who delighted in demonstrating her ability to do the exercises. What she did not know was that the materials we were using were intended for children much younger than she. These were clearly copied from Japanese prototypes, as indicated by the depiction of tatami in household scenes.

26. Davies (2002) explores in great detail the politics of memory about the Cultural Revolution and the memoirs authored by sent-down youth (now entering middle age) that became a publishing phenomenon in 1998, commemorating the thirtieth anniversary of the policies that sent the former Red Guards to the countryside.

27. Zhou Enlai was premier of the People's Republic of China from the time of its establishment in 1949 until his death in 1976. Before 1949, he had been one of Mao's closest allies in the period of the War of Resistance against Japan and the subsequent civil war with the nationalist party. This eulogy commemorates the hardships he endured during those times.

28. My use of this term borrows from Anne Allison (chapter 8, this volume), who looks at how technologies have reconstituted the social world of the child.

29. The fascination with nutritional supplements has led to sometimes unfortunate results. The addition of hormones has caused premature sexual maturity for children as young as six or seven. A lack of legislation requiring the reporting of ingredients and various kinds of consumer fraud has led, in some cases, to fatal poisoning (Yang 2000).

30. If the American teachers had doubts about China's birth policy before their visit, their experience of travel in China, as circumscribed and staged as it was, seems to have pushed them into a state of conviction about the need they (the Chinese people) have to keep their population in check. Here we see a complex exchange between quantity and quality, revealing the way in which neoliberal logics are transforming the teachers' thinking.

31. Paula Fass (chapter 2, this volume) reminds us how this tension lies within the romantic construction of youth, in which youth figures as a source of hopeful dynamism but also potentially disruptive rebellion.

32. In this respect, the fact that Chinese parents invest in the aspiration of their only child attaining the status of a new global superclass may also reflect their belief in China's rise to global transcendence as a superpower. This may stand in marked contrast to how the "crisis of the child" is constructed in post-recessionary Japan. See Allison, chapter 8, this volume, and Arai 2005. In an odd way, the crisis of youth in China and Japan would seem to replicate the divide between belief and cynicism that Constance Flanagan (chapter 6, this volume) describes among working- and middle-class American youth about the market mechanism as a form of meritocracy.

33. Paula Fass (chapter 2, this volume) recalls the important place of the public school in constructions of citizenship and national and community identities in the early twentieth century. Barrie Thorne's chapter 4 (this volume) evocatively demonstrates what has changed since then.

4

"The Chinese Girls" and "The Pokémon Kids"

Children Negotiating Differences in Urban California

Barrie Thorne

On a warm spring day in 1997, a group of fifth- and sixth-grade students from a public school in Oakland, California, boarded a city bus to begin a field trip to a nature area. As the bus lumbered up the long, steep route that goes from the "flats" to the "hills" of the city, the kids' conversations veered in and out of commentary on the sites they passed. Many of them recognized a public middle school, and they talked about people they knew who attended it. Farther up the hill, the bus passed the spacious campus of a large and expensive private school. One of the kids called out, "There's that rich private school!" Others, leaning toward the window to get a view, chimed in, "Look at the tennis courts!" "They also got a swimming pool!" Students at the "rich private school" were mostly white and Asian American; all but those with scholarships came from affluent families. In contrast, the students on the bus were mostly from working-class and lower-income families; more than half had immigrant parents, and the rest, except for two white students, were African American.

The distance between these two school worlds exemplifies the deep and racialized social class divide that, over the past three decades, has come to characterize "the new California" (Schrag 2006). Processes of globalization have led to economic polarization, the depletion of state provisioning for families and children, the spread of a market ethic, and a dramatic influx of immigrants from diverse points of origin. This chapter explores the articulation of these structural shifts in the social positioning and daily experiences of children growing up in Oakland. It also highlights a significant historical change. The growing cleavage between affluent and low-income childhoods in contemporary California has reversed a trend initiated in the United States during the Progressive Era a century ago, when the outlawing of child labor and the introduction of comprehensive public schooling and other forms of state support muted class divisions in the circumstances of children's lives (Fass, chapter 2, this volume; Zelizer 1985). Paradoxically, widening gaps between today's rich and poor children tend to be obscured by social distances embedded in patterns of residence and schooling and by two other changes related to global economic restructuring: the spread of children's consumer culture and high rates of immigration. This paradox relates to a more general observation made by Jean Comaroff and John Comaroff (2000a), that neoliberal capitalism magnifies class differences while also undercutting class consciousness. The incident on the bus, when the public school kids noticed and talked about the "rich private school," was a rare sort of occasion.

This ethnographic study of children negotiating social differences in urban California starts with processes of globalization, an abstract idea seemingly distant from kids' daily lives and experiences. To bridge the global and the local, I use statistical and historical information to document structural changes, which I then draw together with observations from three years of team fieldwork in Oakland. The analysis attends both to globalized shifts that have altered a local field of social difference and to preexisting cultural and institutional practices, such as US modes of racial classification that kids use and rework as they grapple with rapid social change.

Do kids growing up in Oakland comprehend the varied phenomena that social analysts congeal in the concept of "globalization"? Not, of course, through the lenses of social theory. But children in our key field site, an ethnically heterogeneous public elementary school, encounter complex fields of linguistic and culturally marked difference that are continually being reconstituted through the global circulation of people and converging patterns of immigration. They also make use of globalized forms of commercial children's culture promoted by multinational corporations such as Disney, Nintendo, and Mattel. And, in fragmented moments and highly mediated ways, kids glimpse increasingly polarized social-class divides in the circumstances and organization of childhoods and in the shaping of life trajectories. Much as Cole and Flanagan describe (chapters

5 and 6, respectively, this volume), structural changes associated with glob-alization make class a salient, but newly obscure, experience that young people attempt to sort out. This chapter highlights children's perceptions of and participation in the local articulation of these varied types of struc-tural change.

I begin by describing the research site and the collaborative ethno-graphic methods of this empirical study. Then, stitching the global to the local, I discuss broad structural changes that are reconfiguring the geogra-phies of difference and inequality encountered by kids growing up in Oakland. This discussion provides context for an ethnographically informed analysis of the ways in which kids mark, mute, and negotiate individual and group distinctions. Some social divisions are strongly coded and highly vis-ible; others remain more hidden from view, though their workings are nonetheless consequential.

RESEARCH SITE AND METHODS OF STUDY

I first lived in California when I was a college student in the early 1960s. In the mid- and then late 1970s, I returned with my family on teaching sojourns, and in 1987 we moved from Michigan to Los Angeles. Over these decades, I observed firsthand some of the striking demographic and cul-tural shifts taking place in urban California. As a sociologist of childhood, I had long had my eye on younger folks, and I increasingly began to pon-der what might be called globalization or transnationalism *very much* from below (Smith and Guarnizo 1998). My interest in child-centered snapshots of change—such as rising rates of child poverty and the much cited fact that, by the late 1980s, more than ninety languages were spoken by stu-dents attending public schools in Los Angeles—helped set this project into motion. In 1995, after moving from southern to northern California, I began to organize an ethnographic study of the changing organization of childhoods and the daily experiences of children growing up in a mixed-income, ethnically diverse area of Oakland.

I chose "Oakdale Elementary School" (a pseudonym) as a primary research site because of its unusual ethnic diversity. Located in a middle-class "slopes" transition zone between the affluent hills and the lower-income flatland areas of the city, Oakdale is a place "where peoples meet" across lines of racialized culture and, to some degree, across divisions of social class. In 1996, the first and most intensive of our three years of field-work, half of Oakdale students qualified for free or reduced-price lunch, the one official marker of the social class composition of US public schools. None of the students lived in the upper-income part of the intake area;

about a fourth had transferred to Oakdale from the lower-income "flats" regions of the city. Over the three years of our study, the number of African American students (mostly lower-income, some more middle-class) ranged between 43 and 49 percent. The percentage of white students, most of them middle-class and living near the school, declined from 12 to 10 percent. More than 40 percent of Oakdale students were the children of immigrants, with the largest clusters falling into the pan-ethnic categories of "Asian" (their ratio held steady at around 25 percent of the students) and "Hispanic" (their numbers increased from 14 to 18 percent of the total during the period of our study).

School district racial-ethnic categories gloss enormous cultural variation. For example, Oakdale "Asian" students included the children of immigrants from China, Hong Kong, the Philippines, Vietnam, Laos, Cambodia, and Korea. Most of the "Hispanics" were from Mexico; others had roots in El Salvador, Guatemala, Honduras, or Nicaragua. There were also students whose families came from Yemen, Tonga, Nigeria, and Eritrea. Some of the children had migrated with their parents, but the vast majority living in immigrant households were born in the United States and spoke English at school. Around a third of the students spoke another language at home, more than eleven languages all told, with speakers of Cantonese and Spanish the largest in number.

Oakdale Elementary School takes official pride in its cultural diversity. When the principal took me on an initial tour, she called the school "my little United Nations." A mural painted on the outside wall of a portable classroom building depicts a row of children with faces and clothing of various colors and design. Above them sails a ribbon of words: "Smiling Faces of Different Races." Each June during our three years of fieldwork, an elaborate promotion ceremony for students moving on to middle school opened with a chain of greeters who offered a welcome in as many as seven languages. Each time, an African American student went first, with a welcome in English. These practices invited children to imagine themselves as part of a global order. They also articulated a deeply American, multicultural, and racialized understanding of global flows of people converging in a local site. It should be noted that social class divisions were not represented in school ceremonial displays—one of many examples of the minimal coding of social class, as opposed to codings of racial ethnicity in US cultural understandings and categories of identity (Bettie 2003; Ortner 2003).

To gather data about the everyday lives of children and parents from a range of social class, immigrant, cultural, and racialized backgrounds, I recruited a multilingual group of graduate and undergraduate students. Teaming up in various combinations, we did three years of participant observation in classrooms, in the lunchroom, in hallways, on the playground. We also went on multiple classroom field trips, attended PTA meetings, and hung out in after-school programs, neighborhoods, households, a park, the public library, McDonald's, and other child-related sites. After about six months of observing, we began to complement our ongoing fieldwork with open-ended individual and group interviews. The eighty parents and eighty-two children (mostly fifth graders) whom we interviewed over the next two years came from across the economic and cultural spectrum of the intake area. To document the preceding four decades of demographic and political-economic changes in Oakland, we gathered census, city budget, and other statistical data, as well as material from local history archives. We also invited children to draw and write about their lives. I will discuss one of our data-gathering strategies—a highly inductive approach to the mapping of socially coded distinctions—after I step back to sketch the larger changes that are reconfiguring the contours of childhoods in urban California.

GLOBALIZATION AND THE RESTRUCTURING OF CHILDHOODS IN URBAN CALIFORNIA

Over the past three decades, varied forms of globalized change have altered the structural and cultural circumstances of children growing up in contemporary Oakland. These changes include economic and political restructuring and the creation of polarized extremes of wealth and poverty; accelerated rates of immigration and the convergence of new residents from varied places of origin; and the international circulation and pervasive influence of commercial children's culture, with multinational corporations marketing images and products directly to kids.

Widening Social Class Divides

The past thirty years have seen accelerated immigration and widening economic inequality in Oakland, in the state of California (which has the world's fifth largest economy), and in the United States as a whole (Schrag 2006). These entangled trends are related to global economic restructuring, fueled by the dynamics of international capitalism and guided by neoliberal state policies. In the United States, processes of deindustrialization, the decline of real wages, and tax cuts and other policies favoring the wealthy have amplified the gaps between rich and poor. The already minimal US welfare state has increasingly cut back on various forms of public provisioning for families and children, diminishing the safety net of welfare and leading to the deterioration of public schools and parks and recreation programs, especially in urban areas.

Compared with other industrialized countries, the United States now has by far the largest gaps of income and wealth, and, compared with other states, California has an especially polarized class structure, which is coming to resemble an hourglass. State rates of child poverty have steadily increased over the past three decades to the current figure of 22 percent. At the same time, California has an unusually high proportion of households with annual incomes of more than $200,000, whereas the middle class is shrinking (Palmer, Younghwan, and Lu 2002). In Oakland, 25 percent of children (most of them children of color) now live below the poverty line; the median income of white households is nearly twice that of African Americans, Latinos, and Asian Americans (Gammon and Marcucci 2002). Half of white children in Oakland now attend private instead of public schools, a figure much higher than among families of other racial-ethnic backgrounds (Tucker and Katz 2002).

The deepening, institutionalized cleavage between affluent and low-income childhoods has undermined the earlier efforts of the US welfare state to mitigate the effects of poverty. By law and widespread practice, contemporary US childhoods continue to be organized through households and schools, a transformation consolidated in the early twentieth century with the prohibition of child labor and the expansion of public schooling. But in urban California, many affluent children are now growing up in privatized or gated childhoods, organized through market-based services available only to those who can pay. An infrastructure of private schools and fee-based recreational, sports, science, art, computer, and other after-school and summer programs has burgeoned in metropolitan areas over the past thirty years, a trend that has both paralleled and contributed to the deterioration of public schools and parks and recreational facilities.

Class-privileged children in Oakland, such as those who attend the "rich private school" described in the opening vignette, have much less exposure to cultural and racialized difference than do children from more modest economic backgrounds who attend public schools in ethnically mixed areas of the city (Thorne 2003). This differential engagement with racialized cultural diversity reflects a national trend toward increasing racial segregation of US schools, with white children and youth disproportionately isolated from other groups (for statistical details, see Harvard Civil Rights Project 2005). Students who attend Oakdale Elementary School come from a wider range of income backgrounds, from solidly middle-class to very low-income, than those in many schools in the city. This mix of social class backgrounds is coupled with an unusual cultural and linguistic diversity resulting from high rates of immigration, a second structural shift related to processes of globalization.

Globalized Migration Projects Converging in Oakland

Since the 1965 loosening of US immigration laws, California has received more immigrants than any other state, at a time when class inequalities have steadily widened. Statistics about children provide a striking illustration of these demographic changes. The 2000 census found that 40 percent of children in California spoke a language other than English at home and 46 percent had at least one parent who was born in another country. Although people from virtually every continent have migrated to California over the past three decades, the majority (around 90 percent) are from Mexico or countries in Central America or Asia. The immigrant families who enrolled their children in Oakdale Elementary School illustrate some of the globalized trajectories and the cultural and linguistic diversity of the "new California."

Members of the Assad extended family (all names have been changed) had engaged in more than thirty years of sojourning and then chain migration and transmigration from Yemen to California, resulting in a transnational infrastructure of property and businesses. The family owned and operated two liquor stores in the East Bay and a four-unit apartment building near Oakdale, where, at the time of this study, the grandparents and their three sons, their daughters-in-law, and their grandchildren lived in separate units. The Assads also owned a farm in rural Yemen and an apartment building in Saana. The grandfather had a second wife and a younger set of children who lived in Yemen; he went back and forth. The Oakland-based sons and their wives also nested their childrearing practices in transnational arrangements, occasionally "going back" to live with relatives in Yemen in order to immerse their US-born children in Islamic culture and extended kinship ties. The parents arranged marriages between their children and cousins and others in Yemen. They sent sons back to "straighten them out" if their sons began to smoke, drink, take drugs, or get caught up in the teen romance culture of Oakland public schools (for further details, see Orellana et al. 2001 and Thorne et al. 2003).

One day, when I was observing in a "sheltered English" third-grade classroom, the teacher asked students to imagine themselves as trees whose roots are the places, people, and things that help them grow. She went to the blackboard and sketched herself as a tree with roots anchored to her

FIGURE 4.1.

A landscape "Roots" drawing by a Yemeni American girl that mixes sites of daily living in Oakland with an apartment building in Yemen.

house, the school, and other local places. Responding to the classroom assignment, Fatima, a Yemeni American girl, drew an imaginative landscape that mixed sites of daily living in Oakland with an apartment building in Yemen (figure 4.1). Fatima wrote the narrative at the top of the picture, expressing emotions related to international travel, in response to another classroom assignment.

Randy Phan's "My Roots" drawing memorializes his mother's traumatic journey from Vietnam to Oakland (figure 4.2, the box in the lower left corner). After leaving Vietnam in the aftermath of the US war and spending a harrowing period at sea, his mother reached a refugee camp in Indonesia. Several years later, Catholic Social Services, pursuing its own globalizing strategies, arranged for her to settle in Oakland, where she met and married her husband, also from Vietnam. Randy was born in Oakland. At the time of our study, his father was unemployed, and his mother commuted long distances to work as a manicurist in a nail salon.

Another Oakdale student, Janet Wong, was born in Hong Kong and

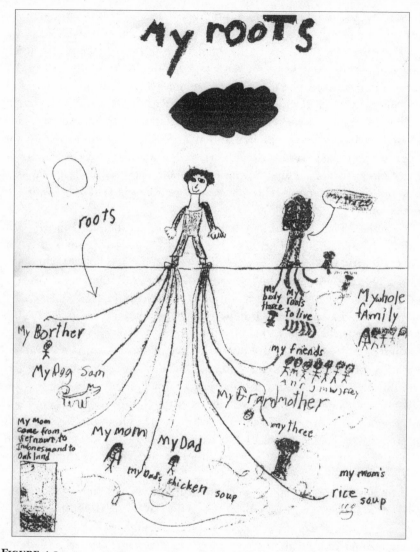

FIGURE 4.2.

A Vietnamese American boy's "Roots" drawing memorializing his mother's traumatic journey from Vietnam to Oakland via Indonesia.

began her schooling there. When she was eight years old, her father's business failed, and, in an effort to recoup their economic position, her parents decided to move to Oakland. They were sponsored and helped by Janet's uncle, who had immigrated to California some years before. When we met Janet, she was in sixth grade. Her mother worked long hours in a garment factory in Oakland; her father was unemployed. Both he and Janet yearned for their more established life in Hong Kong. The family spoke Cantonese and watched the Bay Area Chinese-language television station. An uncle "back home" in Hong Kong regularly taped and sent Janet videos of the latest Chinese versions of *Sailor Moon*, a Japanese anime cartoon show popular among Oakdale students. This family-organized flow of commercial media, originally produced in Japan, translated into Chinese, and purchased in Hong Kong, reached the Wongs' Oakland home before the episodes appeared on Bay area television. Sustaining a sense of dignity in the context of her family's downward mobility, Janet sometimes asserted that not only are schools better back in Hong Kong but there is also better television.

Fatima Assad, Randy Phan, and Janet Wong participated in what the Oakland-based poet Ishmael Reed has called a "callaloo" (gumbo soup) of cultures, with, in Reed's words, "people from an astounding array of backgrounds living and attending school side-by-side" (quoted in McMurtrie 2003). The media often portray this complex callaloo with child-centered statistics, such as the fact that between sixty and seventy language groups are represented in the Oakland public schools. However, as mentioned earlier, patterns of mixing are uneven. Oakland has a history of racial segregation of residential areas, enforced by housing covenants that geographically contained African Americans until the 1960s. In the wake of the civil rights movement and residential and school desegregation, many whites moved to the suburbs or to nearby, mostly white, working-class communities like San Leandro. By the 1980s, African Americans became the majority ethnic group in Oakland, although their relative numbers have begun to decline in recent years.

In contemporary Oakland, economically privileged families live in the predominantly white, residential areas of the "hills," on the eastern side of the city. Lower-income families, who historically have been primarily African American but are increasingly also Latino and Southeast Asian, live in the "flatlands" by the bay. Widening class divides are loosely racialized, with a disproportionate representation of whites among the economically and educationally privileged. As many observers have noted, in the East Bay, altitude correlates with income, and households with the ability to pay (including more affluent immigrant and African American households) increasingly turn to the market to organize their children's schooling and out-of-school activities. The increasing commodification of childhoods constitutes a third major source of structural and cultural change in the lives of American children.

The Commodification of Childhoods

The imagery of global flows has been used to refer not only to people and capital but also to the rapid circulation of products and ideas, including commercial children's culture, which has become a multibillion-dollar industry (see Allison, chapter 8, this volume). In the United States, according to estimates by James McNeal (1999; also see Schor 2004), around $15 billion is now spent on advertising and marketing to children. Many corporations that promote child consumption actively operate across national boundaries. US transnational media empires like Disney, Japanese corporations like Nintendo and Sanrio (makers of Hello Kitty), and European companies like Lego touch the lives, imaginations, experiences, desires, and material resources of children in many parts of the globe. Children growing up in Oakland are no exception. In their daily encounters across a range of settings, the kids we got to know often talked about video games, the plots of television shows, or their favorite cartoon characters; they showed off and sometimes traded baseball and Pokémon cards; at lunchtime, they scrambled to trade up, exchanging portions of the school lunch or food prepared at home for more valued commercial items such as Oreos, Cheetos, and Fruit Rollups (Thorne 2005). They talked about the commercial products they owned or wanted to own; older kids with spatial autonomy to shop in groups unaccompanied by adults had distinctive status.

Dan Cook (2004) has traced the increasing commodification of US childhoods over the course of the twentieth century. This process, along with cutbacks in state provisioning, has altered relationships among households, markets, and the state—the institutional nexus in which childhoods take shape. The expansion of the market into the organization and dynamics of children's lives is a striking trend, but it also needs further specification. Because commercialized children's culture—mass-produced clothing, backpacks, videos, toys—is widely accessible, it tends to obscure class divisions (Pugh 2006).[1] On one hand, this may be a general phenomenon. In chapter 5, this volume, Jennifer Cole notes that young people in Madagascar also claim that mass-produced consumer goods such as clothing are no longer a clear index of class. On the other hand, Oakland parents' differential consumption of services—the affluent turning to the market to organize their children's daily care, schooling, and out-of-school activities, with lower-income families relying on public provisioning and the assistance of kith and kin—amplifies and entrenches income-based inequalities (Thorne 1993).

The increasingly institutionalized and social-class-inflected division between market and public provisions in the organization of childhoods has significant implications for civic and political life, and for the future of democracy. As mentioned earlier, compared with other social distinctions, divisions related to household income and education are only minimally coded in the daily worlds of Oakdale students. Residential and school segregation amplify social distance between households with disparate levels of income, obscuring children's awareness of class inequality. The widespread availability and appropriation of children's consumer culture also mutes the visibility of class divides.

These three structural shifts—widening and increasingly institutionalized class divisions in the organization of children's lives and their access to opportunities, high rates of immigration, and the expansion of commercial children's culture—have altered the local field of differences and inequalities encountered by children growing up in contemporary Oakland. How do kids comprehend and navigate this shifting terrain, positioning themselves and others? How, in their daily practices, do they display, claim, obscure, interpret, and articulate varied social distinctions? How do converging forms of social change emerge or recede from children's awareness?

MAPPING A LOCAL FIELD OF AVAILABLE DIFFERENCES

I began this project with a wide angle of vision, wanting to grasp the changing and interrelated dynamics of US childhoods. Rather than highlight children's school-based constructions of one particular line of difference, such as gender (as in Thorne 1993) or racial ethnicity (as in Lewis 2003; Troyna and Hatcher 1992; Van Ausdale and Feagin 2001), I decided to take a more inductive and open-ended approach. When my collaborators and I observed on the playground, in the lunchroom, and in classrooms, we tried to map the complex dynamics of group formation and dispersal and to be attentive to the ways in which kids and adults talked about boundaries and differences. We paid special attention to moments of identity work, when kids and adults claimed, contested, or negotiated social placement. Rather than supply preset categories in our interviews, we asked open-ended questions, such as "What kinds of kids are there in this school?" which invited informants to put forth their own categories and meanings. Throughout the processes of data gathering and analysis, we took note of the varying salience and sometimes contradictory constructions of multiple lines of difference and inequality. This broad, multifaceted approach is complex and difficult to manage. But it does have the virtue of opening insight into the situated and eclectic difference-marking and difference-mixing practices used by kids and adults, as when we discovered that kids used commercial culture to both bridge and mark racialized, ethnic, age, and gender divides.

Commercial Culture and the Bridging, Etching, and Obscuring of Social Differences

When my collaborators and I entered the world of Oakdale Elementary School, we were alert to markings of cultural difference. I had chosen the school because of its linguistic diversity, and I recruited a multilingual research team so that we could learn about the dynamics of a world where differences had multiplied through several decades of immigration. During our initial days of fieldwork, we took note of the head scarves worn by girls from Yemeni families, the snippets of playground conversation in Spanish, and the Cantonese regularly spoken by a group widely known as "the Chinese girls." But we also noticed that unless they were prodded by adult questions or exercises (such as the "Draw Your Roots" third-grade classroom assignment described earlier), kids from immigrant, as well as non-immigrant, backgrounds mostly talked about subjects anchored in the here and now. On the playground, all but a handful of kids spoke English, and they divided into groups first on the basis of age (a criterion of sorting so basic to school practices that it tends to be taken for granted); then, to some degree, by gender; and then, to a lesser degree, by racial-ethnicity (these patterns have been reported by many school-based ethnographers, as discussed in Thorne 1993). Socioeconomic distinctions inflected patterns of sorting, but these were less overtly coded than gender, age, and racialized ethnicity.

During our first two years of fieldwork, Oakdale offered a Cantonese bilingual class for the lower grades and a Spanish bilingual class for fourth and fifth graders. Both classes also included native English speakers and a few speakers of other languages, such as Vietnamese. This form of classroom sorting and resource allocation irritated some African American parents, who felt that their own children needed extra help that they were not getting. Parents and teachers from a range of backgrounds complained that bilingual classes had the effect of separating rather than integrating kids from different backgrounds, although some parents supported bilingual pedagogies. In June 1998, California state voters passed Proposition 227, which outlaws bilingual education unless parents sign a waiver (this was part of a more general voter backlash against immigrant families and children). The Oakdale principal decided that the school would no longer offer bilingual classes, resulting in more mixing of Spanish- and Cantonese-speaking kids with those from other backgrounds, not only in classrooms but also on the playground.

Even when there were bilingual classes (which, at most, included less than 15 percent of the students in the school), kids often reached across visible and hear-able divisions of language and national background as they formed friendships and organized activities. The salience of crosscutting distinctions of age and gender, widespread facility in spoken English, and the particularities of a shared, immediate world, such as engagement with activities such as basketball or double-dutch jump rope, facilitated interaction across racial-ethnic boundaries—as did experiences outside school, such as having seen *Star Wars* or being hooked on a particular television cartoon show. One day, I watched as an African American fifth-grade boy who was skillful in interacting with younger children helped his assigned kindergarten "buddy" do an art project. The younger boy, who wore the optional school uniform of a white shirt and navy blue pants (almost none of the older kids wore the uniform), had recently arrived from Hong Kong and spoke very little English. The older boy guided the younger one through the making of a collage, demonstrating the needed steps. At one point, the older boy gestured and exclaimed, "Like Ninja turtles!" The younger boy's face lit up with recognition.

In situations like this, commercial children's culture operates as a global lingua franca, supplying forms of knowledge, fantasy, and skills (such as video game playing) that kids carry across national and linguistic boundaries. Some Oakdale students sported backpacks with Chinese lettering and pictures of Garfield, Hello Kitty, or Sailor Moon; the cartoon images were familiar to all the children in the school. On several occasions, I saw mixed-gender groups of Vietnamese, Mexican, Laotian, and Chinese kids trading Sailor Moon, Dragonball Z, Power Ranger, and Pokémon cards on the playground. One spring, a network of fourth-grade boys became so obsessed with collecting, trading, and selling Pokémon cards that others began to call them "the Pokémon kids." When a teacher discovered that one of the boys had earned forty dollars from these school-based transactions, she seized the cards and made a rule that these were no longer to be brought to school. (See Anne Allison's chapter 8, this volume, for insight into the uses and appeal of Pokémon.)

The cultural worlds of Pokémon, Power Rangers, and Sailor Moon are adult designed but directly target child consumers with advertising appeals that heighten boundaries between children and adults (Seiter 1993). Age, similar to and in conjunction with gender, can provide common ground for kids of different racial-ethnic backgrounds. To avoid the disruptions of bragging, envy, theft, and (as in the case of Pokémon) surreptitious exchanges of money, the Oakdale school staff sometimes tried to regulate the toys and objects kids brought from home (children's underground economies of food and objects in schools are discussed in Thorne 1993, 2005). Sometimes teachers tried to steer children's classroom writing and drawing away from characters such as Ninja Turtles or Sailor Moon. But commercial figures continually popped up in daily school life, some of them (Disney's Pocahontas) transient and others (Barbie, Hello Kitty, Power Rangers) more enduring in their presence. Adult ambivalence and lack of full knowledge no doubt enhance the allure of commercial children's culture.

Commercial culture provides a social currency that kids pick up on, interpret, rework, and use in varied ways (Chin 1999). Although Sailor Moon cards are generally understood to be "for girls," some Oakdale boys included them in card collections that mixed cartoon worlds. Hello Kitty, however, was strongly marked as female and also as Asian; the fourth- and fifth-grade "Chinese girls," for example, carried Hello Kitty pencil holders and gave one another Hello Kitty gifts. Nike shoes attracted widespread attention, but African American boys and girls were the most adept in Nike lore. They were familiar with the latest brands and sometimes made drawings of Nikes during class. Among fifth and sixth graders, shoes became a prime marker of the "cool," and the Chinese girls, inscribed with the younger-age-inflected meanings of "cute," knew that they did not qualify (see Cross 2004 for an analysis of the "cute" and the "cool" in children's commercial culture).

In a group interview, which Eva Lam conducted in Cantonese, "the Chinese girls" described and laughed ambivalently about a time when Alex, a popular African American boy, saw that Belinda was wearing a pair of shoes that were "a little pointed" and he observed that she was "like a witch."

> JESSICA: Alex said, "How come Chinese people be all wearing pointy shoes? Look at all the Chinese people. You put a whole class of Chinese people together [the girls laughed], they all gonna have pointed shoes.... You can just see it. They are all witches. You'll probably scream and run away."... Whenever we have something, they think that other Chinese people is the same as us. So if they see us wearing, like, twins or whenever they see...like, she's wearing a tennis shoe, and she's wearing a tennis shoe, and she's wearing a tennis shoe, and I'm wearing a tennis shoe, and Belinda is wearing a tennis shoe, that's all different colors, they start thinking that Chinese people is all wearing tennis shoes, because they all.... And then they be thinking that you

guys probably buy your shoes from Payless because people out here be wearing Nikes and special shoes at the mall. And all you guys do is buy in Chinatown somewhere at a shoe store [laughs, and other girls also laugh], a very not expensive one like Payless. Like, you guys probably buy it for, like [Kim chimes in, "Five bucks!"] five bucks, or eight bucks or something, and they be saying that "We don't have enough money to afford Nikes, or expensive ones like Reeboks and Adidas."

KIM: Why do we need? We don't really need Nikes.

JESSICA: Or expensive shoes, because...

KIM: We just wear them on our feet.

JESSICA: 'Cause it's too expensive. Why spend so much on a pair of shoes when you're gonna run in it and walk in it and break anyway?

The girls clearly understood the dynamics of stereotyping, which in this case linked racial-ethnic divides ("Chinese girls" and the assumed contrast, "cool Black people") with practices and sites of consumption (buying and wearing cheap tennis or "pointy-toe" shoes from Payless or Chinatown as opposed to Nikes from the mall). The girls also understood their subordinate status in the hierarchy of "cool"; they laced this recognition with rueful laughter and with efforts, which seem to echo parental arguments, to rationalize the buying of cheaper shoes ("We don't really need Nikes." "We just wear them on our feet." "You're gonna run in it and walk in it and break anyway."). Thus, kids in Oakland, like the youth Jennifer Cole studied in Madagascar and Brad Weiss studied in Tanzania (see chapters 5 and 9, respectively, this volume), drew upon age-graded consumer culture—within the constraints of family consumption practices—to engage and negotiate processes of self-fashioning.

On one occasion, I heard two of "the Chinese girls" wonder aloud whether kids who wore Nikes were "rich." Most of the kids in these conversations—the wearers of Payless, the wearers of Nike—came from working-class or very low-income families; all five of "the Chinese girls" and Alex, the African American boy who remarked on their pointy-toe shoes, qualified for free school lunch. The clothes kids wore and the objects they brought to school tended to signify household consumer practices more than variation in income, including adult readiness to give in to kids' begging. (In one notable exception, a third grader whose parents were from

Vietnam told me that she was embarrassed by her Pocahontas backpack, which she got as a handout at her church. She knew that Pocahontas was obsolescent and that Little Mermaid, inscribed on the backpacks of other girls in the school, was Disney-up-to-date.)

As noted, the highly affluent were largely absent from these children's daily interactions. The middle-class kids at Oakdale were more likely than lower-income kids to participate in after-school programs, paid tutoring, and organized sports activities, because their parents had enough money to pay the fees and also because they were oriented to a type of child rearing that Annette Lareau (2003) has termed "concerted cultivation." When kids talked about what they did outside school, these distinctions came into view. Rarely, though, in the discourses of difference that sprinkled through their daily school-based encounters, did teachers, staff, and kids talk explicitly about social class. Institutional practices marked income distinctions only by the "free," "reduced price," and "regular" school lunch categories.

In contrast, school discursive and sorting practices highlighted categories of gender, age, and, to some degree, racial-ethnicity. Occasionally, kids would refer to the distant Others at the far end of Oakland's wide spectrum of income—"rich white people in the hills" or "kids who go to the rich private school." Kids implicitly evoked income distinctions when they compared the size of family dwellings or noted that a particular student lacked enough money to go on a field trip. Generally, students from low-income families worked to hide, and teachers deflected attention from, overt signs of poverty. As a result of these many factors, differences of income were often ambiguous and obscured from view.

Although the prevalence and uses of commercial children's culture tend to hide social class inequality at the elementary school level, these commodified forms do emphasize divisions of gender and age (Williamson 1986) and render them in particular ways, as in the exaggerated versions of female and male embodiment signified by Barbie and by GI Joe. Kids were adept at reading the semiotics of "for girls" or "for boys" built into the design of commercial products. They also used clothing and objects to mark varied tempos and ways of growing older, as when a fifth-grade girl wore spaghetti straps to the promotion ceremony, leading other kids and adults to gossip about how "fast" she was. To create new, profitable market segments, designers and advertisers have designated new generational groups, most notably, sexualized "tweens" (ages nine to thirteen but going on sixteen), targeting and framing them with distinctive lines of cosmetics, magazines, and types of clothing. Global capitalist practices of market segmentation reverberated, with local twists of usage, in the social relations and meanings of kids at Oakdale.

The Variable Coding of Distinctions and the Complexities of Racialized Ethnicity

As I mapped the distinctions drawn by kids in their social relations, gestures of labeling and placement, and claims about group and individual identities, I noted a continuum of coding. Age and gender are highly visible and coded in the daily worlds of schooling. As previously discussed, social class positioning is much more ambiguous—muted in close-up school contexts by patterns of institutional segregation (with "rich" kids socially distant), minimally marked in official school practices, glossed rather than inscribed in widely available children's commercial culture, and obscured by the "shame work" (a term suggested to me by Arlie Hochschild) that more impoverished kids and adults undertake to sustain a sense of dignity. Racial and ethnic distinctions lie in between these extremes of the highly marked and the less visible. They have become increasingly complex, contested, and negotiable as speakers of different languages, from multiple places of national origin, and with physical appearances that confound tidy US racialized perceptions, converge in urban contact zones (Pratt 1992) like Oakdale Elementary School.

The availability of differences that may be successfully deployed in the naming of identities and the organization of groups depends, in part, on shared knowledge (Song 2003). When a new Spanish-speaking second grader enrolled in the school, other kids asked him whether he was Mexican. He said no, that he had just come from Nicaragua. The other kids (who had never heard of Nicaragua) insisted that if he spoke Spanish, he must be Mexican, and he soon grew tired of protesting and acquiesced to the highly coded ethnic category. In contrast, to highlight the significance of local demography and knowledge, in the large school in the Pico Union area of Los Angeles that Marjorie Orellana studied in loose tandem with our research in Oakland, most of the students were Spanish-speaking transmigrants from Mexico and Central America. In that context, "Nicaraguan" was a highly coded and therefore available marker of identity, and some kids were even known to be from particular villages.

In the daily school life of Oakdale fifth and sixth graders, the most routinely coded categories of racialized ethnic identity were "Black/African American" and "Chinese," the largest visibly marked groups in the school. Both "Mexican" and "Spanish-speaking" were also well-articulated categories, officially (because of the Spanish bilingual class) and in the repertoire of identity categories shared by kids and adults. But these terms were more ambiguous because of variation in racialized physical appearance. All the Chinese speakers "looked" Chinese, a "look" that sometimes led to the identification of children from Mien (a Laotian ethnic group) and Cambodian immigrant families, both much smaller in numbers, as "Chinese." Those who "looked Black" were "called Black," even if they insisted, as one fifth grader tried to do on several occasions, that they were "mixed" (he wanted to be understood as part Black, part Creole, and part Native American). But some kids who spoke Spanish "looked white," pushing the generic "Mexican" a bit askew, and some kids who spoke Spanish were from the Philippines (others from the Philippines spoke Tagalog).

Institutional practices such as the categories provided on school forms (which reflect a homogenizing yet tangled mix of US racialized, language, and place-of-origin meanings) interacted with local demographics (the proportionately large number of kids who spoke Spanish or Cantonese at home) to sharpen the coding of some racial-ethnic differences while muting others. Nearly everyone seemed to recognize that there were speakers of "Spanish" and "Chinese"; those were, after all, the named bilingual classes. The national-ethnic identities of students who spoke a total of nine other languages and were clustered in "Sheltered English" classes were more ambiguous, and when kids from different backgrounds hung out together, these distinctions were further obscured. But, in general, as Laurie Olsen (1997) demonstrated in an ethnography of the experiences of immigrant students in an East Bay high school, school cultures and practices prodded, "Find your race [in US-based classification systems] and take your place."

The number of white students attending Oakdale rapidly diminished after second grade, when families living near the school began to transfer out of the neighborhood school to "hills" public schools or else "went private." During our first year of fieldwork, only two sixth graders, both girls, seemed unambiguously marked as "white," but we rarely heard students use that word to refer to themselves or to others in the school. Whiteness was most sharply articulated from a distance when coupled with overt class privilege, as when kids referred to "the rich white people in the hills." But kids rarely claimed or deployed "white" as a local marker of identity; it operated through present absence and had vaguely pejorative connotations.

The present absence of "white" was sustained by the racialized authority structure of the school. Half of the Oakdale teachers were white, although only a tenth of the students were in that category, and visitors from the district office were often white, as was the leader (me) of the multiethnic research team from the nearby university. I became known as the "teacher" of the other, much younger fieldworkers, an occupational positioning that, along with my race and age, created a wide social gap between the kids and me. In contrast, my collaborators had more relaxed and comfortable access to the kids' worlds.

Kids who "looked white" claimed other ethnicities whenever they could. For example, a "white-looking" girl said that she was "Hispanic" because one of her grandparents came from that background. Two fifth-grade girls actively claimed the stand-alone category of "mixed," a category that kids seemed to use only when referring to people with one white parent and another "of color." Thus, the girl who was widely acknowledged as "part Black and part Mexican" was not referred to as "mixed." The two girls who successfully embraced the stand-alone category of "mixed" had college-educated parents and were good friends. The father of one of them was Jewish; her mother was third-generation Chinese American. The other girl had a mother who was generically "white" with Irish roots and a father who was an immigrant from Egypt. In interviews, these girls talked about using their "mixed" identities to avoid fights, because "mixed" spared them from having to choose sides in ethnically charged group conflicts. They also deployed other identities in order to negotiate alliances. Soheir, the girl with an Egyptian father, usually called herself "mixed," but at one point when she wanted closer ties to a group of Black kids, she told them, "I'm Egyptian, and that's in Africa, so I'm African American." Later, one of us overheard a group of Black boys trying to decide whether Soheir really was African American.

Group Identities and Boundaries

Kids' negotiations of individual identities sometimes assumed protracted and complex forms, whereas the naming of group boundaries veered in a simplifying direction. It should also be noted that, in the daily organization and marking of differences, patterns of group formation and dissolution are especially consequential for public articulations of identity. In our fieldwork, we were alert to processes of "borderwork," a concept drawn from the work of Fredrik Barth (1969). This refers to interactions across ethnic (and gender) boundaries that sustain a sense of difference (see Thorne 1993). The ebb and flow of borderwork gives socially constructed lines of difference a fluid quality; a difference that counts in one context may be less salient in another, and boundaries may shift as contexts change. However, when group boundaries are sustained across time and social contexts, a particular distinction may become highly significant.

In daily school life, kids and adults constructed racialized and ethnic differences within the context of other sorts of grouping, drawing distinctions with varied purposes in mind. In an interview, Jessica, one of "the Chinese girls" (and an especially observant and articulate informant) described how teams were chosen during physical education classes:

> And so, whenever there are two Black people and they are choosing teams, usually it's the fat people and the Chinese and Mexicans who would stand on the side, and the other people, like those who know how to play and the tall ones, are chosen. We, usually the four of us [her friendship group, "the Chinese girls"], don't play well, but the teacher says they need to choose some of the other people. And then the captains are all quiet and ask the teacher if they really have to, and the teacher says they have to. So it's, like, nobody wants to choose us.

This enumeration of groups mixed racial-ethnic categories—those (other than gender and age) most often articulated in the school—with categories related to body size, height, and level of skill. Jessica clustered these lines of difference around a dichotomy: being good or bad at sports. In another sort of context, Latoya, an African American fifth-grade girl, first pointed out the groups who gathered during lunchtime at the outdoor picnic tables, and then she shifted gears to generalize: "Black kids hang out together, and Chinese. Unfortunately, that's how it is. The races are separate. See that group? They're all Black. Except for that one girl is Mexican. Sometimes that happens."

Indeed, that year, among fifth and sixth graders there was a sharp and frequently named divide between "Black" and "Chinese" girls. In the fifth- and sixth-grade classroom where I did extensive observing and where students had chosen their own seats around several long tables, there was a predominantly African American area, with much interaction between girls and boys; a predominantly Asian area, with more gender separation; and two tables of Mexicans, Yemenis, Filipinos, and Cambodians, which also included the two "mixed" and the two white girls. Kids from quite different racial-ethnic backgrounds hung out in several close friendship groups, but these groups mostly went unnamed.

During our first year of fieldwork, "the Chinese girls" was the most consistently bounded and racially and ethnically defined of all the named groups. Four of the girls were US born and fully bilingual; Janet, the fifth, had emigrated with her family from Hong Kong three years before, as mentioned earlier, and was not fully fluent in English. In every setting, "the

Chinese girls" maneuvered to sit and hang out together, and they often switched from English to Cantonese, speaking loudly and with animation, which led other children to worry that they were being talked about. Eva Lam, the fieldworker who spoke Cantonese, asked the girls how they decided when to speak in Cantonese or in English. Jessica replied, "We speak Cantonese when we want to talk about someone, and when it's more personal, and when we don't know some words in English." The exclusionary gestures of "the Chinese girls" gave them the reputation of having "an attitude," and other kids sometimes mocked and made fun of them, imitating Cantonese with phrases such as "ching chong" and, as detailed earlier, making fun of their "pointy-toe" shoes.

"The Chinese girls" stuck together, in part because of discomfort with and fear of African Americans, both in the girls' spatially dispersed flatland neighborhoods and in the school. The girls, and their parents, talked about Blacks as a primary source of danger. Belinda, for example, said that she would now be dead if she had attended the predominantly Black school near their house. "The Chinese girls" engaged in sustained conflict with a group of Black girls who, for part of the year, set themselves apart by calling themselves "the Looney Tunes Club" (another example of a local deployment of popular culture, in this case to exclude other Black girls who wanted to be in the club). Near the end of the school year, group tensions erupted into episodes of mutual name calling. This protracted conflict compounded the salience of racial-ethnic categories and group identification in the school lives of these students.

In contrast with the overtly bilingual "Chinese girls," the fifth- and sixth-grade Cantonese-speaking boys always spoke English at school, and they often hung out with African American, Latino, Mien, and Vietnamese boys in a large, somewhat fluid network of kids who played basketball at recess and during the lunch hour. Jessica, the insightful social observer, commented during a field trip, "Chinese boys get along better with African American boys because they can do things together, like playing games." And during Eva's group interview with four of the "Chinese girls," Belinda observed that the Chinese boys had a "masculinity thing." The shared activity of basketball playing, and the commonality of gender, lessened the salience of immigrant and ethnic identities for these boys. One of the Chinese boys was fluent in Cantonese and often translated for his parents, but he never spoke Cantonese in school. He told Eva that once when he had spoken Cantonese in public, some kids teased him. Ever since, he had been reluctant to speak it outside his home. Thus, in a process often involving shame work, some dimensions of potentially marked difference may be deliberately suppressed. However, because Janet, an immigrant from Hong Kong, spoke English with a strong accent, she, unlike the other Cantonese-speaking fifth and sixth graders, had little choice about being marked as an immigrant.

The division between Janet (the immigrant) and the other (US-born) Chinese girls widened the next year when they moved on to a nearby middle school known for racial divisions and "fights" between "the Blacks, the Asians, and the Mexicans." Pan-ethnic categories and racialized group boundaries consolidated in the larger, more anonymous world of the middle school, compared with the smaller, relatively more fluid and personal world of elementary school. Jessica, Belinda, Kim, and Sheila developed close ties to a girl (not ethnically Chinese) whose parents came from Vietnam, and they all developed an interest in wearing "teen cool" feminine fashions. They began to call themselves "Asian American" and stopped speaking Cantonese in school. Although Janet became steadily more fluent in English, she spoke with an accent and had neither the interest in nor the means to buy "cool teen clothes." She went through a painful period of feeling excluded and then began to hang out with a group of girls who had recently emigrated from Hong Kong and who, like Janet, had been placed in the middle-school ESL track.

CONCLUSION: LOCAL ARTICULATIONS OF DIFFERENCE AND INEQUALITY

Over the past thirty years, processes of global economic restructuring have amplified cultural, linguistic, and (in American perceptions) racialized differences in urban California. But children's experiences of diversity are unevenly distributed because of another globalized shift: widening gaps between rich and poor that have become increasingly institutionalized in a division between affluent, privatized childhoods and the more racial-ethnically diverse childhoods that are organized through public institutions. As the class-privileged have pulled out of the "public," they have left middle- and lower-income children to do the work of democracy—making sense of and negotiating lines of difference and commonality in local contact zones like Oakdale Elementary School. As this ethnography suggests, these negotiations have creative, conflictual, and constraining dimensions.

The language of "restructuring," "flows," and "forces" portrays globalization as an inexorable, world-remaking process. A more situated approach (as theorized by Tsing 2000) brings heterogeneity and the open-endedness of the present more fully into view. Attention to the remaking of local geographies can also bring attention to children's agency, for example, in helping to shape processes of immigration and transmigration (Orellana et al. 2001; Thorne et al. 2003), in reworking racial-ethnic categories, and in making use of commercial children's culture.

Will the massive influx of immigrants from Mexico, Central America, Hong Kong, China, Vietnam, Laos, Cambodia, Korea, and the Philippines decenter the racialized polarization of white and Black that is deeply rooted in US culture, history, and institutions? Are other groups "whitening" or "darkening" as they become part of US society? Aihwa Ong (1999) has observed that San Francisco Bay area immigrants from Hong Kong, especially those from privileged educational and class backgrounds, may be "whitening" and that Cambodian refugees, who are more impoverished than any other ethnic group in the United States, are "darkening." This generalization fits some dimensions of our case study; however, it obscures varied and changing inflections of "whiteness" related to demographic changes and to widening gaps of social class. And it may too quickly foreclose the ongoing, contingent, and open-ended processes through which social relations and divisions are remade.

As children navigate a local field of available differences that is being reconfigured by changes related to globalization, how do they articulate multiple and power-laden distinctions? As I have demonstrated, highly coded differences of age and gender may, in some situations (as with "the Chinese girls"), compound and, in other situations (the "masculinity thing" of the Cantonese-speaking boys), cut across and mute boundaries of racialized ethnicity. Class distinctions may alter racial-ethnic meanings, as in perceptions of "rich white people in the hills." But perhaps the most notable conclusion I draw from this effort to map and untangle diverse and crisscrossing lines of difference is that the most significant structural change—the increasing polarization of rich and poor—tends to be hidden from the active awareness of the children in our study. Social class divisions are more extreme now than at any time in US history, but extensive residential and school segregation, widespread consumption of commercial children's culture, and the amplification of racialized cultural differences divert children's attention from these tectonic economic shifts.

Acknowledgments

The research for this chapter was supported by a grant from the John D. and Catherine T. MacArthur Foundation Research Network on Successful Pathways Through Middle Childhood and by the UC Berkeley Center for Working Families, funded by the Sloan Foundation. The UC Berkeley Institute for Human Development also provided support. I would like to thank the graduate and undergraduate students who helped me gather and analyze data: Wan Shun Eva Lam, Hung Thai, Eréndira Rueda, Nadine Chabrier, Allison Pugh, Eileen Mears, and Ana González. Brad Weiss, Jennifer Cole, Marjorie Orellana, and Dan Cook provided valuable comments on earlier drafts of this chapter. Conversations with Hanne Haavind, Arlie Hochschild, and Peter Lyman have nourished my thinking and writing. I am also grateful to the children, parents, teachers, and school staff for their cooperation with this project.

Note

1. The relationship of kids' consumption practices to social class varies by level of schooling. Kids at Oakdale Elementary School did not, by and large, mark class divisions with stylized choices of dress or cosmetics, in contrast with the presence of highly visible and named subcultures such as "skaters," "homies," and "preppies" at local public high schools. US elementary schools tend to be smaller and more personal than the much larger, more anonymous worlds of public middle schools and high schools, where academic tracking (which tends to reproduce racial and class hierarchies) is often practiced. Processes of racialization, entangled with class hierarchies and meanings and often solidified in group boundaries, intensify in middle school, in part because sexual meanings also become more salient at that age. Older kids have more autonomy as consumers, and some earn their own spending money, which gives more latitude in their purchases. In an ethnography of Mexican American and white girls in a working- and middle-class high school in the Central Valley, Julie Bettie (2003) documents alternative, highly stylized versions of gender performance inflected by and helping to constitute an inseparable mix of race and class meanings. Developing an argument that resonates with themes in this chapter, Bettie observes that class is discursively invisible, its meanings often displaced onto or read through other categories of difference, such as race or gender. Social class, nonetheless, has powerful effects.

5

Fashioning Distinction

Youth and Consumerism
in Urban Madagascar

Jennifer Cole

Poverty sits on your skin no matter where you go. It is like the clothes that you wear. Whatever you do, it is because you are poor.

—*Mamy, fifteen-year-old girl*

In the summer of 2004, while talking to a Malagasy historian, I asked her about a problem that had come to plague me over the course of my research on youth in Tamatave, a large port city on Madagascar's east coast. How should I conceptualize the nature of social class in Madagascar, given the rapid changes that had accompanied economic liberalization since the early 1990s? Looking perplexed, she responded, "I don't know how to think about social class anymore. Now that everyone dresses up, you can't tell the difference." I recount this anecdote to introduce the themes of this chapter: the relationship between youthful fashion practice, social distinction, and globalization in urban Madagascar.

Madagascar's move from state socialism to a liberalized economy has changed the country in many ways over the past seventeen years. Economic liberalization has brought increased access to foreign media and commodities and, for the lucky few, new economic opportunities. But these transformations have also been accompanied by increasing economic disparities, within cities and between the cities and the countryside. Recent changes have simultaneously sharpened existing economic disparities and offered people new media—in the sense of images and of things—for imagining the nature of social relations.

These changes raise the question of how social distinction operates in the contemporary moment. My friend and I shared an understanding of the word *class* loosely based on a Marxist definition of one's standing as determined by the kind of labor he or she does and its relation to the means of production. After all, not only was my friend highly educated, but also she had lived through the socialist period, when the use of Marxist language to understand social relations was common (see Ratsiraka 1975). Her confusion about class and "dressing up" suggests that this older understanding is no longer relevant to Malagasy intellectuals or, at the very least, has been undergoing change.

These changes are not restricted to Madagascar. In a discussion of millennial capital, Jean and John Comaroff suggest that, at present, class tensions are expressed in personalized terms: "Its contrasts [are] mobilized in a host of displaced registers, its distinctions [are] carried in a myriad of locally charged…signs and objects—from the canons of taste and desire, to the niceties of language use" (Comaroff and Comaroff 2000a:306). Efforts to rethink class as a social science analytic substantiate this observation. For example, in Mark Liechty's discussion of middle-class culture in Kathmandu, he draws on Judith Butler's (1999) notion of performance to argue that the middle class is best conceived of as a "constantly renegotiated cultural space—a space of ideas, values, goods, practices and embodied behaviors in which the terms of inclusion and exclusion are endlessly tested, negotiated, and affirmed" (Liechty 2003:15).

These recent discussions stand at theoretical odds with each other, the Comaroffs continuing to draw on a Marxist tradition by decrying the fact that new registers of identity mask the reality of socioeconomic inequality, Liechty drawing on Butler to rethink class in more Weberian terms. Nonetheless, I want to highlight two similarities in these otherwise very different approaches. First, both studies emphasize the importance of consumption instead of production in creating contemporary social distinctions, thereby continuing a trend that began much earlier (Bourdieu 1984[1979]). Second, both works single out youth in an effort to understand social distinctions in contemporary terms. The Comaroffs (2000a:306) suggest that, at present, "generation is an especially fertile site into which class anxieties are displaced." Liechty (2003:37) argues that the middle class's efforts to constitute itself in cultural practice bring youth into existence as a category.

There are good structural and historical reasons to use youth as a lens through which to understand the changing nature of social distinction at this particular moment. Structurally, youth are located betwixt and between: not yet adult and not having acquired a significant burden of responsibility, they are more able to take advantage of new conditions (Cole 2004; Mannheim 1993). As a result, they have been associated with mobility in many times and places. Because of this association with mobility, youth is also the age group in which the tension between reproduction and change is most likely to be visible. Consequently, youth very often becomes a flash point for wider social anxieties.

As several of the chapters in this volume also make clear (see chapters 6 and 9 by Flanagan and Weiss, respectively), these structural tendencies have become exacerbated in the current moment because the particular social and economic conditions of contemporary capitalism have created contradictions for youth by simultaneously targeting them as consumers and making them particularly vulnerable to socioeconomic exclusion (Cole 2004; Comaroff and Comaroff 1999, 2000a; Ruddick 2003). At the same time, many aspects of contemporary consumerism accentuate the allure of youthful qualities.

In Tamatave, one medium through which these tensions play out is fashion. Though people of all ages care about what they wear, contemporary socioeconomic changes have made fashion increasingly associated with youth. During the nineteenth century, members of the Malagasy elite dressed in European clothing, a privilege that was forbidden to those of lower rank (Ellis 1867). During the late colonial period and then during the first ten years after independence, married women followed the fashions, which were usually borrowed from France (*lamaody*).[1] Today, however, people unequivocally associate youth with fashion. In fact, youth and fashion are so closely linked, that one is often explained or imagined in terms of the other. One young man commented, when I asked him what it means to be young, "That means you pursue your pleasure. That is to say, youth don't do what is important. They do whatever pleases them, for example, fashion. Not everyone is forced to follow the fashions, but youth act like it is the most important thing."

In a sociocultural milieu in which the majority of the population is young—the average age is 21.7 years, and roughly one-third of the population falls within the age range considered "youth"—youth's fashion practices have come to embody important social changes for everyone. At the very least, a certain select section of this demographic group, particularly the young women (referred to by the French term *jeunes*), has come to do so. Emerging out of the tension between prolonged education, scarce employment opportunities, and consumer desire, all jeunes, male and female, find themselves facing an uncertain future. Previously, young urbanites achieved adulthood by going to school, finding a job, marrying, and setting up a household of their own. Previously, they also assumed that schooling would guarantee upward social mobility. For educated urbanites at least, adulthood was linked to upward mobility. The modernist assumption that third world peoples would move from rural to urban, from traditional to modern, was reflected in the ideal life trajectory for individuals as well.

This idealized life course no longer holds. The increasing uncertainty about what constitutes adulthood, what the future will look like, how it should be achieved, means that youth seek new ways to reach their goals. They do so, in part, by drawing on the consumerist culture surrounding them. In particular, female youth perceive fashion as a route to what they refer to as *fivoarana*. Youth use the word to connote, simultaneously, aspiration—a kind of reaching beyond oneself, not for transcendence but for self-perfection—and the kind of labor on the self that is required in order to achieve that state.[2] To achieve fivoarana means that an individual has made social and material progress through an individualized labor on the self.[3] Specifically, women use fashion to gain access to wealthier men who may enable them to leave Madagascar.

Although this group of jeunes may be numerically in the minority, they have come to carry a much wider cultural significance than their numbers would imply, much as the hippies of the 1960s did in the United States.[4] Their fashion practice has become a key site through which social mobility, as well as social and economic difference, is imagined and performed for all to see. The association of fashion with social mobility is not merely symbolic. Rather, youth use fashion to try to change their social positions more substantively. They do not always succeed. But, because of fashion's ability to project a desired future and to draw in the past, it works as a metaphor and mechanism for establishing socioeconomic distinctions. As the Comaroffs (1997:273) observe for the missionary encounter in southern Africa, style not only reflects existing realities but also is part of their very making. With an eye to how Tamatavian practice might illuminate the contemporary workings of social class, I trace how jeunes' use of fashion works to create social distinctions in the contemporary moment.

SOCIAL HIERARCHY, MOBILITY, AND YOUTH IN MADAGASCAR

Contemporary Malagasy ideas about social and economic hierarchy are complexly interwoven with older ideas about hierarchy and space. Many words that Tamatavians use to refer to social distinctions have the connotation of a social gradient that maps onto space, so the young people cited earlier speak of "people above" (*olona ambony*) and "people below" (*ambany*). They also refer to people with "different regions of life" (*farapianana*) to describe people with different incomes and lifestyles. But Tamatavians also use the term *kilasy* to refer to social and economic standing.[5] Richardson's (1885) dictionary defines *kilasy* as "class" in the sense of a classroom of children, suggesting that people's use of the word *kilasy* to refer to socioeconomic class may be drawn from their historical experience of schooling as a way of creating social distinctions. However, it is also possible that Malagasy youth use *kilasy* in the socioeconomic sense that emerged in mid-century political discourse, in part because of the early presence of the Communist Party in Madagascar (Randrianja, personal communication, March 15, 2004).[6]

This general framework of a social gradient mapped onto space is closely related to older ideas in which different groups were identified according to the territories they inhabited. In central Madagascar, which had a kingdom, the king or queen gave each group its ritual privileges. Where one's ancestors lived determined one's ranking in an overall social hierarchy. Though there was no kingdom in the area around Tamatave, similar ideas prevail within the context of local relations among lineage elders. At the same time, within each group, people consider elders more powerful than juniors because only elders have ritual control over ancestors in relation to the land. Given these associations, rootedness in place signals power: juniors move toward seniors to request ritual blessing, not vice versa (Cole 2005). Although the kinship system is bilateral, central east coasters give kinship traced through men more weight than that traced through women. Women generally go to live with their husbands when they marry (Cole 2001). Consequently, according to official ideology, men are associated with stasis, women with mobility, though this is always tempered by a woman's right to be buried in her father's tomb. One woman remarked, "People like to have boys because they 'make many people.'"[7] By bringing wives to live with them and have children, men increase the number of people in a given ancestry, thereby increasing the ancestry's power.

Youth occupy an ambivalent position within this framework (Cole 2005). On the one hand, they are furthest away from the ancestors, who are ideologically constructed as the legitimate source of power. Even when peasants gain power through economic ventures such as growing new cash crops, they use rituals of cattle sacrifice to reinterpret that power as having originated in ancestral blessing, rooted in particular pieces of land (Cole 2001). Because youth are supposed to ask ancestors for blessings, they remain dependent on their elders for access to their ancestors. On the other hand, precisely because youth are less closely related to ancestors and to the land, they are more able to move in search of new sources of economic wealth.

The way this movement is enacted, and what its ultimate consequences are, differs for men and women. Men are expected to go out and seek their fortunes while they are young. Ideally, they then return to their ancestral land, thereby reproducing the system and supporting the association of men with stasis. In practice, many young men find fortunes elsewhere. When they have built up enough social and economic power, they enter into a ritual cum practical battle in which they try to move the ancestors, as well as the ancestors' tombs, to them (Cole 2001). Kinship ideology emphasizes female youth as a source of discontinuity because they marry away. In practice, though, tensions and anxieties about social reproduction versus social transformation focus primarily on male youth.

This system continues to operate in rural contexts. Because many people who live in Tamatave retain ties to their rural ancestral villages, this same set of associations around socioeconomic hierarchy and age also operates in the city. But it has been partially displaced by ideas about social and economic hierarchy that originated in the context of colonialism. During the colonial period, education, which was closely associated with the Christian missions, became the key route through which Malagasy could ascend the social hierarchy. Gaining access to schooling enabled one to find a job in the colonial government, as a subaltern functionary.

In the colonial context and during the years following, schooling, a government job, and a more Western lifestyle were all considered highly prestigious. Many rural east coasters sought to gain education for their children as a route to social mobility (Ledoux 1951).[8] Young men became still further associated with mobility in the new colonial context because it became important for families to place at least one son in the colonial administration. In the cities, urbanites were so aware of the close connection between schooling and class privilege that equal access to schooling was one of the primary demands of those who brought down the First Republic (1960–1972) and instituted the Second (1975–1992) (Covell 1987). Students, angry because their chances for social mobility were blocked, were key players in the socialist revolution (Covell 1987). During the state socialist period, from approximately 1975 through 1991, government policy sought to downplay social distinctions, introducing slogans such as "We're all Malagasy" (*samy gasy*) and words such as *saranga*, an old term associated with rank, in efforts to foster national solidarity. The state's plans for development failed. Ironically, however, the impoverishment of the Second Republic over the course of the 1980s meant that as Madagascar became one of the poorest nations in the world, social and economic disparities decreased. Everyone was poor together, though distinctions remained.

Discontented urbanites ousted the Second Republic and supported a new government that liberalized the economy. As in 1972, youth in 1991, frustrated by their blocked social mobility, advocated these changes. Their fashion practice also became central to how people imagine social distinctions and social mobility. To understand why this is so, we need to consider local ideas about clothing and fashion.

CLOTHING, CONNECTIONS, AND CONSCIOUSNESS

Cloth and clothing play an integral role in social relations, working to bind people together and to set them apart (Bayly 1986; Cohn 1989; Tarlo 1996; Weiner and Schneider 1989). In Madagascar, cloth provides a significant metaphor for thinking about the fragile yet enduring nature of social relations. At the same time, weaving, as well as the exchange of store-bought cloth, is important in the production and reproduction of relations among the living and between the living and the dead (Fee 1997, 2002; Feeley-Harink 1989, 2003; Green 2003). In both respects, clothing is a meaningful vehicle through which people project a future and invoke a past.

Both historically and today, the clothing one wears communicates what kind of person one is—or hopes to be. It enables members of groups to signal their solidarity and to distinguish themselves from others (Bourdieu 1984[1979]). Tamatavians assume that how you dress embodies what kind of person you are. For example, members of new evangelical churches use dress to signal adherence to a Christian lifestyle, focused on the hereafter rather than on worldly concerns (figure 5.1). These youth dress in a modest (*maotina*) manner in keeping with their Christian morals. For men, this means forgoing the popular Pistons shoes and wearing long-sleeve shirts. For women, it means wearing skirts that cover their knees and shirts that cover their shoulders. Dominique, a young man who was a member of the Assembly of God Church, remarked, "There are those Pistons which are respectful, but there are some that point up in the front with metal. I want to be a model for my friends, and if I wore those kind of shoes, then all my friends might follow. Since I pray, if I were to do something that didn't fit my status as a Christian, that wouldn't do." Dominique's comment indicates both urbanites' use of clothing to mark groups off from one another and their belief that what one wears has the power to influence others.

FIGURE 5.1

A Malagasy pastor and his family display a modest dress style.

Just as clothing marks distinction, it also indicates solidarity. For example, a family carrying out a ritual will commonly buy similarly patterned wraps for the event (Feeley-Harnik 2003). Some high-school-age girls I knew all pitched in to buy the same fabric with which to sew sports uniforms, hoping to avoid the distinctions and social tensions caused by having access to different quality clothing. In the end, their plan was foiled when individuality reasserted itself and some of the girls chose to have the fabric sewn in different styles. However, their intent to use clothing to signal solidarity, instead of difference, was widely shared.

Clothing practice in Madagascar is not only symbolic. It is also substantive: clothing can partake of the wearer's physical and spiritual substance. People believe that clothing absorbs the qualities of another's skin, including not only bodily effluvia and diseases but also fate or destiny.[9] So intimately is clothing tied to the identity of the wearer, that a person's clothing "virtually speaks for the wearer" and can be used to stand in for a person in ritual contexts—as when invoking ancestral blessing (Feeley-Harnik 2003:70). Rural east coasters may take a piece of a mother's clothing to comfort her crying child when the mother is absent, as I learned when a friend asked me whether I did that with my own daughter when I left her to conduct fieldwork. This sense of the way in which one's self becomes bound up in one's clothing is profound. One young man I knew commented that if he lent his clothes to his brother, he would not ask for them back: "We each have our own skin, even if we are brothers." Some prostitutes I knew believed that certain clothes brought them good luck by attracting wealthy clients; to lend these meant potentially giving that luck to another. As a result, they rarely did so. When they did, it always caused fights. To exchange clothing was a sign of intimacy, so many men said that they would never trust a girlfriend who lent clothing to a friend. The act signaled that her loyalties belonged more with that friend than to the man. Such is the power of clothing to signal one's loyalties and connections.

Precisely because of these associations, giving clothing is one of the most important ways that people indicate their love and loyalty. I was most often praised and told that I was a "good, wise child" (*hendry*) when I brought new clothes from abroad to the family with whom I lived. One time, when I had brought a new wrap to my adoptive mother, she insisted on putting it on and going visiting around the village in a not-so-subtle display of how much I loved her.[10]

Conversely, many east coasters interpret a failure to give clothing as a lack of love. In a fit of anger at her stepfather, one girl remarked, "My step-father hates me. He won't even buy me a dress, though he's lived with us five years." The repudiation of clothing is also regularly used to mark breaks in social relations (see also Feeley-Harnik 2003). One woman, who had grown up in a rural area but then moved to Tamatave, had borne her first child out of wedlock. The boy's mother came bearing clothes ostensibly from the boy. Offended that the boy himself had not bothered to come, her father refused to put these on the child. She recounted:

> When the month of May came, I gave birth, and my mother sent word to the baby's father, but only his mother came. She brought clothes for the baby. And my father said, "If the child's father doesn't show up, we aren't going to put those clothes on our child, but you can take them home." He was so proud, my father, because the father of my child had been so disrespectful. Eventually, the baby's father showed up, and that is when we finally put those clothes on her.

Among lovers, taking back clothing that one has given is the clearest way to signal a rupture in social relations (see also Fee 2002). Traditionally, men give women gifts of clothing in order to establish sexual relationships.

In contemporary Tamatave, however, women who earn money from their long-term relationships with European men often buy gifts of clothes and give money to support their young Malagasy lovers (see Cole 2005). In many women's narratives, the end of the relationship almost always took place when the woman found the man spending her money on another girl, usually by buying clothes for the other girl. She would then mark the rupture by ripping off, or demanding the return of, the clothing she had bought for him. Tearing off someone's clothing or ripping someone's clothing in a fight is one of the most violent ways in which people seek publicly to shame each other and convey the rupture of a relationship.

ECONOMIC LIBERALIZATION, FASHION, AND FIVOARANA

Powerfully imbued with the ability to signal difference and sameness, to embody a person's essence, and to make and break social connections, clothing has many of the properties required to build a social world. In the contemporary context, however, these properties have taken on a new set of associations because of the rise of consumerism and the influx of images from abroad. Young people read other people's clothing to indicate how much money a person has, even though the actual economic basis behind this performance is fragile and ephemeral. This ambiguity makes fashion a particularly compelling idiom through which to imagine social and economic distinction in the current context. It also makes fashion central to some young women's efforts to improve their social and economic standing.

Like elite Malagasy in the past, jeunes take their ideas about what is fashionable, and therefore socially valued, from foreign places, particularly American popular culture (figure 5.2).[11] They try to achieve fashions set by pop stars (such as Celine Dion, the Spice Girls, Britney Spears, and the Backstreet Boys) whom they see in music videos on TV or read about in teen magazines like *OK Podium*. The channels through which young people learn about fashion are embodied in many of the words used to describe what it means to be well dressed: *mikata*, from the French "catalogue" (see also Weiss, chapter 9, this volume); *miposiposy*, from the French "to pose"; and *migenty*, from the English "to gentlemen."

Young men's fashionable clothing consists of a T-shirt, jeans, and shoes referred to as Pistons, which resemble thick-soled Dr. Martens.[12] Young women's clothing is more elaborated, in the double sense that they have more styles to choose from and that the social propriety of many of these styles is more debated. Young men and women widely agree that "sexy clothes"—those that hug the body and show off a girl's thighs, chest, or

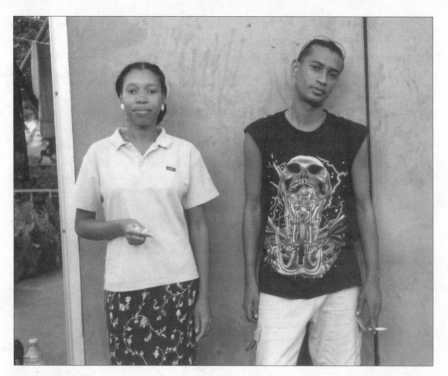

FIGURE 5.2
Two Malagasy jeunes display their style.

navel—are most fashionable in Tamatave, precisely because these fashions reveal a girl's body. Such clothes include the *"je m'en fou"* ("I don't care") top, a tiny top that shows one's belly; the "Marimar," a backless halter dress named for the heroine of the soap opera; and the *"maladià legon"* ("Come quickly, boys"), a form-fitting dress that buttons all the way down the front, so named because it implies easy sexual access for men. One young woman explained, "Girls like fashions that really cling to their body! That way, people can really see your figure. The objective is to seduce men to look at you." Yet dressing in such a scantily clad manner is in explicit violation of certain Malagasy norms of propriety and bodily decorum, which hold that one's upper arms, back, and knees should be covered. The production of a modern, youthful identity is built through the flagrant violation of older norms.

Jeunes believe that a relationship exists between the kinds of clothing one wears, how much money one has, and a person's social value. Economic worth constitutes personal value; one's status in this hierarchy is publicly indicated through fashion. One young man commented, "For youth who don't pray, they like shirts that have a picture of things that scare you and shoes that are very expensive. They think that if something is expensive, it is good, but if it is cheap, then it has to be bad. And they pursue everything that is expensive and do whatever they can to get that." Jean Aimée, a high school student who was quite fashionably dressed, noted, "It is mainly girls who compete over lamaody. The way I see it, the reason is that they want to show people that they have money, that they can buy many things that are expensive. Here, only people who have money have weight or importance. The old proverb 'Better to lose money than friendship' no longer holds. Now it is the reverse."

The use of fashion to signal economic wealth means that Tamatavians increasingly read other people's clothes to learn not only what kind of people they are but also how much money they have access to. Jeunes repeatedly described meeting others as a process of mentally totaling up the worth of their clothing (one imagines dollar signs in the eyes, as in the cartoons) to read what kind of economic power they possess.[13] These attitudes are captured in Veblen's (1992[1899]:118–119) observation that "expenditure on dress has this advantage over others: that our apparel is always in evidence and affords an indication of our pecuniary standing to all observers at first glance." He further notes: "Since the consumption of these more excellent goods is an evidence of wealth, it becomes honorific; and conversely the failure to consume in due quantity and quality becomes a mark of inferiority and demerit" (Veblen 1992[1899]:64). Tamatavian youth would agree.

Yet jeunes are also keenly aware that the relationship between fashion and one's pecuniary status, to use Veblen's words, is more complex than this model allows. Earlier in Madagascar's history, sumptuary laws may have made it relatively straightforward to guess status from the clothes someone wears, but, in contemporary Madagascar, this is not the case. Youth often say that economic power and fashion go together and that following the fashions is, transparently, supposed to signal one's access to money. But they are also well aware that fashion conceals as much as it reveals. Tamatavians regularly remark that the exterior signaled through fashion does not always correspond to the interior of the person. Among evangelical Christians, this concern with the potentially duplicitous nature of clothing is evident in the belief that people can appear like Christians but secretly harbor bad thoughts and motives. One fifteen-year-old member of the Assembly of God Church remarked, "There are some people who are modest [in dress] but have a bad character. Just because you dress modestly does not mean that you are well behaved."

Among those jeunes who followed the fashions, the concern was most frequently expressed in the idea that men, though well dressed, might not have a penny in their pocket. Explaining the term *manindry* (literally, "to press down on"), which youth used to refer to the status competition that takes place among them, one young woman remarked, "Manindry is someone who shows off for no reason. He shows off the clothes he is wearing, but maybe he is just showing off and he doesn't even own those clothes. Maybe he has just borrowed them." Though people hesitated to lend clothes to one another (at least in theory), they can rent clothes at the small bazaar. Much as commoners in Antananarivo at the end of the nineteenth century rented European clothes in order to appear at the Merina court (Raison-Jourde 1991), people today occasionally rent clothes to make a particular impression and thus achieve particular social goals. As a result, keeping up with the fashions does not always mean what it appears to signal.

Fashion's association with youth and the rapidity with which people become aware of new Western fashions also mean that fashion increasingly conveys novelty. To some extent, the necessity of being up-to-date marks the distinction between clothes and fashion: fashion, while retaining many of the characteristics I sketched out for clothing, emphasizes the importance of contemporaneity. Not only do jeunes use pricing and commodities to talk about human relationships and human value, but also they use fashion to talk about people's relation to time, which is, in turn, geographically situated.[14] Jeunes regularly comment that they are or are not "late" in respect to Western fashions. Although this temporal element of fashion was, no doubt, present during the colonial era, it has been heightened in the contemporary period because of the increased rapidity with which urbanites have access to foreign media.

These factors converge to make fashion central to how Tamatavians imagine and talk about social and economic differences. For example, referring to the ubiquitous social competition among students, a young woman at the university noted, "People fight to be of the same social class [*miady kilasy*]. Everyone tries to get the hat on *Marimar* [a soap opera] or the new fashion from *Le Coupable* [another soap opera]. Everyone wants frizzy hair like Aube [the heroine]. They want her purse as well. Whatever is good and beautiful in the film of the moment is what people want to get." In a similar vein, a young man described his hometown, using the colloquial expression "clean" to refer to being well dressed:

> In my neighborhood, the people divide in two. The rich people
> live up high in the town, and there are those who are high func-
> tionaries or doctors, and then we who live below and are still

struggling. If there is a child who is playing with a ball and he happens to go into the courtyard of someone who is rich and he goes to get his ball, they will treat him like a dog if they see he is the child of someone who is poor. *But if he is clean or has money,* they aren't mean to him. [emphasis added]

Another girl, whose widowed mother earned a living selling snacks, commented, "Me and my friend, even if we are the same social class [*farapianana*], she is very jealous, for she wants to be on top for everything. Here in Madagascar, we are always jealous of each other. There are fashions, but only those who have [*izay manana*] can follow the fashions."

In all these cases, being of a desirable "province of life" is repeatedly associated with having the right clothing, a condition that is sometimes expressed as being "clean" (as in the young man's statement above) but often expressed in talk about one's ability to keep up and follow the fashions. Jeunes' emulation of Western fashion, as well as the comment above about not being "late" in relation to Western fashion, suggests that the use of fashion to talk about socioeconomic distinctions also situates their conception of social distinction in relation to a wider world system. This point becomes particularly visible when we look at what female jeunes do with fashion.

GIRLS' FASHION, ASPIRATION, AND EUROPEAN MEN

Writing of fashion at the turn of the century, Simmel observed:

> The fashionable person is regarded with mingled feelings of approval and envy; we envy him as an individual but approve of him as a member of a set or group. Yet even this envy has a peculiar coloring. There is a shade of envy which includes a species of ideal participation in the envied object itself.... The moment we envy an object or a person, we are no longer absolutely excluded from it. [Simmel 1971(1904):304]

One reason that youth use fashion to talk about social and economic distinctions is that, like fashion, they feel a more desired socioeconomic position to be always just out of reach. Yet viewed from their perspective, it also seems potentially obtainable. Simmel's observations about the peculiar form of participation provided by envy captures an important aspect of fashion practice in Tamatave because the envy that young women feel for other people's clothing motivates their efforts to improve their own socioeconomic position.

I became aware of the complex relationship between aspiration, fashion, and male/female relationships when person after person told stories like the following. Olivina was a high school student whose father had worked as a gendarme and whose mother stayed at home. She recounted:

> There is a lot of competition [among youth] because, like everyone else, youth, too, want to improve their situation [*tia hanjary*]. When I was still in the Classe de Troisieme [the equivalent of ninth grade], I didn't think about it and wore my torn-up flip-flops to school, and all the students would make fun of me. And they kicked my shoe ahead of me, and I was so ashamed to go and get it, but I had to. I wasn't much bothered by it, but some youth, they couldn't stand that. Because people treat you like you're *soldes* [the French word for "sale," meaning cheap, worthless]. Because our parents' social class [*farifianana*] can't afford what youth want to buy, yet youth feel lower and less worthy in front of their friends. They start to look for ways to become like their friends. Whether boys or girls, we're all caught up in this. And so youth start to do bad things—like they get a boyfriend and get money from him to use to become like their friends.

As Olivina explained, in order to avoid feeling ashamed in front of their peers, many young women seek older, wealthier lovers who will give them the money or clothes they need in order to keep up with the fashions. Girls just starting out—often as young as fourteen or fifteen—may go with any man who has money as a way to obtain fashion, in a version of the "sugar daddy" relationship that has been documented throughout Africa (Hunter 2002; Nyamjoh 2005). Over time, this strategy means that these girls are less invested in schooling, choosing instead to use fashion to attract wealthy men. Sometimes, young girls make these choices because they have to, because their parents cannot afford to pay for their schooling. In other cases, girls' parents can afford the schooling. Either way, many young women perceive themselves as torn between two—sometimes three—choices. They can drop out of school and try to earn a living as best they can; they can struggle to complete school and undergo the difficulties of finding a job in a stagnant economy; or they can take the risk of finding wealth via the sexual economy. Although many young women go with any man who has money, they are well aware that the real path to success is to find a European (Cole 2004). One young man explained:

> There is a song by Doctor J. B. called "Love for Self-Interest" ["L'amour par intérêt"]. His song is really true! Nowadays, if one girl studies and one girl marries a European, it is the girl with the European husband who wins. Because the girl who marries the European can have a cement house, a car, and go in planes frequently. So she can really show off in front of the poor students who are still in school!

Finding a European to marry is the most popular way in which young girls from a variety of social backgrounds seek to improve their social and economic standing. There is an important temporal dimension to this process.

Among the young women who choose this route, finding a wealthier man or European is integrally tied to their self-conscious performance of being jeunes. The adjective used to refer to these girls is *mietsiketsika,* or someone who "moves." Young women I knew who fell into the category of mietsiketsika used the term positively to refer to someone who follows the latest fashions and knows how to search for money—by forging liaisons with, preferably, European men. By contrast, my conversations with unemployed or underemployed young men suggested a more ambivalent reading of mietsiketsika.[15] On the one hand, like the women, many of the men defined mietsiketsika as a girl who dresses well, tying it both to prostitution and to possible marriage. One young man remarked, "Those girls who move, it is to seduce men's eyes. When the man is seduced, he might marry her if he really likes the girl." Another commented, "To me, a girl who moves is someone who follows the fashions. Often, they are prostitutes [*makorelina*]. Where else would a girl get money to buy clothes and jewelry if it isn't from selling herself?" By using a local word for *prostitute* (*makorelina*) that has a pejorative connotation, this man signaled his critical view of girls who are mietsiketsika.[16] But other young men tied the term *mietsiketsika* to the image of a young woman who is responsible and knows how to search for money.

This ambivalence reflects the possible consequences—success and failure—associated with being jeunes, following the fashion, and looking for men. One young woman, who came from a poor rural background but had married a German, summarized what happens when a girl successfully uses the link between fashion and men to improve her socioeconomic standing:

> We all know that if you marry a Malagasy, you'll suffer, unless

maybe you both have big diplomas and great work. But I only have my CEPE [grammar school] diploma, and so it is better for me to marry a European and leave my suffering. I look at my friends who've been married to Malagasy men for years, and I outstrip them in terms of possessions. None of them have cars, and I have one. I've seen overseas, and they haven't. I know how to speak German, and they don't know any language but Malagasy.

For women like this one, dressing well and finding a European man *is*, in fact, a way to be responsible in social life, in her household, and to her family, precisely because it allows her to improve her social and economic status. In all fifteen interviews I had with women who had managed to fulfill the dream and forge close relationships with Europeans, creating a relationship with a European had a striking effect on their family's situation. It literally enabled the young women to become part of a global middle class. One young woman gave a particularly vivid sense of the social and economic advantages:

When you marry a European, you give birth to the descendents of Europeans, and the child's future will be much better because they'll have access to a foreign nationality and they can go to a good school in Europe and don't have to just stay here in Madagascar. They have much more of a chance to go far in life! Our children have gone to continue their studies in France. The younger one is still at the Lycée Français here in Tamatave. There are very few Malagasy who study at that school! That is already one huge advantage. And another advantage is that people respect you.

Still others described how they built houses, gave money to their parents, or were able to finance their younger siblings' education, thereby making it more likely for members of their families back in Madagascar to "jump tracks" as well. In each case, the successful women were able to translate the short-term performance of a desired status through fashion into long-term relationships with the potential to provide opportunities for their children and their natal families.

Yet girls who use fashion and "move" run the risk of failure: the mobility that is structurally associated with youth applies to both directions on the social ladder. The passage of time is an important part of this process.

Young women, who are relatively unencumbered, are most likely to succeed in their quest to find a European and "jump tracks." Often, however, the use of fashion and the attempt to forge relationships with men lead young women down the slippery slope toward stigmatized, hand-to-mouth prostitution. It takes very little to knock someone from the status of doing okay to a situation of real vulnerability: having a baby and being abandoned; having that baby get sick and not being able to pay the hospital bill; losing clientele because of political upheaval (something I watched happen after political unrest in 2002). The distance between comparative wealth and terrible poverty—the cusp of hope and failure—can be treacherously small. Young women who gain success by forging lasting relationships with Europeans are admired, but those who do less well and slip toward prostitution are despised and cruelly mocked, as implied in the man's critical comment about prostitutes, cited earlier (Cole 2004).

Moreover, for those girls who do not find a European, it becomes increasingly unlikely, although not impossible, that boys from their own neighborhood will want to marry them. Florien, a young man who wanted to set up a business but lacked the capital to do so, remarked, "If people didn't know that a woman had been a prostitute, they might marry her. But for me, I would never want to marry a girl who I'd known had been a prostitute, because I would fear the diseases I might catch from her." This man's comment about disease was unusual; many others talked about the loss of honor associated with marrying a former prostitute. Corroborating the pattern described here, several other young men commented that women who were prostitutes married people from "elsewhere," not boys from the same neighborhood. In other words, when a young woman moves from the category of "jeune who moves" to that of "prostitute," she almost has to marry a European—or a Malagasy from another part of the country—because local men will be less likely to marry her. And if she is unable to create a stable relationship with a man, she inevitably has fewer resources to work with, making movement down the social gradient all the more probable.

FASHION AND MOBILITY: TWO LIVES

What distinguishes between these two possible scenarios? According to jeunes, the difference is one of fate or luck.[17] According to the scenario sketched above, another important difference is time, the ability to maximize on desirable qualities of youthfulness. To begin to answer this question more thoroughly, however, let us consider the relationship of fashion to social mobility in the lives of two young women. I start with Zana, whom I first met in 1992 when she was only eight years old.

Zana

Zana's kinship network was entirely rural, with the exception of an uncle who worked in the army but lived in Antananarivo. Zana was the last-born daughter in a family of ten, and all the rest of her family farmed rice in a village to the south of Tamatave. At the age of seventeen, with the bare minimum of a grammar school education, she left the village to seek her fortune in Tamatave. When I first arrived in Tamatave, Zana was working as a maid for a Malagasy family. She was paid 35,000 fmg a month, about seven dollars at the time. Like all maids, she was allowed to go out on Sunday afternoons, when she would go strolling down at the beachfront to pick up men (Cole 2004). During my fieldwork, she stopped by my house to show off her new clothes and how "clean" she had become in contrast to her rural life. Zana used her new clothes to find a boyfriend, who gave her still more new clothes. She ended up pregnant, however. When a botched abortion left her dangerously ill, her parents sent her brother to bring her back to the village.

Anita

Anita was a strikingly pretty woman in her early twenties. Like Zana, she came from the countryside. Her father had abandoned her and her siblings at an early age, and she was raised by her mother. Unlike Zana, Anita parlayed her use of fashion into connections that enabled her to change her socioeconomic position and help her family.

While still in high school, Anita moved to Tamatave to live with her aunt. She went to school but quit and began selling clothes. She also started to covet the fashionable clothes that she saw people around her wearing, much as Olivina, cited earlier, described. On the advice of a friend, she started to go with men as a way to get the money to buy clothes. The men gave her clothes and money, some of which she sent home to her mother in the country. Despite her rural origins, Anita had connections in the city. Her aunt was employed at an import-export company, where, for a brief time, Anita worked as a secretary. It was there that she met the European who became her boyfriend. He took her to France to live, but she returned home of her own choice. On her return to Tamatave, she met one of his friends, also a European, who became her lover. They were contemplating marriage at the time I met her.

PAST CONTEXTS: KNOWLEDGE AND FAMILY

Zana's and Anita's stories suggest that luck and time are certainly important but that other factors also shape the possibility of success, factors that take us back to fashion as a way of conceptualizing socioeconomic distinctions. Jeunes mietsiketsika may use fashion to signal their aspirations, but how they use fashion—the places they wear it and the social networks that it implies—links them to past contexts as well. I turn to two aspects of the past that are embodied in clothing and help determine whether a girl's use of fashion is successful: knowledge and personal connections. These two aspects of the past are intimately related. Through personal connections, young girls often gain knowledge; by using their knowledge, they can make new personal connections. For the sake of analysis, however, I separate the two.

In multiple ways, particular kinds of cultural knowledge increase the probability that a young woman will be able to use fashion to achieve the socioeconomic mobility she desires. First, it takes a certain amount of cultural knowledge to be properly fashionable in the first place. As mentioned earlier, fashion rests on the premise of newness and the constant creation of obsolescence as new styles become fashionable. Because young people take their models of what is fashionable from Western media (contemporary American TV shows, magazines, the Internet), knowing what is fashionable requires access to certain forms of global knowledge. This association between fashion and knowledge is particularly evident with regard to the discourse about girls like Zana, who come from the countryside to work as maids in the city. The local slang word for these girls is *ambassady*, from the term *ambassador*, because they represent their families back in the countryside. As Zana's story illustrates, the first thing these girls do when they get their pay is to buy new clothes and go out strolling on Sunday afternoons, their only time off. As Zana's story also indicates, these girls are very proud of their sartorial transformations, and they use their clothes to make themselves appealing to boys who may give them money.

But urbanites mock the ambassady for failing to achieve up-to-date fashions, a failure that people largely attribute to lack of knowledge. Gilda, an eighteen-year-old girl who lived with her uncle and aunt, explained:

> Ambassady are people who come from deep in the countryside and move to town. There is a new fashion that comes out, and they want to follow it, but they don't know how to do it. Because they don't talk to other people and get their opinions, but just talk among themselves. There are those who wear denim overalls, and they put on a belt, but the fashion is to wear it loose! They don't get enough progress because they work in houses and don't go out. They only get to go out one day a week, so their thinking is really behind.

Strikingly, the representation of knowledge evident in Gilda's quote does not suggest a conception of knowledge as embodied dispositions and habitus in the sense defined by Bourdieu (1984[1979]). Rather, she is referring to a kind of knowledge that *can* be acquired by country girls *if* they build the social connections needed to acquire it. Just by being in their employers' homes and watching TV—something I often observed maids doing with the families for whom they worked—these young girls do begin to acquire these models. In this sense, these girls may have less access to global forms of media than Gilda, who could spend her time after school as she wished, but over time they do acquire the rudiments of modern fashion.

In other cases, however, the accumulation of knowledge relies more on long-term social connections, including modes of interaction and styles of self-presentation acquired by inhabiting the city and possibly attending school. This is particularly true about the knowledge girls need in order to use fashion as an entrée into the worlds they want to become a part of. For example, girls who attend the university (usually from more affluent families, with parents who work as shopkeepers or in government administration) often use the Internet or correspondence services to attract a husband. In many cases, a Malagasy woman, or a couple in which the woman is Malagasy and the man is French or Belgian, circulates a list of men who want "African wives." The girls submit their photos; ideally, a correspondence and then a meeting and marriage ensue. These women are thus able to bypass the potentially stigmatizing act of streetwalking or going to nightclubs to look for men. Also, many use the correspondence agencies secretly at the same time they are involved with Malagasy men. These "matrimonial agencies," as they are called, share the view of jeunes that it is luck or fate, not one's family background, that shapes a girl's chances.

In practice, however, knowledge plays an important role, particularly knowledge of European men's desires. I learned this when I went with a woman, Eudoxie, to take her friend's photo to a marriage agency for placement. Eudoxie came from a modest rural background and had long worked as a maid, but she had an aunt who had managed to marry a European. She was also a close friend of a woman who ran a hair salon and whose two sisters had married Belgians. Though Eudoxie did not have much education, over time and partly through working for Europeans and living in the city, she learned about their habits. By contrast, the friend whose photo we were carrying was newly arrived from the country. The photo showed a young girl dressed in white ruffles, clearly startled by the camera. Eudoxie and another young woman who accompanied us repeatedly commented on how inappropriate the photo was, how it would not be pleasing to men.

Even among those women who do end up working at nightclubs, knowledge about what European men want and how to make oneself desirable plays an important role.

If knowledge is crucial in shaping how a young woman uses fashion to achieve her goals, then so are social relations of various kinds. As mentioned earlier, it is difficult to separate the two because the possession of one often leads to the other. What is clear from my interviews with women who had actually married Europeans is that, in most cases, young women find Europeans, in part, because family connections or friends provide them with contexts in which to meet European men. In some cases, like the one mentioned above, a young girl might bypass the stigmatized version of streetwalking within the local neighborhoods, where one was likely to find only poor Malagasy men like herself, in favor of the fancier nightclubs because she had friends who were already used to going there and could show her the ropes. In other cases, family connections enabled young women to work in a place that made it easier for them to meet Europeans. In almost every story I heard, the richer branch of the family provided the social connections and capital necessary for a poorer member to achieve social mobility. In turn, the young successful woman became a focal point for her siblings' aspirations.

CONCLUSION

I could tell many more stories about how young women try to use fashion to improve their life circumstances. To conclude, I emphasize three general points.

First, the Malagasy jeunes' idiom of fashion *does*, in fact, provide a powerful analytic for conceptualizing how class works in the contemporary moment. It does so because, in the Malagasy context, the performance of fashion explicitly signals a person's aspirations *and* encompasses "a sense of self enmeshed in ties with others" (Feeley-Harnik 2003:70). As a result, it has the power to signal future hoped-for contexts and past ones. In this regard, the Malagasy idiom of fashion speaks to some of the issues raised by Liechty's (2003) and the Comaroffs' (2000a) efforts to theorize the nature of class in the contemporary moment. Recall that Liechty (2003) argues in favor of a consumption-oriented, performative conceptualization of class but that the Comaroffs bemoan the tendency, visible in both everyday life and scholarly accounts like Liechty's, to dissolve more enduring inequalities into lifestyle choices and consumption. Liechty builds an account of class rooted in personal experience, an experience that may inadvertently erase the conditions of its possibility; the Comaroffs highlight the experiential dimensions of class but argue that any analytic must move beyond experience to consider a wider frame.

Part of what I have argued here is that because jeunes' fashion practice simultaneously signals aspiration, personal performance, and broader social links, it provides a way out of this contradiction by explicitly signaling the dialectical relationship between the two theories. The Malagasy idiom of fashion highlights consumption and the particular conditions of possibility that enable some young women to transform ephemeral performance into more enduring structures of privilege. At the same time, jeunes' use of fashion to achieve mobility provides important insights into the nature of contemporary social hierarchies by highlighting the temporal and gendered dimensions of social mobility. Specifically, as Madagascar has moved from a neocolonial independence, to state socialism, to a liberalized economy, jeunes argue that schooling no longer provides a route to socioeconomic mobility. Young men and young women agree on this point, but only young women can use fashion to try to improve their socioeconomic position.

What my ethnography suggests, however, is that their ability to do so is profoundly limited by time. Girls are most likely to be able to use fashion to improve their socioeconomic position while they are chronologically young, as my discussion of "youth who move" implies. The ability to perform "youth who moves" relies on youthful bodies, bodies that inevitably age. Fashion practice may provide the means for a few girls to achieve social mobility, but it cannot replace more enduring mechanisms of mobility such as education. Youth, at least the bodily condition of youth, is fleeting, but the skills bestowed by education last well beyond the context of their initial production and can be used in multiple contexts. Though I have not investigated systematically the relationship between education and social mobility, my anecdotal experience after eight years of conducting research in Tamatave suggests that education still provides a route to mobility within Madagascar, despite what jeunes say.

This observation leads me to a final insight into the dynamics of class gained from looking at jeunes' fashion practice: the emergence of two tracks, one that is "world-class" and situated beyond the confines of Madagascar, another that is, to borrow James Ferguson's (2006) phrase, "second-class" and situated locally. When jeunes succeed in using fashion practice to achieve socioeconomic mobility, it is not because they have moved up the social gradient in Madagascar. Rather, it is because they have literally jumped tracks by finding a European to marry, thereby becoming part of what might be called a global middle class. Only a tiny minority can do so.

The rest are likely to slide down the economic ladder within Madagascar. The divergence between those who "jump tracks" and those who remain within Madagascar suggests that, in the context of globalization, any analysis of class must continually take global inequalities into account.

Acknowledgments

The fieldwork on which this article is based was carried out in 1999, 2000–2001, and again in 2002, 2003, and 2004. I am grateful to the Fulbright Program, the Wenner-Gren Foundation for Anthropological Research, and the American Philosophical Society. A fellowship from the Radcliffe Institute for Advanced Study enabled the writing of this material, which benefited greatly from comments by members of the Cambridge Writing Circle, 2003–2004: Smita Lahiri, Anne Marie Leshkowich, Ajantha Subramanian, Karen Strassler, and Christine Walley. I would also like to thank Anne Allison and Paula Fass for their helpful comments. As always, I am grateful to Debbie Durham for helping me think through my youth-related material.

Notes

1. For example, see *Loharano Malagasy*, no. 39, Février 1952, located at the Bibliothèque Nationale, Paris.

2. Derived from a word that during the nineteenth century meant "to arrange to build, to make ready" (Richardson 1885), *fivoarana* acquired the meaning of an inner spiritual work on the self in the context of Protestant teaching in the early twentieth century.

3. The idea of fivoarana exists alongside that of *mandroso*, which denotes more collectively oriented progress.

4. Several scholars have noted the tendency for the characteristics of a comparatively small group of people to come to stand for the larger whole. Karl Mannheim (1993), for example, argued that town youth, who have access to various forms of public culture, would more likely come to stand for generational culture. Similarly, Barrie Thorne (1993) observed that, among schoolchildren, the behavior of a few kids is habitually generalized, or reified, into a characteristic of the age or gender of all the kids.

5. People can also use the word *kilasy* in the same sense as "classy" in English, for example, "high-class" (Malanjaona Rakotomalala, personal communication, July 14, 2005).

6. Occasionally, people would also mention the word *saranga* in these contexts.

Traditionally used to indicate height and rank, *saranga* was adopted during the socialist period to replace the word *class* in the government's efforts to abolish class differences (Malanjaona Rakotomalala, personal communication, July 14, 2005). Richardson (1885) says that the word *saranga* comes from the word for bird feathers of unequal length.

7. In Malagasy, the expression she used was *Lehilahy mahamaro olona*.

8. They also expressed keen awareness that education could change people by making them more prone to anger and therefore unfit for ancestral practice. As a result, many rural families would invest in one child by giving him access to education, and another child might be chosen to take over ancestral responsibilities.

9. See Bayly 1986 for a discussion of similar ideas in the South Asian context.

10. This observation holds for other groups as well, as both Feeley-Harnik (2003) and Fee (1997) note for the Sakalava and Antandroy, respectively.

11. The use of metropolitan—or, in this case, North American—models for fashion is not simply a product of the post-colonial period, as much current theorizing might imply. Rather, it stems from long-standing ideas about the power and prestige that come from incorporating foreign power. See Rutherford 2002 for a comparative example from Indonesia.

12. During my fieldwork following 9/11, the faces of Osama Bin Laden and Bush set against an image of the two towers collapsing was a favorite T-shirt among young men. They chose the T-shirt because it symbolized the clash of two powerful men, both of whom were *supposed* to be powerful (*masiaka*).

13. This was particularly true of how young women regarded men as they sized them up as potential lovers. One young man recounted:

Really, we compete over fashion! Girls compete over clothes, and men compete over shoes. Even if a man's clothes aren't that good, they wear shoes that are worth 450,000–500,000 [around ninety dollars and as much as a functionary might earn per month]. Then the girls will notice him. For example, if I walk around and flirt with women, the first thing they notice is my face. Then, if they look at my face, they look at my clothes, then at my pants. And if they are pretty clean, then they look at my shoes. If I was wearing flip-flops, they would leave and never look at me again!

14. For example, people use the word *soldes* (Fr: sale) to indicate worthlessness and the expression *pointure* (Fr: shoe size) to express the fit of a particular relationship, as in "He's not my shoe size!" (*tsy pointurko*).

15. The one way that young men might be able to acquire a mietsiketsika girl is to become her *jaombilo*, the relationship formed when a girl earns money from prostitution or a long-term relationship with a European and uses that money to support a

younger Malagasy man (Cole 2005).

16. Local views about sex-for-money exchange are complex. Although it is considered standard for women to receive gifts or money in exchange for sex, views about women who actually make a living by sleeping with many partners are mainly negative. If a woman manages to achieve financial security and move out of prostitution, however, people will overlook how she earned her money (see Cole 2004).

17. Young people use the term *anjara*, which can be translated as "fate," "lot," or "portion," depending on the context. It is frequently used in discussions of marriage. They also talk about "trying one's luck" in the context of explicitly searching for a European partner.

6

Private Anxieties and Public Hopes

The Perils and Promise of Youth
in the Context of Globalization

Constance A. Flanagan

Consider the following excerpts from Richard Sennett's book *The Corrosion of Character* (1998):

> Adjustment and change is woven through human history. Natural disasters, wars, economic depressions have upset the status quo and engendered anxieties. But what's peculiar about uncertainty today is that it exists without any looming historical disaster; instead it is woven into the everyday practices of a vigorous capitalism where instability is meant to be normal. [31]

> A larger sense of community, and a fuller sense of character, is required by the increasing number of people who, in modern capitalism, are doomed to fail. [135]

Sennett's observations capture the dilemmas that younger generations face as they imagine futures in the context of globalization. His suggestion that the current moment is filled with personal anxiety yet demands a new sense of community frames the two sets of youth narratives discussed in this chapter. In the first set, youth imagine a world where they are on their own to manage lives made precarious by flexible capital. They accept the rules of a neoliberal order as a given, tie their hopes to the happiness it promises, believe that their commitment to education and hard work will pay off, but worry privately about whether the system will deliver. Drawing from Sennett, I argue that there are psychological costs in anxiety and self-doubt for individuals who imagine only private solutions to the uncertainties that global capital and the privatization of risk have normalized. In the second, alternative set of narratives, activist youth are making public and political the private anxieties they share, challenging a world organized on market principles, and seeking a fuller sense of character than jobs alone can furnish (see also Cole and Durham, chapter 1, and Weiss, chapter 9, this volume).

The period of youth offers a unique lens on the future because, more than other times in life, the late adolescent/early adult years are a time to take stock, to assess the "adult" world one is entering and the niche one might carve in it. Some psychologists contend that youth is a period for experimenting, for pushing boundaries and exploring different identities before settling into social roles (Arnett 2004). The argument is that even poor choices made at this time can be illuminating because, unlike older adults, young people have time to change course and, for some, life offers second chances. Other scholars contend that the luxury of a moratorium to explore identity varies by class and that what may appear as a lack of role commitment may really be a lack of opportunity (Côté 2000; Nakkula 2003). Typically, youth are less committed than older adults to roles that constrain the futures they envision. They also are more intellectually and psychologically flexible and more socially mobile. Thus, it is easier for them to accommodate, as well as contribute to, social change. Because they are at the brink of adulthood, it is also more incumbent on them to do so.

The lens of youth is a good vantage point for framing what the future portends because the collective decisions of younger generations are what constitute the future (Flanagan et al. 2005; Youniss and Yates 1997). Visions of the future and the possibilities young people imagine frame the personal choices they make today, and class and race differences in the paths young people take are, in large measure, shaped by what they imagine is possible for people "like them" (Flanagan and Campbell 2003).

Figuring the future through the "youth" lens also amplifies intergenerational disjunctions. For contemporary youth, the rules of the "social contract" in America have shifted considerably since the days when their parents came of age. I use the metaphor of a social contract as an interpretive frame for understanding how young people theorize and try to make sense of their social order. What do they think are the rules by which we live, the ties that bind us together? And what are the psychological tensions and prospects associated with changes in those principles?

In using the term *social contract*, I am evoking a long history of moral and political theory that tries to explain the foundations on which individuals join together to form civil societies. Early versions of social contract theory posited that people surrender certain rights as individuals to a government that, in turn, guarantees their liberties. Implied in this exchange is a belief that those who live by the rules of a social order (and, as critics of the theory have noted, make the rules of that order) also reap its benefits.[1] In modern welfare states, the formulation of this contract meant that governments protected citizens from the volatility of a free market while at the same time supporting the expansion of the market.

In recent decades, a new social contract has been evolving, one that reflects the ascendancy of markets and the decline in government's role in curbing their excesses and protecting citizens against their vagaries. The new deal with which younger generations now grapple as they come of age also reflects a devolution in responsibility for risk, from a model in which risks were socialized, to one in which risks increasingly are privatized (Hacker 2006). Finally, the facts of life with which younger generations must contend include a restructuring of the nature of work that portends more episodic and insecure jobs with fewer lifetime benefits and guarantees. In light of the increasing uncertainties associated with the transition to adulthood, perhaps it is not surprising that the period of youth itself— that elastic period in the late adolescent and emerging adult years—has become protracted (Fussell and Furstenberg 2005; Settersten, Furstenburg, and Rumbaut 2005).

From the early nineteenth century through the 1950s, the transition to adulthood became progressively more standardized and orderly, especially for white men. By the mid-twentieth century, they could assume that they would complete school, get a job, marry, and start a family, all in a somewhat orderly sequence (Shanahan 2000). The links between developmental tasks, institutional preparations, and social roles were clear. For young people today, the job market is less predictable, and training is a matter of constant retooling for the market's shifting demands. It is increasingly incumbent on individuals to manage uncertainties (Hacker 2006). As a developmental and social psychologist, I am interested in what meaning this new order holds for youth. Toward that end, I have employed the psychological concepts of social representations (Deaux 2006; Moscovici 1988) and lay theories (Levy, Chiu, and Hong 2006). Both refer to the socially constructed beliefs that are shared by groups (in particular cultures or at particular historical moments) to explain phenomena, reduce uncertainty, and guide decisions. When considering child and youth development, it is important to remember that both social representations and lay theories shape the practices of formative institutions such as schools and, in turn, are reinforced by repeated enactments in those settings.

In the first part of this chapter, I draw from the words of high school students in the United States to illustrate that, in the insecure world of flexible capital, (a) they perceive the increasing competition among individuals for a shrinking supply of jobs; (b) they believe that individuals should work harder, be more vigilant, and regularly retool; and (c) the new social contract exacts a heavier burden on working-class youth because their families are less able than middle-class families to substitute for the state's eroding safety net of programs. The central theme in these interviews is about the self-made individual who works hard, jockeys for position, and rises above hard times. If, as Sennett argues, instability is a normal state of affairs, then uncertainty is the future. I maintain that it is futile for individuals to resolve the tensions of flexible capital in private, because they will bear the costs in increased anxiety and diminished trust.

In the second part of this chapter, I suggest that new forms of youth political activism offer individuals collective alternatives. Like the young people quoted in the first part of the chapter, young political activists are aware that opportunities and resources are becoming scarce and that individuals have to be creative and use their imagination to resolve problems. However, in contrast to the first group, they do not expect individuals by themselves to resolve the tensions, and they do not accept that a neoliberal social contract is a given. As the slogan of the World Social Forum suggests, they believe that "another world is possible."[2]

Historically, youth have revitalized political organizations and social movements, in part because they tend to be more idealistic, adventuresome, and willing to take risks than are the adults in those movements (Halberstam 1998; Watts and Flanagan 2007). The new forms of activism reflect youth's awareness of the global scope and interconnections of political issues, their sense of shrinking resources, and their blurring of private and public in lifestyle and consumer politics. Young activists are creating political identities that are fluid and flexible and organizational forms that are inclusive and take advantage of the democratic potential of the Internet. Taken together, these developments suggest that youth's images of the evolving social contract constitute a key site through which we can witness the emergence of new political forms. By focusing on the various ways that those who are coming of age in the context of globalization are resolving its tensions, we can imagine possible futures.

THE EROSION OF SAFETY NETS

Risk, as Jacob Hacker (2006) points out, is a social condition that creates variety in human experience. To deal with risks, a society can create political and market institutions that pool risks associated with the human condition (health of family members, natural disasters, factory closings, old age). Alternatively, a society can decide that individuals and families alone should manage the uncertainties and bear the burdens of risk. *The Great Risk Shift* refers to the transfer of responsibility for managing risk that has occurred in the United States over the past thirty years, from a network of government and employer programs, to individuals and their families.

For earlier generations, states socialized the risks associated with unpredictable markets through social insurance programs. With unemployment compensation and poor relief programs, states ensured that contingencies such as industrial downturns, economic depressions, and personal hardships due to aging and disability would not fully determine the life chances of their members. The social welfare system in the United States, established in the Social Security Act of 1935, was based largely on a male "breadwinner" model. Gordon (1996) has referred to the US model as a two-tiered system: The first tier of social insurance programs included Social Security and Unemployment Insurance, with Workers' Compensation and Medicare added later. Women, the poor, and many people of color were not in jobs covered by this system and therefore were excluded. The second tier of welfare (Aid to Families with Dependent Children, originally ADC) was reserved for women and children whose livelihoods were not provided by a breadwinner. Compared with other welfare states, the US government provided little insurance against risk. But, as Hacker (2006) points out, private workplace benefits such as health care, unemployment compensation, and retirement pensions were part of the safety net to which many American workers and their families were accustomed.

The transfer of risk management to individuals and families has occurred during roughly the same period as a radical restructuring of the US economy. In the decades after World War II, unemployment was cyclical, following the rhythms of contraction and expansion in industry. The new unemployment is structural and therefore more permanent.

Analyses of US work and earnings trends since the 1970s show that more of the jobs in the new economy are contingent (part-time, of shorter tenure, with fewer benefits). Job instability is especially acute for African American men (Bluestone and Rose 1997). Compared with the years between 1946 and 1972, when changes in a person's employment typically reflected promotions and raises, changes in employment today are more likely to be associated with demotion, unemployment, and displacement to other careers (Carnavale 1995). Since the 1970s, family incomes have become more volatile, and access to employer-provided health insurance and pensions has fallen for the average worker, making it more difficult for families to plan their futures (Danziger and Gottschalk 2005; Hacker 2006). To fully appreciate the changing context for working families, declines in union membership over the past four decades also should be noted: In 1953, 36 percent of private sector workers were unionized. That figure is less than 8 percent today, and younger workers are less likely to be organized.

The social contract of the neoliberal state—less reliance on government and more reliance on the self—is reflected in remarks that Margaret Thatcher made in an interview in 1987:

> I think we have gone through a period when too many children and people have been given to understand "I have a problem, it is the Government's job to cope with it!" or "I have a problem, I will go and get a grant to cope with it!" "I am homeless, the Government must house me!" and so they are casting their problems on society and who is society? There is no such thing! There are individual men and women, and there are families and no government can do anything except through people, and people look to themselves first. [Keay 1987:9]

How should young people respond to this neoliberal social contract in which, as Thatcher advises, people should look to themselves first? The answer they have been offered is to get more education. In the vernacular of economists, the returns to more years of education are in better-paying jobs. In fact, post-secondary education is now considered essential for obtaining jobs that can support families. Yet it may not be enough. Paul Krugman (2005) notes that when the technology bubble of the late 1990s burst, so did the notion that American knowledge workers were invulnerable. Maximizing their competitive edge is clearly on the minds of young people. High school students hire professionals to coach them through the college application process. They pad their résumés with advanced placement courses, extracurricular activities, and community service hours. College students hedge their bets by accumulating credentials, juggling double and even triple majors. In North America and Europe, credential inflation and qualification accumulation appear to many to be the right strategies to ensure their marketability (Roberts 2003).

At the same time that more years of education, training, and retooling are needed, government is paying less. Individuals are incurring more of the costs in tuition, living stipends, and loans. Besides the financial costs of education, they have to deal with an uncertain job market, making their best guess about which sectors will be hiring when they have completed their schooling. The extended period of education and the burden of individual debt associated with it are some of the major contributors to the protracted period that the transition to adulthood has become.

THE PROTRACTED PERIOD OF "YOUTH"

In late modern societies, the period between adolescence and adulthood has lengthened. During the mid-twentieth century, it was common for white males to complete their education, start at the bottom of a career ladder, and work their way up (Côté and Levine 2002). There were normative patterns and a predictable sequence and thus some clarity about the connection between choices made in the present and future life trajectories. Compared with that relatively orderly sequence of roles, the trend for today's youth includes longer periods of schooling, combinations of work and education, delayed marriage, and lower lifetime fertility (Fussell and Furstenberg 2005). Gone is the typical career paradigm characterized by lifetime employment and a pension upon retirement. A growing share of the jobs on which people's livelihood depends includes independent contracting; temporary, on-call, day labor; self-employment; and part-time work. Analyses of national trends in 1995, 2001, and 2005 reveal, respectively, that 32.2 percent, 29.3 percent, and 30.6 percent of the workforce were employed in such "nonstandard" jobs. Compared with full-time jobs, nonstandard work is characterized by lower pay, fewer benefits, and less job security (Mishel, Bernstein, and Allegretto 2007).

It is noteworthy that colleges and universities have done little to help younger generations deal with these new realities. Although educating younger generations for the labor market is one of the main goals of postsecondary education, the elusive nature of the job market makes it difficult to predict those sectors that will be in demand when an entering freshman class graduates. Increasingly, individual youth must define their own path to adulthood and identify and pay for the training and opportunities they will need in order to achieve their goals.

The family is the main backup system that scaffolds young people during this period, but there are class differences in the financial resources that families can offer. Furthermore, the experiences that many, particularly working-class, parents had as they entered adulthood do not serve as a useful guide for their children. Consequently, as in the past, class differences in family resources and social connections contribute to the diverging pathways that youth's adult lives will take (Kerckhoff 1993; Osgood et al. 2005). During their late teens and twenties, 40 percent of American youth now move back to their parents' home at least once after leaving (Goldscheider and Goldscheider 1999). Economists estimate that American parents provide $2,000 annually to their eighteen-to-thirty-four-year-old children (in 2001 dollars), with the households in the top 25 percent income bracket providing at least 70 percent more assistance to these offspring than the 25 percent with the lowest incomes (Schoeni and Ross 2005). As Beck argues in his book, *Risk Society* (1992), the gains and risks associated with the transformation from an industrial to a new modernity are unevenly distributed: "Like wealth, risks adhere to the class pattern, only inversely: wealth accumulates at the top, risks at the bottom. To that extent, risks seem to strengthen, not abolish, the class society. Poverty attracts an unfortunate abundance of risks. By contrast, the wealthy (in income, power, or education) can purchase safety and freedom from risk" (Beck 1992:35).

How do young people interpret this new social contract? How do they explain the implications of deindustrialization? What, if anything, do they expect the state to do if people lose their jobs? Do youth view the loss of jobs in the United States as part of a larger global picture? How much control do they believe individuals have over the changing conditions of the workplace? What do they think individuals should do to maximize their chances for success?

Such questions have been at the heart of my program of research on adolescents' interpretations of the social contract. In this work, I have explored the psychological underpinnings of what political scientists refer to as diffuse support for the system, that is, the widely shared belief that our system is just. In the United States, this means that, in general, people have to believe that everyone has an equal opportunity to succeed, that the playing field is level, and that differences in income and status reflect individual differences in performance. The belief in a level playing field is a commonly held cultural script in the United States (Crocker, Major, and Steele 1998) and is tightly linked to our shared conviction that the American dream of financial success and independence is achieved largely by individual determination and hard work (Hochschild 1995). This social representation of the American system as a meritocracy is so strong that we tend to legitimate existing social arrangements, even at the expense of personal and group interest.

Jost, Banaji, and Nosek (2004) have advanced a psychological theory of *system justification* to explain people's motivation to legitimate the status quo. They contend that both the historical record and a host of psychological studies show that there is more evidence that disadvantaged groups acquiesce to and defend the status quo than rebel against it. In part, this is because people have a need to maintain a favorable self-image, to feel validated in their actions, and to perceive their behaviors as consistent with their beliefs. Disadvantaged youth who apply themselves, studying hard in high school and aspiring to college, have to believe that their efforts will pay off—that the rewards of a meritocratic system will accrue to people "like them," who follow the rules.

The notion that we live in a meritocracy is absorbed by most children in the United States as they grow up, but I contend that the success of disadvantaged youth especially depends on an ardent commitment to this belief. For people "like them," with few connections, safety nets, and second chances, there is no other way to succeed except through intense self-reliance and hard work. Cultural psychologists argue that we develop our identities and beliefs via the accumulated enactment of "selfways"; that is, relationships and interactions we have in everyday contexts form the contours of our lives (Markus, Mullally, and Kitayama 1997). Building on this point, I contend that youth's interpretations of the social contract reflect the particular contexts they and their families have known and the selves they have enacted. Furthermore, their views reflect an intimate understanding of the way the principles of their social order, its opportunities and constraints, apply to people "like them."

In the mid-1990s, I set out to learn more about how young people interpret the evolving social contract in America. I was particularly interested in their theories about inequality, which I investigated by asking students in high school social studies classes how they would explain to a hypothetical foreign visitor why some people in our country are poor, some are unemployed, some homeless, and some rich (Flanagan and Tucker 1999). I emphasize that schools were the site where the study was conducted, because that is an important part of the story: the views reported here are those of high school students and not their peers who had dropped out of school.

The high schools were located in communities in Michigan, part of the rustbelt that had been accustomed to a steady supply of jobs in auto and steel for generations but in the final decades of the twentieth century experienced deep cutbacks. As the hub of the American automobile industry, Detroit is a prototype for the old social contract that bound workers and management in a pact in which economic risks were socialized. For several generations, families in these communities had enjoyed the legacy of good jobs in auto and auto-related industries. Furthermore, communities in the region benefited economically from the tax base and large number of working families. Jacob Hacker describes this in *The Great Risk Shift*:

> The old contract—never enjoyed by all workers and almost always implicit, yet still a powerful private standard whose influence belied its less-than-complete reach—said that workers and employers shared the risk of uncertainty in the market as well as the gains of productivity from skills and innovation....On the worker side, shared risks meant a certain degree of loyalty to the firm, a certain degree of commitment to the pay and welfare of fellow employees, a certain degree of restraint in demanding benefit and pay increases when times were good so that the fallout would be less painful when times were bad. On the employer side, shared risks meant an emphasis on the development of workers' skills, the provision of generous workplace benefits like health care and pensions, and the buffering of workers from the risks of fluctuating demand. The bargain held because it worked for both parties—workers received job security, guaranteed benefits, and good pay; employers got loyal, productive workers who invested in skills specific to their jobs and didn't jump ship when times got tough. [Hacker 2006:65]

The psychological implications of deindustrialization are palpable in communities where the customary rhythms of everyday life were organized around assumptions that no longer fit reality. Restructuring of the auto industry and the massive layoffs associated with it, as well as the rollback of unions, were well under way in the 1980s, when I conducted a two-year study on the spillover of parents' job loss and demotion on family life and children's adjustment at school. These declines in parents' work lives caused increased conflict with adolescent children (Flanagan 1990) and also manifested in the children's behaviors at school. Over the course of the two years, teachers (who were unaware of which families were impacted by layoffs) reported poorer adjustment for those students whose parents had, in fact, been affected (Flanagan and Eccles 1993).

In the context of the economic restructuring that was affecting their communities, I was interested in learning more about the younger generation's theories about economic change. I purposely sampled in schools whose students came from a broad spectrum of class backgrounds. Some youth in this study had parents who were doctors, lawyers, and executives in the auto industry. Other parents were on-line workers, domestics, or were unemployed. More than four hundred high-school students participated in the study. Fifty-six percent of the participants self-identified as Caucasian, 17 percent as African American, 13 percent as Arab American, and the rest with other ethnic minority groups.

Regardless of their age or background, the most common theme young people expressed was the individual's responsibility for his or her fate and the imperative in childhood to work hard in school in order to succeed in adulthood: "The reason why people have good jobs is because they work for seventeen to twenty years in school." People who are unemployed "probably didn't think of their future as youngsters, but they now should pay back by being unemployed." In contrast, they asserted that people are rich because they "worked hard, got what they wanted, had a good education, wanted to be someone, not a nobody." The meritocratic ethos taken to its logical extreme is captured in this high school student's explanation for poverty: "In every society, there are going to be poor people. Darwin's theory holds true, survival of the fittest. The smartest and most motivated earn the most money."

The importance of staying in school, of personal motivation, of applying oneself and delaying gratification in order to obtain a good job later in life, was echoed again and again in the teens' statements. But their assertions contain an even bigger comment on the character of those who make it or fail. Those who succeed had a goal—to be "someone, not a nobody"— and they studied and worked hard to achieve that end. No benefit of the doubt is given to those who lose their jobs. Rather, unemployment is considered a just desert, a consequence or "payback" for failing to "plan ahead" as a child and develop the qualities of character that lead to success.

Young people also located success and failure in the character of families, rather than in a wider structure of social and economic relations. One white male high-school student remarked, "Most of these people were born into poverty. Their fate can be blamed on their ancestors," whereas people who are better off "obviously take education, motivation, and intelligence very seriously. Somewhere in the family, someone had to work hard to get where they are—a trait that should and is passed down in the family." Although being born into poverty could be perceived as an indication that the playing field is uneven, families (ancestors) are still held accountable: motivation and hard work are transformed into traits of character passed on as a legacy to future generations. These themes of family responsibility echo those found in national opinion polls in which the American public holds parents, and especially mothers, responsible for how children turn out (Hochschild 1995).

It was the adolescents from privileged backgrounds who were more likely to critique the system as one of unequal opportunities. For example, they observed that one reason people may be rich is that they "have connections, got the right breaks, exploited them, and made the most out of what they could." Youth from more privileged backgrounds also were more likely to hold the government accountable: "The government wants to cut help for the needy, won't increase the minimum wage, and our educational system in some places is not that good, so they don't have the skills to get decent jobs." They also noted how policy contributes to inequality: "A lot of rich people are successful in what they do, but they also benefit from the US government. There is not enough focus on homeless people, and also the government doesn't make it better for them."

In contrast, rather than criticize inferior schools or government negligence, less privileged youth more commonly held individuals accountable. One young man whose father was a steelworker said, "I would say that the unemployed didn't get an education and they don't want to work, because anyone can get a minimum-wage job." He explained that people are homeless because "they are lazy and don't want to get a job. They just want people to feel sorry for them." Similarly, a female from a poor urban area, whose vocational goal was to go to "hair school," said, "People are unemployed because they are lazy and think jobs should come to them." Another female from this same community explained, "Poverty is something that has been going on for years.... If you *choose* to be poor, then that is a decision that you have to either change or deal with." She also believed that people are rich because "sometimes people have dreams and set goals and that is what happens." In the picture these youth portray, inequality is a natural state of affairs, and the sorting process by which people succeed or fail is a matter of personal motivation.

Why would those who are disadvantaged by a system embrace its tenets and legitimate it? As system justification theory predicts, legitimizing the system restores a sense of confidence and control, especially for those who are confronted by uncertainty and have no other ways to manage it (Jost and Hunyady 2005). In the case of the young people in my study, justifying the system provides some consistency between their actions and beliefs. Their decision to stay in school, despite high levels of dropout in their school districts, is consistent with their belief that individuals are responsible for their fates. Conversely, if the system is the problem, then ultimately they will be its victims. Furthermore, contesting the status quo would exact a heavier burden on their futures than on the futures of those who are privileged by the system.

Several studies of ethnic minority youth are relevant in this regard. Although most Americans espouse the promise of the American dream, African American youth are more likely to harbor doubts that its specific tenets apply to members of their group (Hochschild 1995; Mickelson 1990). At the same time, young people make different choices, and those decisions tend to be consistent with their beliefs. Whereas disadvantaged African American youth who give up on their education are more likely to blame "the system" for the job ceilings African Americans face, those who are committed to getting an education are more likely to internalize beliefs consistent with the economic and sociopolitical systems that schools promote (Ogbu and Fordham 1986). However, the choices are rather bleak. Lacking an alternative, those who are marginalized by the current system can choose to criticize it and suffer the consequences, dropping out of school and making the best of minimum-wage jobs, or they can buy into the values of the system and criticize others for their motivational failures.

Based on the reports of the young people in my study, their parents' advice was quite clear. When asked what their parents told them about making it in America, the African American students were more likely than their European American peers to say that they were told they should work twice as hard as others if they wanted to get a good job, they should not expect people to hand them opportunities, and if they did not succeed in life, then they would have only themselves to blame. In addition, although White and Black youth were equally likely to hear that it was wrong to judge others, the parents of Black youth also warned them that there would be times in their lives when they would be the objects of prejudice. In summary, young people's lay theories about the social contract are informed by the everyday realities of how its tenets play out for people "like them."

We can compare the views of the less privileged youth quoted in an earlier passage with the sophisticated and critical but detached perspective of one white female whose father teaches college. She explained that unemployment exists "because it is a capitalist economy and is healthiest (for everybody else) if at least a certain number of people are unemployed. In a rich country, our wealth is not evenly divided." When asked about her plans after high school, she responded, "Go to college, see how I like it. Maybe transfer colleges, spend a year abroad as a student. Graduate school? Depends on what I want to do."

The thought of dismissing a college education would be anathema to a young person from a less privileged background. The children of privilege, however, have more safety nets and second chances. Their schools are not the inferior ones. If they decide to take time off from school, their families can afford to support them while they explore various interests and identities. But the theories of the poor reflect the realities of lives without safety nets, that is, an intense belief that people's fortunes turn on their own efforts. Their views of the social contract are reinforced by their families, who tell them to work twice as hard as others if they want to get a job and that they should not depend on the system or other people to bail them out (Flanagan et al. 1997; Flanagan and Tucker 1999).

The personal fates of privileged youth are disconnected from poverty, but economic hardship is a concrete possibility, not an abstraction, for youth living in low-income communities. These class differences in beliefs about individual success and failure have been found in other contemporary studies. For example, Dalbert (2001) found that youth with lower levels of education were more likely to feel that the system was fair, that individuals just had to work hard, and that those who did not work hard deserved what they got. He reasoned that their commitment to meritocratic principles reflected the fact that they had to cope with the "randomness and unfairness encountered in the world" (Dalbert 2001:62). Crosby and Mistry (2004) report similar results from their interviews with elementary-school-age children. Those whose families had lower incomes and those who attended a predominantly low-income school were more likely than their middle-class peers to say that individuals bore the blame for economic failures because they were unwilling to work hard or could not manage money well.

Notably, these class differences in theories about economic inequality contrast with those reported by Robert Leahy in the 1970s. In that earlier period of relative prosperity and lower inequality, Leahy (1983) reported that older children, regardless of their social class background, were more likely than younger ones to believe that individuals were responsible for their own fate in life. He explained that as children matured, they would learn to endorse the meritocratic principles on which the American economy was based. In contrast, I maintain that with changing economic conditions, children's views of the social contract vary by social class, specifically, that they vary according to how that contract plays out for people "like them."

During the 1960s through the early 1970s, economic growth lifted all boats. In fact, in the twenty-five years after World War II, the American economy experienced sustained economic growth, rising real wages, and low unemployment that benefited most Americans. In the 1960s, President Johnson even declared a federal war to end poverty. Since that time, however, there have been significant changes in the economy and in policies toward the poor. Compared with other industrialized nations, the United States has never spent as much of its gross domestic product on social programs to reduce poverty (Smeeding, Rainwater, and Burtless 2001). In the 1990s, our pecuniary tradition took a more egregious turn when the Personal Responsibility and Work Opportunity Reconciliation Act reformulated welfare policy. The sanctions and time limits in this legislation sent clear messages that government support to needy families was not an entitlement, that personal responsibility was the rule, and that there were no long-term guarantees. The message, much as Margaret Thatcher had suggested, was that people could not rely on the government and would have to look to themselves.

In summary, economic restructuring and changes in welfare policies have increased economic disparities and radically changed the social contract for younger generations. A major contradiction of the new global economy is that, while many businesses, stockholders, and members of the upper middle classes prosper, the healthy economy does not lift all boats, as an older wisdom had it. The new social contract means more uncertainty and fewer safety nets for individuals and exacts a greater burden on the least privileged.

THE THEME OF SCARCITY IN YOUTH'S NARRATIVES

While the class position of youth in my study shaped how they thought about personal responsibility and social inequality, youth from all classes referred to job scarcity and increased competition for a shrinking supply of work, revealing their perception that contemporary capitalism had, as Sennett contends, normalized uncertainty.

> "There are a lot more people in this country than there are jobs. The unemployed are unable to compete in the modern-day workforce."

> "There are so many people here and so little jobs. Everyone is in competition, and there are not enough jobs to go around. Those with less education and training get shut out and are unemployed."

> "Not many people are qualified for the jobs in our country. The job market is very strict, and it helps to have connections. There is a lot of competition out there and not many places to fill."

This is how one female whose mother is a cosmetologist said that she would explain unemployment to a foreigner visiting the United States: "I would tell them, for unemployment, that some people didn't graduate high school. Therefore, it is hard to get a job, and jobs here are becoming scarce." A high school student from an upper-middle-class community explained: "It is difficult to find jobs in this country that are lucrative. Jobs created since 1970 are mostly poverty-level wages which cannot secure a person's welfare." Although both students refer to a shrinking pool of job opportunities, note that the privileged youth's analysis is more abstract, historical, and institutional. In contrast, the daughter of the cosmetologist talks about jobs "here" becoming scarce and, in the same breath, about the implications for those who drop out of high school. As Bettie (2003) points out in her ethnographic study of an American high school, students tracked into vocational classes are less likely than those in college preparatory classes to learn about and analyze economic, social, and political institutions. Their lay theories reflect a more intimate interpretation of how these systems play out in people's lives.

Job scarcity and the global threat to "American" jobs were common themes among youth from advantaged and disadvantaged backgrounds alike. Some perceived a world where flexible capital jeopardizes the competitive edge of the American worker. Unemployment is "the fallout of the new global economy," one youth claimed. People are out of work because "their companies move to different states or countries," said another. A third explained that competition and profit as a bottom line were the reasons that loyal workers had become redundant: "In a place where everyone is trying to get ahead of everyone else, people will let a hard, long-time worker go in order to hire someone for less pay." But more commonly, youth blamed immigrants and foreigners for undercutting "American" jobs: "There are too many foreigners who are taking our American jobs for less money."

These youth share concerns with Sennett about the new global contract; that is, the "no long-term" rules of flexible capital loosen bonds of trust and commitment, making both skills and people disposable. In their minds, the new economy not only means fewer *good* jobs but also fewer jobs altogether and an oversupply of workers competing for a shrinking piece of the pie. Loyalty and hard work are outdated virtues, replaced by company greed and threats from "foreigners" who undercut the American standard of living by working for less pay. For those who cannot find a way to be needed, anxiety gives way to self-doubt and a loss of private hopes.

WHAT CAN BE DONE

The competitive, contingent, and elusive nature of the job market and the mismatch between the human capital/supply side and the demand side of the economy were echoed many times in the youth's statements. They said that success depends on finding the right match between what one is trained to do and the jobs that need to be filled at a particular time, "that some people work really hard or are in the correct job that is in need." People who are poor "have not found the way they can be needed for a job, and they don't have the education because of bad decisions." An African American female whose father had a temporary job packing auto parts explained that people are homeless because "they took for granted that what they had was secure. Some invested all their possessions into something that failed." Another adolescent who empathized with the unemployed reflected, "Some people fall on hard times and they lose their job, and it is really hard for them to get another job. So they quit looking. They have given up hope in themselves." Those who were more optimistic believed that individuals who fall on hard times can turn their fate around, can make a comeback by dint of hard work: "Due to rough economic times, they were laid off, but, in time, if they are persistent, they will find another job." "They might have had a bad break in life. Maybe they lost their job and couldn't get back up on their feet. But homeless people still need to work hard and come back."

Whether the outcome they pictured was that people would lose hope in themselves or would find a way to get back on their feet, images of insecurity and apprehension about an unpredictable future were integral to their narratives. As Sennett suggests, instability is meant to be normal. And the only advice for how to deal with it is to persist in the face of adversity. The young people recommended that individuals should deal with job loss or even homelessness by working harder and being persistent. In fact, their advice is embodied in the new industry of career coaching in which the unemployed are told to become more aware of their identity capital (Côté and Levine 2002; Ehrenreich 2005), that is, their talents and resources, and to deploy them strategically by networking and by reframing and selling themselves. The demands of the ever-changing workplace mean that individuals must be prepared to retrain and retool and to be "proactive in reframing their very identities" (Giddens 2000:65).

Personalities, values, and belief systems evolve as people negotiate the rules of their social contract at particular historical moments. In an era when industries were located in and identified with particular communities, loyalty to the company was a virtue, symbolized by the gold watch at retirement. Today, the image of a career ladder is gone, and loyalty to the company serves neither managers nor entry-level workers. In a recent study of low-wage workers, economists Andersson, Holzer, and Lane (2005) found that "moving on" to different employers is a more remunerative strategy than staying with the same company and gradually, in small increments, "moving up." In this regard, we can see the way in which the tenets of neoliberal capital shape every level of the system. Flexibility and reinventing oneself have replaced loyalty and authenticity as virtues to cultivate, and networking has replaced a self anchored in stable, long-term relationships with co-workers.

The following quotes from two high-school students capture a shared perception that capitalism affords individuals both opportunities and risks and that a true American takes the gamble:

> The US is a capitalistic society. While we try to avoid unemployment, it is inevitable. It is true of any nation. Due to new technology and global competition, some unemployment is inevitable. Our society is built so you can make your own life. The way a democracy was formed is to make your own life.

> No country has no unemployment. America is no exception. America is a capitalistic country. There are the poor and there are the rich. There are also those people in the middle. But the poor do not have to stay poor, and if they work hard enough, there are many avenues to success that can be taken by many. That is part of the American dream.

But when asked, "When you hear on the news about a company or a plant closing down, what is your reaction?" this same youth (quoted second above) replied, "I feel more tense about the reality of the increase in unemployed workers. I also feel worried about the effects on the economy and perhaps my own employment in my future if it was a company or a plant I was interested in. I also would feel the shock of reality in a capitalistic society."

Political views are the languages of explanation we employ to account for problems in society. In the past several decades, psychologists have engaged in a popular discourse that categorizes youth, or at least certain youth, as "at risk."[3] The term refers to those young people presumed to be destined for failure because of their social background, disabilities, or imprudent choices. Disproportionately, those classified as "youth at risk" come from families that are poor, female-headed, or ethnic minorities. By pathologizing individuals and transferring risk onto their shoulders, the "youth at risk" paradigm fits well the terms of the new social contract of neoliberalism. Rather than critique a system that has individualized problems generated by social and global forces, this paradigm frames the problem in individual terms. The discourse lacks a sociological imagination, which appreciates that "personal troubles are very often also problems shared by others, and more importantly, not capable of solution by any one individual but only by modifications of the structure of groups...and sometimes the structure of the entire society" (Mills 1959:186).

Anxiety, self-doubt, and distrust are personal troubles for individuals who can imagine only private solutions to the public problems engendered by flexible capital. The modern-day workplace, as the adolescent quoted earlier described it, is ever changing, and everyone is in competition for a shrinking pool of jobs. No amount of personal retooling will resolve this dilemma, and, in the context of the rollback of trade unions, collective identity and actions around work have been delegitimized. What alternatives are left? As Sennett poses the current dilemma, how are we to organize our life histories in a capitalism that disposes us to drift?

ENGAGING HOPE: COLLECTIVE FUTURES

In this second part of the chapter, I focus on another narrative of the future, imagined by youth engaged in various forms of political activism. Here I draw from the distinction that C. Douglas Lummis (1996) makes between private and public hope. By private hope, he means an individual's belief that his or her own life will go well, that he or she will earn a good living and achieve personal success, even if others do not. Public hope, in contrast, reflects a belief that people, if they pull together, can effect change that will benefit all. To have public hope, one has to invest one's time and energy in building a larger sense of community.

The current generation of young Americans grew up in the years when public goods and services were eroding. Currently, public schools in many states are threatened by government-supported voucher programs that enable families to buy private schooling. Since the enactment of the Personal Responsibility and Work Opportunity Reconciliation Act, social welfare is now considered a personal instead of a public responsibility. And deregulation of media, airlines, and the health-care industry has undermined the government's role as guardian of the public welfare. Despite this erosion of a public consciousness in government policies, many members of the younger generation are investing in public hope by engaging in collective actions that benefit society, not just themselves. I discuss several characteristics of these new social movements, noting at the outset that some reflect forms of privilege, including access to the Internet, money and time to travel, and infrastructures provided by institutions such as universities.

Based on conventional political indicators (voting in elections, keeping informed by reading newspapers, joining trade unions or professional organizations), the younger generation appears to be politically disengaged. In part, this is because they consider the electoral arena ineffectual (Galston 2001) or perceive that elites are the only voices in mainstream political discourse. In addition, political issues increasingly transcend the borders of states. The transnational reach of multinational corporations and of institutions such as the World Trade Organization (WTO) and World Bank means that they are less likely to be held accountable by the classic mechanisms of representative governments in nation-states. In recent years, there has been an increase in the number of organizations and public protests that target transnational instead of national and local political entities (Imig and Tarrow 2000; Smith 2004). Compared with their elders, youth are more likely to engage in such movements (Norris 1999).

The political narratives of younger generations involved in transnational activism turn a spotlight on the gap between the power these institutions hold over people's lives and the lack of accountability to the very people affected by their policies (see also Weiss, chapter 9, this volume). Transnational activists are contesting the inequalities and lack of accountability inherent in the new world order by, to borrow from C. Wright Mills (1959:188), insisting that "all power to make decisions be publicly legitimated and that the makers of such decisions be held accountable." They challenge multinational corporations and governance and focus on three justice themes: fairness in labor, environmental, and procedural practices (Juris 2006).

Contemporary political movements also combine utopian sentiments with pragmatism. They believe (borrowing from the slogan of the World Social Forum) that "another world is possible" (Ponniah 2004). At the same time, a pragmatic attitude of getting things done manifests in a willingness to build coalitions across groups that share some common goals but may differ radically in their ultimate political agendas. For example, if environmental preservation is the goal, then animal welfare activists have to partner with hunters to preserve open spaces, even sometimes with developers to preserve the dwindling supply of green spaces. The politics of younger generations also reflects an awareness of scarcity. Words such as *stewardship* and *sustainability* figure prominently in the discourse, and there is a recognition that natural resources are limited, that there is an unequal distribution of access to and utilization of those resources, and that profligate actions can squander them. In this regard, activists may differ from the modal youth of their generation. National trends in high school seniors' attitudes over the past three decades point to precipitous declines in beliefs that resources are scarce and in behaviors to conserve resources, as well as simultaneous increases in materialist values, consumerism, and beliefs that science and technology will solve problems of scarcity (Wray and Flanagan 2006).

Not surprisingly, youth also are cognizant of the political implications of their personal decisions, especially in consumption (Bennett 1998; Stolle and Micheletti 2006). The so-called lifestyle politics of younger generations reflects an awareness that individual choices—of what to eat and wear or which modes of transportation to use—have moral implications for the environment, public resources, the health of the oceans and animals, and the well-being and safety of labor throughout the world. According to surveys in the United States, consumer politics is a method used by about half of fifteen- to twenty-five-year-olds (as well as about one-third of their elders) to voice their political views. They boycott companies whose policies they do not support and buy from companies whose policies they approve of (Keeter et al. 2003, available on CIRCLE website, www.civicyouth.org). Similar trends have been found among youth in Canada and Europe (Stolle and Micheletti 2006). Consumer politics may also reflect youth's sense that their actions can have a greater impact on the market than on national politics. As noted, globalization has weakened the ability of nations to hold corporations accountable. Political consumerism is a way that individuals can act locally in a global marketplace, and more "glocal" organizations (Wellman 2001) are helping people understand such connections.

The United Students Against Sweatshops (USAS) is a good example. On US university campuses, students have contested the labor practices of multinational corporations operating in the developing world where their university's logo wear is produced. Students press their university administration to contract only with sites where proper monitoring of labor practices is enforced. USAS members educate fellow students by appealing to the identity of the alma mater and revealing the affront that sweatshop conditions are to their values and reputation (Ballinger 2006). USAS has expanded its efforts to include fair labor practices at home in its campaign challenging Wal-Mart and educating consumers about the working conditions and wages of its employees.

Another example of political activism that exposes inauthentic corporate appeals to consumers is the work of the truth® campaign, the youth-engagement arm of the American Legacy Foundation, an independent public-health organization. With innovative technology and in-your-face, hard-hitting ads, the truth® campaign exposes corporate tobacco's targeted appeals to young people and urges youth to take a stand against it. Apparently, the truth matters. The campaign has been acknowledged by Monitoring the Future (which tracks teen trends in alcohol, tobacco, and other drug use) as one of the reasons teen tobacco use has declined in recent years (Scheve and Syvertsen 2006).

Culture jamming, or adbusting, is a tool used by anti-corporate, animal rights, and anti-sweatshop activists to educate consumers about corporate duplicity. Culture jamming utilizes a company's marketing strategy to satirize the company's values by revealing the truth behind its practices. The prototypical culture jam was the political use of Nike's invitation for customers to personalize and customize shoes by ordering a unique logo on them. Then MIT graduate student Jonah Peretti ordered a pair with the word *sweatshop* on them. The new youth politics also takes advantage of cultural forms such as hip-hop that thrive on morphing, as well as technologies that enable the autonomous reconstruction of meaning. The structure of these forms enables more voices and perspectives to be included in the political process. For the past decade, an independent media movement (IndyMedia) has been active in using alternative avenues to mainstream media to ensure that other voices are heard. Also, the increasing reliance of mainstream media on "citizen journalists" using cell phones to record historic moments points to the porosity of the borders between alternative and mainstream.

With respect to organizational style, young activists tend to encourage direct democracy and take full advantage of the democratic potential of the Internet to share information, network, and organize (Ponniah 2004). Many have been inspired by the Zapatista Army for National Liberation (EZLN). Rooted in the struggles of indigenous peoples in Chiapas, Mexico, the Zapatistas use twenty-first-century technology, such as faxes, cell phones, and computers, to draw attention to the impacts of free trade on indigenous people (Constantino 2006). The egalitarian structure and gender-conscious practices of this movement also herald a new organizational form that transnational activists try to emulate.

Transnational activists have educated the public about new multinational entities such as the G-8 and WTO by timing public protests to coincide with their meetings and by using highly visible street theater to gain attention from the mainstream media. Their new style of politics encourages autonomy, creativity, and entrepreneurship, traits that flexible capital itself celebrates. In contrast to the centralized and hierarchical organizational structures of political parties and trade unions, transnational activists choose to work in loose networks with flexible memberships. They are united by values and worldviews rather than by organizational membership and rules.

Leadership is dispersed instead of centralized, and decision making is horizontal instead of vertical. One organization, the Movement for Global

Resistance (MGR), once referred to itself as a movement without members (Juris 2006). In fact, the episodic and spontaneous character of many new political forms may be one of the attractive features of this style of activism. Individuals can move in and out of groups freely; one is mainly accountable to oneself. With creative use of the Internet, more organizing can be virtual instead of face-to-face. Although large events such as demonstrations require planning by a committed core group, with instant messaging and the Internet, massive numbers can be rallied on relatively short notice. It is too early to tell whether a movement can be sustained with virtual connections, flexible memberships, and accountability only to oneself. E-mail may make it easier to inform and organize large numbers in a short time, but Internet anonymity may exact costs in organizational recruitment and commitment. Typically, social activism depends on a core group; the Internet may broaden the space for fellow travelers. It also is worth noting that media are most effective when intrinsic motivation for particular actions is high. For example, when Penn State's 2007 spring break meant that students would be absent for the annual St. Patrick's Day drinking celebrations, Facebook provided the means for rallying thousands to celebrate an early, alternative version of the holiday.

The themes of public accountability, scarcity, and the erosion of public goods and services also are evident in youth activism in poor communities. Whereas transnational activists are more likely to be young adults and often college students, young activists in impoverished communities are more often teenagers working in collaboration with adults. Like those students in the rustbelt who are trapped in inferior schools, these young activists also attend inferior schools. But rather than deal with those inequities in private, they are raising these as public issues, in part because they are channeling anxiety and frustration into analysis and action through programs in which they partner with adult mentors. Groups such as the Educational Opportunity Gap Project in New York and New Jersey, youth organizing communities in California, the Philadelphia Student Union in Pennsylvania, and Students 4 Justice/Colorado Progressive Coalition are organizing, often with teachers, to improve facilities, fight budget cuts, insist on more accountability and student voice in the public schools, and challenge inequalities in the allocation of resources (Torre and Fine 2006). In fact, many of the causes youth take up reflect a fight for basic needs, such as textbooks in public schools, travel subsidies for students who use public transportation to get to school, and green spaces near public housing. But the activism itself heralds a new form of youth development program.

In these new models of community youth development (CYD), young people's frustrations and anger are channeled toward social change. Rather than press youth to accommodate to the status quo, rather than identify risk-laden youth as the problem, youth organizing and activism encourage young people to contest the way things are (Watts and Flanagan 2007). To do so, youth learn how to gather information and dissect the issues, including the power dynamics and politics underlying them; as a result, they become more strategic thinkers (Larson and Hanson 2005). Groups such as Youth in Focus and SOYAC (Serving Our Youth and Communities) train underrepresented groups in youth-led action research techniques, including collecting and critically analyzing information, evaluating policy decisions, and planning and executing action plans (London 2006). The process of political commitment occurs as young people develop a sense of solidarity with others, appreciating the connection between their own experiences of oppression and those of other youth and realizing that collective action is necessary to bring about change (Pearce and Larson 2006).

When young people learn how to analyze the political and economic bases of social issues, they develop a political consciousness that helps them deal with personal experiences of oppression (Watts, Griffith, and Abdul-Adil 1999). Adults who are sensitive to age-based inequities of power and knowledge partner with them, serve as their mentors, and connect them to resources. The new youth–adult partnership models present challenges, however, even for those who contest the more common, asymmetrical relationships of power between generations. To make these partnering models work, training of and support for individuals and practice guided by regular reflection between the youth and adult partners are essential (Camino 2000; HoSang 2001).

Youth activism and organizing are part of a larger change in mainstream youth development and community-based organizations (part of the trend focusing on positive youth development), which increasingly feature young people in authentic leadership and decision-making roles. Examples include youth-led community organizations, public policy consultation, community coalitions for youth development, and decision making in nonprofit organizations (Camino and Zeldin 2002). Many of the young people in these programs are similar in age and background to the marginalized youth featured in the first part of this chapter. But the very experience of being connected to other youth and adults in an organization provides a larger sense of community, and the experience of being part of the decision-making process in these organizations enables youth to see how, collectively, they can solve the public problems we share (Kirshner in press).

In contrast to therapeutic interventions that target youth as "risky" (deficient, dangerous, or needy), the newer models reframe youth and the notion of risk. They begin with the assumption that youth are assets to their communities and that, given opportunities, they will contribute to rather than drain community resources. Indeed, youth's greater willingness to take risks is an asset that can revitalize organizations and communities. Historically, youthful risk taking, idealism, and commitment have invigorated movements for social change. For example, in the struggle against apartheid in South Africa, it was the militancy of youth that rejuvenated the African National Congress (Ngomane and Flanagan 2003). In the United States, the risks taken by youth in the Student Nonviolent Coordinating Committee (SNCC) revived civil rights organizations such as the NAACP (Oberschall 1989).

Perhaps because youth insist on authenticity, their involvement in contemporary youth–adult partnerships appears to bring both the adults and the organization back to their core values (Zeldin et al. 2000). These new institutional models provide spaces where young people are free to explore alternative selves and to evaluate the challenges and choices before them with a fresh lens. Rather than encourage young people to capitalize on individual assets for private gain, these programs promote the power of collective identity and shared leadership (Kirshner in press; Lewis-Charp et al. 2003). In certain ways, these models differ from the more fluid and flexible forms of political activism discussed earlier. Although egalitarian forms of leadership are common in both, community youth development organizations are more likely to be based on face-to-face contact and thus may engender more accountability to one another than activist groups with fluid memberships organized in virtual space.

In summary, the new narratives and forms of youth civic engagement reflect an awareness of globalization and the interconnection of local and global issues, as well as new organizational forms that encourage the kinds of inventiveness, flexibility, creativity, and change that global communications portend. Political action helps to make public the private fears associated with uncertainty. It provides sources of social connectedness and support, the "larger sense of community" and "fuller sense of character" to which Sennett alludes.

RE-GENERATIONS

In any historical period, youth embody the collective anxieties of their society and its hopes for the future. Each new generation contributes to social change by reinterpreting the social contract that is the legacy of earlier generations (Mannheim 1952[1928]). More than their elders, youth represent the possibilities of the future instead of the patterns of the past. And, more than their elders, the choices young people make today are linked to their images of what the future holds and the possible selves they envision. Thus, the tensions in the narratives sketched in this chapter are a good barometer for society. Focusing on youth helps us appreciate the new set of choices that globalization presents us and the kind of world those different choices portend. We can choose private or public hope.

In *Radical Democracy*, C. Douglas Lummis reflects on Rousseau's conclusion that the social contract is the basis on which human beings can live in an orderly community and still be free. Lummis concludes that democratic faith, a belief that people will choose public over private goods, is essential for that contract to work.

> Democratic faith is the decision to believe that a world of democratic trust is possible because we can see it in each person sometimes. It is the decision to believe in what people can be on the basis of what they are sometimes. It is the decision to believe that each polity and each person contains the possibility of a democratic version of itself. It is the belief that as people are free, they are free to become that, too. None of this has been proved, but neither can it be disproved. One is free to believe either way.
> [Lummis 1996:154]

Understanding the anxieties, risks, and hopes of youth as they imagine the future is an essential part of this picture.

Notes

1. It also should be noted that social contract theory has been criticized for its gendered and racist assumptions (see Fieser and Dowden 2006).

2. There is an asymmetry in the two parts of this chapter, based on the empirical basis for the claims in each. The first part is based on primary data collection with high school students. The second is based on secondary analyses of contributions to a volume on youth activism that I co-edited (Sherrod et al. 2006), supplemented with interviews with student activists.

3. A keyword search of the PsychInfo database revealed no articles using the term in the 1970s, but in the early 1980s there began a steady climb from 1 percent to more than 9 percent of the youth articles in the database in 2005 referring to "at risk" youth.

7

Apathy and Agency

The Romance of Agency and Youth in Botswana

Deborah Durham

Youth have agency. This claim is repeatedly offered as an argument in books and articles on youth. But what kind of agency do youth have? And what does it mean for us as anthropologists to go out and seek to identify youth agency in various places around the world? These questions have troubled me in my research and writing about youth in Botswana. As Laura Ahearn (2001:109) noted, the term *agency* "has become ubiquitous in anthropology"; it has become, seemingly, a basic human right that everyone should be able to exercise. Most recent approaches to agency see it in the exercise of free will against the oppressions or constraints of social structures and cultural hegemonies (Ortner 1996). Perhaps, then, in recognizing the agency of youth (or children, or women, or the poor and oppressed), anthropologists are engaged in an act of liberation, of restoring to those who seem powerless their individual rights to act effectively upon the world. But it may also be that, by examining youth agency more closely, we can free the concept of agency from its narrower association with free will and liberalist autonomy.

Youth agency is sometimes depicted as the same kind of agency that can be wielded by all kinds of people in all kinds of cultures. Youth participate in the "creation and negotiation of value" (Nieuwenhuys 1996:237) and the "practices through which culture is produced" (Bucholtz 2002:526) alongside their seniors. This kind of universal and uniform agency descends from Enlightenment philosophy and privileges individual capabilities, especially the capacity of individuals to resist inequality and unreasonable cultural expectations. In this form, agency is aligned with subjectivity, but a very particular kind of subjectivity. It is individually rationalist, seeking independent self-determination, and at least a bit self-aware and self-reflective, critically detached from its environment. (Accounts that posit a more complex subjectivity, or intersection of subjectivities, for youth tend to yield more ambiguous accounts of youth agency [see Lave et al. 1992; Willis 1977].) For example, one author defines agency (here, for women) as "the exercise of any measure of resistance and self-determination used by an abused woman to regain control of her life...agency is usually opposed to victimization" (Connell 1997). The politicized schoolchildren in Madagascar described by Lesley Sharp (2002) are such agents: admirable for their capacity for self-reflection, their keen judgment on the contours of their society and their own actions, and their competence in evaluating and executing a range of oppositional and self-interested political acts.

Interestingly, although it seems to be a universal quality, such agency is often represented *quantitatively*; people have more or less agency. (One must assume the uniform nature of a thing, such as time, in order to divide it in this way.) This measured, quantitative agency can be a yardstick of liberatory politics, as the following quotation suggests: "Children's *agency increases* as market relations alleviate intra-household linkages," allowing them more space to "negotiate and strategize" or be independent agents (Porter 1996:17, emphasis added; the full article suggests more complexity to youth agency than this quotation shows). Or it can substitute for the distribution of power in a society, with some people having more agency and some less. Ironically, the quantifying of agency allows children and youth to be depicted (problematically) as "incomplete social actors, or subjects less able to exert agency" (Maira and Soep 2005:xxii). People then "gain" agency as they mature and acquire knowledge, critical thinking, and skill, through the increasing choices set before them and through their increasing independence from parents and indoctrinators. Typically, it is this quantitative idea of agency, as well as the assumption that youth have less of it, that is roundly attacked in the claims that "youth have agency," even as the universal ideal is upheld.

As Katherine Frank (2006) noted, these approaches to agency, which counterpose the individual to society, culture, and other people, tend to smuggle in a variety of unexamined psychological assumptions. Agency is often tied to an independent selfhood, as well as the liberation of the individual as a "self" from cultural or social constructions, and is measured against the ideal of a Western individualism. It is also, as we shall see, vested in the specific narratives of family and ontogeny of the person of Western society. One historian of slavery has written that, in his field, "agency" has become "a master trope...which overcodes...complex discussions of human subjectivity and political organization" (Johnson 2003:114). All of this suggests that it is important to go beyond a recognition that youth have agency. We must ask what kind of agency they might have, how they come by it and exercise it, and how their agency relates them to others and to their society.

In this chapter, I examine more closely ideas about the person and about sociopolitical organization in Botswana to develop a more nuanced understanding of youth as agents within their own society. In doing so, I also raise and examine critically ideas about youth agency that are implicit in much recent interest in youth but are different from the quantifiable yet universal agency I have critiqued already. These ideas are also problematic. Out of Western Romanticism, the historical companion of Western Rationalism, we sometimes draw upon the idea that youth have special roles in their society, that their youth and adolescence give them privileged transformative cultural powers. In Botswana, some of these Western ideas of agency—in the form of empowerment programs, certain discourses on citizenship, and Western education systems—are being engaged with somewhat incommensurable local ideas of youth, personhood, and sociopolitical action. First, I would like to set out the problem of Botswana's apathetic youth and give three vignettes from my fieldwork.

APATHETIC YOUTH IN BOTSWANA

In the summer of 2000, I met with program officers at the Botswana National Youth Council (BNYC), with organizers and officers at other youth programs in the capital city of Gaborone, and with members of the youth wings of political parties. (The BNYC is an NGO that coordinated nongovernment and government youth development efforts in the country and also ran programs of its own.) As our discussions and their many brochures indicated, the program officers were concerned to "empower" youth in the country. This project echoed government rhetoric emerging in the late 1990s about "empowering" the general citizenry of Botswana. Heard frequently in the speeches of politicians and state officials and in certain development programs, most of this rhetoric aimed to empower Botswana's citizens economically by providing loans, grants, and some training to set up businesses. The idea of empowerment clearly was picked up from international development programs originating in the West, filtering through the many global and international organizations active in

Botswana and through the postgraduate university programs in the United States and UK attended by people with government grants. But the idea of empowerment is promoted in Botswana by local government and NGOs, so it is inflected through local concerns and local visions of what empowerment might be. These visions are, as I noted, skewed not just toward economics but also towards the empowered ideal of being a business owner and manager. Starting a business is one way to achieve some of the qualities of mature adulthood, the ability to command the labor of others and not respond to the demands of others, as children and youth do. Such a notion of empowered citizens is also geared toward fears, sometimes very xenophobic, that noncitizens are more successful in business and, with globalization, are dominating the business possibilities in the country.[1] Such fears continue earlier concerns of a decade and more before, that noncitizens from neighboring countries were taking up land, school positions, and jobs that belonged by right to Botswana's citizenry. Although these earlier fears were related primarily to regional politics and migrations, the newer concerns, that Batswana (citizens of Botswana) are unable to compete for business opportunities, are responses to globalization. News articles often invoked the term *globalization* in this context after the turn of the millennium.

The efforts of government and NGO officers to empower youth economically through programs training them in home enterprises and business skills seemed determined to make youth over into unmarked—that is, nonyouthful—citizens (inasmuch as citizens had been successfully "empowered"). I have written about this economic project elsewhere, as well as its intersection with official democratic liberalism and a conflicting ethos of work and care that creates and binds households (Durham 2007). An empowered young person, in their plans, would be one who no longer depends on his or her family and would not, through familial neglect, be tempted into crime, dropping out of school, transactional sex leading to disease or early pregnancy, and homelessness. This list of youth problems largely reproduces the 1996 description of youth problems published in the government's National Youth Policy (Botswana 1996). That document suggested that people who are outside the official youth age range of twelve to twenty-nine and share some of these characteristics (unemployment, criminality) might be included as "youth" in the policy's recommendations and planned programs, thereby implying that criminality, dangerous sexuality, and unemployment for those out of school were almost definitions of youth. (The age range of people who can claim to be youth is highly contested in Botswana, where youth can be age forty or more, in spite of government policies: see Durham 2004 for a full account of claims to be, or assignment of people as, youth.) To counter these forms of youthfulness, government officials and NGO youth officers repeatedly urged young people to start businesses.

There is another aspect to youth empowerment in Botswana: the encouragement of their direct participation in the political sphere (that is, the politics associated with elections, parties, political debate, and governmental policy). To some extent, youth political activity is thought to be hampered by ignorance, as in the case of business empowerment, but many people decry youth apathy as well. The voting age in Botswana was lowered from twenty-one to eighteen in 1994 (students studying outside the country were also given the right to vote) after much agitation by university students and political commentators.[2] By 2000 the Botswana National Youth Council identified as a central concern the apparently extremely low turnout of youth in elections and was formulating strategies and programs to enhance youth political "empowerment." Some people said that only 3–4 percent of youth had voted in recent national elections (these figures were not substantiated, but that the percentage was very low was agreed upon). Only a small group of university youth and children of politicians were active members of political parties, mostly in the youth wings. As I discuss further below, BNYC officers wanted to get youth into the political domain through parades, youth days, and conferences, which dovetailed better with some youth subjectivities than did hopes for youth going to vote. The BNYC efforts for youth echoed the efforts of others in Botswana to gain political recognition, especially "minorities" (non-Tswana citizens) agitating for permanent representation in the advisory but influential House of Chiefs and cultural recognition in the public sphere.

Members of youth wings of the main political parties with whom I spoke in 2000 made fuller and somewhat different statements about youth's lack of political interest. Unable to get a face-to-face meeting, I spoke by cell phone to the chairman of the ruling Botswana Democratic Party's (BDP) youth wing as he played golf near a large, high-cost housing project (associated with more than a whiff of political scandal with his family). He had become chairman of the youth wing after the preceding, much older, chair lost his membership in a 1996 age restructuring that excluded those over thirty-nine from the youth wing. In 1995 that chairman had discussed Botswana's youth with me. He saw a role for them as part of the BDP youth wing in educating the rural population through agricultural, small business, and fund-raising projects (and in having fun with fund-raising concerts, where everyone could be youthful). This older chairman, a graduate of a British university, smoothly conversant in Western political events over the preceding thirty years, had entered into politics soon after Botswana's independence (1966). In 1995 he noted difficulties in recruitment to the party's youth wing; its membership was largely rural and had joined fifteen to twenty years before. He attributed the agricultural demonstration projects' lack of success to broad popular disinterest in agriculture, not to a failure in youth in particular. But he also spoke of what he saw as waning youth interest and engagement in his party. His sense of waning interest may have reflected a general idea in Botswana that urban areas, to which youth were flocking and where unemployment was high, were leaning politically toward the BNF, the main opposition party (discussed below). The BDP is often perceived to draw support from rural areas. But he spoke, too, of a broad inability to recruit youth, rural and urban. Now, in 2000, the new, younger leader was telling me, partly distracted by his golf game and by phone calls on a second cell phone, that older people understood voting and politics but youth were apathetic and uneducated. Their apathy, he implied as he spoke, could be traced to laziness, inability to pursue economic ventures (such as the real estate ventures he pursued), and lack of ability to assume roles (as he had done) in established political organizations such as the BDP youth wing.

The BDP youth wing chairman was part of a privileged elite, but the opinions he voiced—that political participation and economic success are simply a matter of will—are often repeated by impoverished villagers and struggling, unemployed urban young. These views carry implications for new structures of class and inequality. Botswana was one of the world's poorest countries at its independence in 1966, but with the help of diamond discoveries and prudent and fairly responsible government, by 2002 the GNP per capita was $3,500. In those terms, the country is portrayed as solidly middle-class. In the context of the growth in the 1960s–1980s, social mobility was pronounced. Through the rapidly expanding education system and, indeed, hard work, many rural poor secured well-paying government jobs and access to modern housing. The rate of economic expansion has slowed, however, and unemployment rates are high. Income in Botswana is now highly skewed, and a middle, or upper middle, class has been consolidating itself around opportunities and privileges made available through its parents' success and children's future. The new chairman was a clear example of that class process.[3]

Less privileged members of other political youth groups perceived apathy in their midst as well. A university student who belonged to the main opposition party's youth wing told me, in a long chat on campus, how young people in his party were (politically) uneducated and seemingly uninterested in becoming politically engaged, in short, he said, apathetic. Nostalgic for a previous generation of BNF youth who had read and discussed Lenin and African socialism, he described how his fellow youth wing members refused to participate in political reading groups or to work to formulate policy positions to present to party leaders. Even as the party reduced youth participation to what he called "support tasks," he complained bitterly that his (university) cohort formed choirs and joined associations simply for what he called "social" reasons. Other young people I talked to were, indeed, as this young man suspected, more interested in the choirs than in policy or protests.

The idea of apathy invoked by these youth program officers and youth wing members is related to specific ideas of agency, or potential agency. These assessments—that youth were not voting, that they were not joining political parties, that they were politically uneducated and politically uninterested, and that they were denied meaningful roles but also were more interested in "social" activities such as choirs or opportunities for fraternization—reflect strongly the ideas of the education-oriented, liberal elite. These assessments also may echo the government youth policy's expectation that youth not attending school or working in formal jobs were engaged in problematic activities (which include "play" and "social activities," the orientations described by the BNF youth member). They envisioned youth as empowered or effective agents in Botswana society when youths acted in certain ways, that is, when they were informed and able to think and act on their own and were willing to use their education to make decisions that would affect others. Independence and leadership are not, however, the forms in which most youth in Botswana find their agency in society; many negotiate a variety of forms that leave their positions and actions contested and uncertain.

BOTSWANA YOUTH IN ACTION

In the following sections, I describe three "scenes" in Botswana from the 1990s in which youth political agency is ambiguous, complicated by different forms of agency converging on them. Botswana's apathetic youth are, perhaps, enacting other forms of agency. To understand their agency, we cannot rely upon unexamined Western models of youth or agency.

Empowered by Youth Day

On June 16, 2000, a small parade of young people in their late teens and early twenties, flanked by older youth organizers and police cars, marched through the center of Gaborone. All wore T-shirts featuring a weeping African continent protesting sexual violence against children. Health campaigns in Botswana have often used T-shirts to publicize sexually transmitted diseases and tuberculosis and to encourage people to use clinics and hospitals. In villages, such T-shirts can be seen on people of all ages (who get them from relatives working for the Ministry of Health, or the like), as well as on laborers living at cattleposts, who often wear cast-offs. No one pays much attention to the writing on these shirts or most other logo-bearing T-shirts. The T-shirts seem to mark the wearer as a recipient (not a bad thing), but not an espousal of the motto. Chatting and laughing amongst themselves, the young marchers headed to the Inter-national Fairgrounds, where a ceremony for Youth Day in Botswana would take place. The ceremony was delayed for hours because the keynote politicians arrived (typically) late, explaining that they had been in important meetings. The *kgosi* (chief) looked around at empty chairs and asked where "the public" was. The young marchers, who were not "the public" he was looking for and who were not invited to sit in the chairs, had not waited around but left soon after the end of their march. The few school-age young people at the ceremony, dressed in skimpy costumes for choral and other performances that would punctuate the speeches, shivered and complained in the winter cold. During the long wait, an older woman chided them for "looking unhappy" and urged them to be happy: "It is your day." Meanwhile, women and men from various agencies, who carried printed invitations and had chairs reserved with their names and positions on them, drank tea and sat under a canopy or drifted off to return to work.

June 16, now the "Day of the African Child," commemorates the slaughter of schoolchildren in Soweto, South Africa, in June 1976.[4] Those children were protesting apartheid policies of "Bantu" education, especially the curtailment of instruction in English in favor of Afrikaans, which would restrict their access to the world outside South Africa (Hirson 1979). Their slaughter prompted international protest and boycotts. Some twenty-five years later, the heroic activism of those South African schoolchildren was little in evidence in the parade and ceremony in neighboring Botswana. Instead, the parade told a much more subtle and complex story about youth and their political agency. Officers at the Botswana National Youth Council told me that the event was to promote youth political "empowerment." It takes considerable interpretive skill, however, to discern any empowerment of the fifty to seventy young marchers organized and dressed by youth program officers and flanked by police cars in their march, or in the confinement of youth to choral and dramatic performances in the main ceremonies, or in the long wait for dignitaries busy with other, apparently more important, issues. Nonetheless, the officers were sincere in seeing the ceremonies as a form of youth empowerment. The idea of youth as an important part of the nation was presented through the parade and dances, the speeches, and the assembly of bureaucrats engaged in various youth development and education programs. Still, the young people followed a script written by someone else, be it the march organizers or the long-standing traditions of school choirs and drama groups. If there was any sign of youth acting on their own and for their own political and social interests on that Youth Day, it was in the rapid abandonment of the ceremony by the young marchers. But what was unclear was whether those youth were ever intended to stay. No one noted their disappearance during the long wait for the speakers and dignitaries, and there was no place for them, either in chairs or in performances, at the ceremony.

Mmankgodi Burns

Youth in Botswana are not always so indifferent to their politicians and bureaucrats, nor so unlike the Soweto schoolchildren. Whether this makes them "more agentive" is another matter. On April 16, 1997, a *Botswana Gazette* article announced, "Mmankgodi Burns." The article was posted on the Internet discussion list botswanacf,[5] used mostly by students abroad and (at that time) increasingly in Botswana, and discussions of the event continued for weeks among list participants. (The discussions of deadwood mentioned below were held by the same list participants also following current Botswana media accounts.) Mmankgodi is a fairly rural village of four thousand just outside the growing outskirts of the capital, Gaborone (see Townsend 1997).

> Government workers fled their homes half naked Saturday night when a mob of riotous youths—demanding the safe return of a five year old girl who disappeared mysteriously two weeks ago—went on the rampage burning almost all government buildings in the village.
>
> Eye witnesses say the whole village was lit like a Christmas tree as exploding gas cylinders shot up balls into the sky and the flames leaped from the huge Kgotla [chief's public court, now often including government office buildings] structure at the centre of the village.... The only two primary schools were doused with petrol and set on fire.... A police patrol car trying to get out of

the besieged village was assailed by the mob at a barricade outside the village and set alight.[6]

Along with the teachers, an agricultural officer and an agricultural
demonstrator were attacked, as was the village headman (who "thank[ed]
his hunting rifle that he [was] still alive"), and the headman's restaurant
and his sister's bar were burned down. When the SSG (Special Support
Group of the police) came in and arrested forty people, one of those
arrested was wearing a T-shirt stating "Segametsi Day—An injury to one is
an injury to all." This T-shirt, unlike the T-shirts produced by an NGO and
worn by the Youth Day marchers, bore a message that people would read
and announced the convictions of the wearer. Segametsi Mogomotsi was a
young girl whose murder in 1995 prompted riots and the burning of huts
and businesses in her home village of Mochudi, as well as riots in the capital by university students and others, who also stormed into Parliament.[7]
Both Segametsi and the missing child in Mmankgodi were suspected of
being victims of "ritual murder." The attacks against bars and businesses
were attacks against those suspected of using body parts in their pursuit of
wealth. They were also a demonstration against the failures of government
to catch and punish the suspects. One Internet commentator, referring to
Segametsi's death, mourned the "little boys and girls [who] bled to satiate
the ravenous appetites of mindless, hard-to-please material monsters."[8]

Kenneth Good (1996) has noted the unusual entry of schoolchildren
into the *kgotla* of Mochudi after Segametsi's death, where they spoke elo-
quently and demanded answers from government ministers. Generally,
however, Botswana's students have made political protests in the form of
boycotts and, more rarely, the kind of violence reported in Mmankgodi.
Such protests are often against the mistreatment of the young by elders
who are seen as greedy, actually consuming young people's bodies for their
own enrichment or refusing young people the means to well-being and
growth. Many school boycotts, especially at the secondary school level, have
protested school food, which is often very basic and "rural" in nature, and
demanded that rice (a Western luxury food) or other specific food items
be served. Other boycotts have protested the seduction of female students
by faculty and administrators, which may result in girls having to drop out
of school because of pregnancy or may expose them to HIV. These protests
are also explicitly about the inability of young male students to compete
with older sugar daddies for the girls' attention.

When I asked adult and (older) youth residents of Mahalapye, an
"urban village" of nearly thirty-five thousand located on the main highway,

about student riots a few months after they occurred, they seemed not to remember, were unimpressed, or, very often, appeared simply indifferent. Some suggested that the rioters were "just playing," a phrase often used for children and youth's activities that do not contribute work to the household or community. School food continued, during my field period, to consist of sorghum or maize porridge and small amounts of meat or vegetable. Young women continue to enjoy the attentions of older men (a twenty-six-year-old married schoolteacher told me that her female students taunted her with their superior ability to capture older men's attention; government elite blame the men). And children like the young girl of Mmankgodi continue to disappear. Most (like that child) probably fall into wells or get lost as they walk long distances in the bush to get to cattleposts or scattered hamlets in situations of neglect and hunger. A very few (like Segametsi) are murdered for their youthful body parts.

Let Us Give One Another Our Hands

At Christmas 1994, a farewell salutation and ceremony was held at the Herero kgotla in Mahalapye, where the Herero Youth Association (HYA) formally told assembled members of the ward that they were going to Namibia (figure 7.1) to greet Herero there and to learn. (Herero in Mahalapye are descended from refugees of the German–Herero War in South-West Africa [Namibia], who fled the genocide of 1904.) The women of the HYA were dressed in their best Herero-style uniforms, long Victorian-styled dresses made voluminous with petticoats and puffed sleeves; the men wore suit coats and ties. Some members were as young as their mid-twenties; most were in their thirties or forties. Singing, they crossed the open area around the kgotla and then stood and sang a short, concert-like series of songs to the women and children sitting on the ground under the shade of an acacia tree and to the half-circle of men on chairs, stumps, and cinderblocks. One by one, the older men stood and addressed the youth, sending them off with God, urging them to remember that they were Herero from Mahalapye, reminding everyone that these were their children. The elders told them to learn well and to return home and tell what they learned, or similar exhortations. All the while waving in what could be a good-bye or a greeting, the HYA repeatedly sang songs, coming back again and again to the following one:

> *ngatu pasaneye omake,*
>
> *ngatu pasaneye omake,*
>
> *ngatu pasaneye omake,*

tu tje alleluja, tu tje alleluja

[Let us give each other our hands. (Repeat three times.)]
[We say, Hallelujah!]

The chairman of the HYA made a short speech about the group's trip. Then the choirmaster, who had recently been learning Herero traditions and was experimenting with "deep Herero" in songs he wrote, delivered a praise performance. This surprised and delighted the audience, as well as me, for I had never heard such a performance in my time in Mahalapye. But apart from those two contributions, the HYA only listened (although not always attentively) to the older speakers and sang.

There was an undercurrent of tension, however, in spite of the many ululations at the songs and the urgings of the speakers for the youth to go with God and to come back. The trip coincided with the marriage of one of the HYA members, so a large portion of the group was unable to go to Namibia. Because many of the HYA members worked, mostly in government jobs, the trip had been scheduled between Christmas and New Year's, which are official four-day holidays in Botswana. At no other time of year could the travelers find so much time to drive across the Kalahari to the Atlantic Ocean (a highlight of the trip), visit Herero monuments and people in Windhoek and Okahandja, and join a Herero New Year's ceremony at a cattle-herding area where there were several relatives of Mahalapye Herero. But weddings, too, were often scheduled at Christmas. What was more, many believed that the bride's family, who disapproved of the HYA, had purposefully scheduled the wedding to conflict with the tour.

Complaints about the HYA and scheduling had circulated the preceding August as well. The HYA had scheduled the major annual meeting in which it holds elections for the same weekend that Otjiserandu held its annual "August games." Otjiserandu is a Herero commemorative society with roots extending back to the nineteenth century when Herero consolidated into a political-ethnic group under German colonialism. Now Otjiserandu has branches across southern Africa. Every August, ceremonies remembering the dead and celebrating Herero identity are held, as well as an annual business meeting. Often, different branches celebrate together, and this year the Mahalapye branch was going to visit a branch in South Africa.[9] Some of the HYA members were also in Otjiserandu. Their absence was obvious because they were among the few members with cars and were unable to participate in or to help others attend the games in South Africa. That summer, Otjiserandu members complained repeatedly and loudly in public of how the HYA was "junior" to Otjiserandu, how

FIGURE 7.1

The Herero Youth Association performs a song on a tour of Namibia.

Otjiserandu had helped the HYA when it was starting, and that HYA behavior was breaking up the community, among other things. Those accusations hung over the Christmas farewell ceremony, adding to the grumbling of the many Herero youth who could not join the trip because of the wedding. Some of them worried that the particular HYA members who could go on the trip (eight, in the end) were interested only in singing and not in the "educational" aims that had originally been the rationale for the trip. Those who stayed behind would dress in (western-style) HYA uniforms and cook, serve food, and clean plates at the wedding, as well as fete and tease the bride and groom with songs. Unlike the violence of the school-age rioters, which Mahalapye Herero barely remembered and voiced no concern over, the HYA's trips, meetings, parties, and endless choir practices were a constant concern to many parts of the Mahalapye Herero community throughout my fieldwork period.

During the "educational tour" of Namibia, we waded into the Atlantic Ocean (in case it had healing powers), took a tour of a Russian freighter, tried but failed to visit the graves of famous Herero chiefs, successfully visited the Botswana embassy to Namibia, learned songs, histories, and place praise-names associated with the specific families of those on the tour, and met up with relatives and friends in Windhoek and other places who had returned to Namibia years or decades before. Everywhere (except the freighter), the group performed some of its much practiced songs. One of the favorite songs during the trip, which was performed on Namibian radio and TV (and also at the farewell ceremony), had the refrain "*me zemburuka Muharapse wetu* [I remember our Mahalapye]." When we returned to Botswana, another ceremony was held at the kgotla. During the song "*ngatu pasaneye omake*" (quoted above), the returners clasped hands warmly with the HYA members who had stayed behind and with others who came out to greet them, and the trip was pronounced a success. Quietly but insistently, though, a few voiced suspicions that the travelers had done more singing than learning.

THE ROMANCE OF YOUTH AGENCY

It is tempting to look for evidence of youth agency in the riots and disruptions in the schoolyard of Mmankgodi more than in the songs urging people to take one another's hands and to remember their home village while visiting relatives. It is tempting to note the grumbling of schoolchildren in the cold drizzle at Youth Day, refusing to smile for "their day," the rapid abandonment of the festivities by the T-shirt-wearing youth, more than their cheerful march along the streets of Gaborone, planned and framed by adults, and the lively performances of traditional dances, modern music, and familiar song-drama skits of bad behavior and its consequences that punctuated functionaries' speeches. It is tempting to look at the contests over who would organize which activities during the extended holidays more than at the serving of food and cleaning of plates at the wedding. In my presentations and writing, fellow anthropologists and other Africanists are invariably more interested in my accounts of riots and murdered children than in young people serving food at community celebrations or debating for years, as Herero Youth did, the precise shade of blue fabric to be used for women's uniforms in their youth group choir. Poor Botswana's youth, the vast majority of whom are said to be apathetic, can inspire apathy in others as well.

In part, this is the legacy of how Africa, in general, has come to be represented, and African youth in particular. As Karen Hansen (2005:4) notes, the idea of youth and youth's agentive role in public culture has become focused iconically on "young soldiers, paramilitary, rebels, counterinsurgents...militia, township gangs, and youth...who helped propel political shifts in Senegal and Mali." (To this list we should add purveyors and victims of sexually transmitted disease and sexual social disorder.) Lost from sight are the "more mundane dimensions of everyday life" for young people, where "physical violence is not the daily fare" (Hansen 2005:4). The consolidation of images of violence and despair in studies of African youth coordinates with the sense in anthropology that agency is fundamentally oppositional, standing against structure, hegemony, and routine to build expectations about where and what youth agency might be there. We easily find youth agency, then, in the burning of public government buildings in Botswana. We see it in the apparent refusal of the young performers to smile in the cold on "their day." We might look, too, at the T-shirted marchers quickly abandoning the Youth Day ceremonies when those ceremonies turned to center on adult, government officials. These are obvious examples of the small refusals, the foot dragging, that James Scott (1985) suggested are the "weapons of the weak" against domination. Indeed, the situation in Mahalapye is a veritable contest of such small but telling oppositional and resistant agencies—youth association trips scheduled against weddings, conference against conference.

These examples look at youth agency as the assertion of independence and self-interest against impositions of power and cultural hegemonies that support it. Such agency is not restricted to youth: James Scott's peasants, women, slaves, all who are subordinated to others, exercise it in large and small ways. Another strand of thought, intertwined with but also distinct from such a rationalist and universal agency associated with Enlightenment liberalism, focuses on the special qualities of youth agency. Coming out of Romanticism, this strand steers us to locate a liberatory youth agency in the oppositional and the inventive and to endow it with powers particular to youth to, as both Ahearn and Niewenhuys put it, create value and produce culture. Ironically, Margaret Mead wrote her groundbreaking (if problematic) *Coming of Age in Samoa* (1964[1928]) against the idea that youth are inherently rebellious. Nonetheless, youth creativity, resistance, and rebellion remain the hallmarks of interesting—and agentive—anthropological youth, and these qualities seem to inhere in being young, indeed almost to define it. The work of the Birmingham Centre for Contemporary Cultural Studies celebrated the mods, punks, rastas, and teddy boys, as well as the more middle-class hippies, of post–World War II Britain for rebelling against, and subtly commenting on, the sociocultural codes of their socioeconomic system by creating new dress, music, and leisure styles (Hall and Jefferson 1976; Hebdige 1979). Their work became a major point of reference for youth studies at the end of the millennium, directing attention to rebellion and resistance, along with creativity, as hallmarks of fulfilled youth agency.

One common idea about youth feeds both these considerations of youth agency (youth's rebellion against structures of power and their creation of new cultural and social forms). This is the idea that youth are marginal or, in highly significant terms, liminal. Youth are marginal when depicted as powerless, subject to the determinations of other groups in society or to the organization of society around centers and means of action to which they have little access. For example, youth do the work of the chief or for a senior male's agricultural interests; they listen to music that has been marketed to them by a capital-infused media industry. This marginality can sometimes be seen to give youth a sharper view of the inequalities and hegemonies upon which those in power rely, prompting youth resistances and rebellions.

One reason youth marginality often produces insight, rebellion, and creative reworking of society and culture is that youth marginality has been assimilated to liminality, as liminality has come to be understood in anthropological literature: a distinctive social and subjective state in the "ritual process." Victor Turner's development of van Gennep's tripartite nature of ritual emphasized the power of the liminal phase to remake persons into new social beings in a process that allowed considerable creative ferment and offered the possibility of social and cultural invention, or the remaking of a society's core values as conveyed in the liminal phase (Turner 1967, 1969, 1974). Turner's work and that of others who studied the liminal phase frequently took initiation rituals as case studies, and liminality and the movement of children and youth into adulthood have become naturalized in anthropological thought. The parallels between the ritual process and youth are also promoted through the idea that the liminal subjects have had their social roles lifted in order to make new roles and relationships in the course of ritual transformation. Youth are often analyzed as being "freer" to be open to new ideas, creative or critical of their society, because they are less invested in or committed to particular social roles, either through the length of certain roles' performance or because of material interests tied up with those roles. This model risks the implication that youth are unsocialized or are marked by "lack" (see Wulff 1995), but also it underlies the more powerful insights of Karl Mannheim (1952[1928]) in his classic essay on generations, in which he suggests that young people have "fresh" contact with the values of their societies. Even the phrasing echoes Victor Turner's description of young people encountering the symbols of their culture's values in the liminal phase.

Youth in the mid-twentieth-century West have long been seen as "betwixt and between" (Turner's term for the liminal phase), moving between one set of statuses in the natal home and a new set that marks adulthood. Classic psychosocial accounts of youth and adolescence, such as those of Erik Erikson (1965, 1968) and S. N. Eisenstadt (1956), put youth in a narrative in which, as children, they developed a limited but well-defined status or identity within the home. As they grew older, however, they developed another set of statuses at school, in peer groups, and in the wider interactions they experienced outside the home. For Erikson, this was a time of experimentation, imagining oneself in various identities and espousing various values (or "ideologies" such as communism and Catholicism) but not committing to them. This was a period of "identity crisis" for some, but for all, adulthood arrived when a youth settled on one sexual partner, one vocation, and one ideology. The Eriksonian adult married, established a household, got a job, and made commitments to a political party and a church. For Eisenstadt, the period of flux after childhood introduced the developing person to new flexible forms of identity suited to a modern society; the move by individuals both facilitated and recapitulated the move from a traditionalist society to a modern one.

This twentieth-century theory of youth is distinctly romantic. In part, it is romantic because it poses the young person as hero of a narrative in novelistic form, characterized by challenge, crisis, and resolution and by attention to human interiority. Katherine Ewing (2006) notes this narrativity in German media images of daughters of Turkish immigrants: the girls are deemed heroic for separating themselves from (oppressive) Turkish homes and embracing new identities in German society. What the narratives ignore is the range of other social issues surrounding the girls' lives. The twentieth-century romance of youth was built up out of motifs developed in the Romantic period of the eighteenth and nineteenth centuries, in the bildungsroman (a novel about the psychological development of character). In a bildungsroman, a young person constrained by the limited, and typically backward, society of a rural home and by the lack of opportunity for development provided by local education moves to the city, with its diverse, uncertain, and perplexing opportunities. There, he confronts the moral shortcomings of contemporary life and finds his imagination freed to explore and experiment. In the end, the youth finds his walk in life (or career) by bringing together his imagination, a new self-consciousness (often painful), and the wider society he has entered (Buckley 1974). Developed in the context of industrialization, the bildungsroman links personal growth with social change; focuses attention on the interplay of experience, identity, and imagination; and makes youth the historical linchpin of such processes. As the young person finds a personal agency—

individuality, the ability to choose among options and to exercise an imagination—he also becomes the agent of social change.

What these ideas of youth share is a sense that youth is a time of personal or individualized identity making accomplished through a movement that is both liberatory and developmental. As well as shaping the romantic youth, the nineteenth century reformed the idea of the child, such that childhood was to be protectively encapsulated in the home. Youth was the period of mobility between two homes, but such mobility had to be achieved by a rupture. Hence, for Mannheim, "fresh contacts play an important part of the life of the individual when he is forced by events to leave his own social group and enter a new one—when, for example, an adolescent leaves home, or a peasant the country-side for the town, or when an emigrant changes his home" (Mannheim 1952[1928]:253). (Mannheim goes on to note that the youth experience is more radical to society because of its generational character.) To understand youth agency in Botswana, we must shake ourselves loose from both notions—that of increasing individualization and independence and that of youth as a period of movement away from a stifling home and into a fresh one.

YOUTH MOVEMENT IN BOTSWANA

Much as in American Samoa, as analyzed by Mead in her critique of adolescent rebellion, childhood in Botswana is a period of more mobility for most children than in the middle-class West, and that mobility continues throughout life.[10] (Unlike Mead's Samoans, however, children in Botswana are usually not the ones to choose their residences.) From infancy, children are cared for by various older relatives, including siblings (primarily sisters), mothers, aunts, cousins, and more distant female relatives—but especially by grandmothers. (It is not uncommon for children to call their mothers "*sisi*" or "*ausi*" [sister] and their grandmothers "mother.") Grandmothers and the other caregivers are, themselves, often very mobile between village, cattlepost, and city. Villages are the sites of much community social activity and are where schools are located; cattleposts are thought to have more nourishing milk and meat available; and cities have hospitals and income-earning relatives. Children are also moved between these caregivers, going to live with a mother or an uncle in town for a few months, then back to a home village to stay with grandmother, then out to an arable agricultural site or a cattlepost for weeks or months. Children's interactions take place primarily within these multiple households and in surrounding yards and streets with their neighbors and relatives. Yet the households are so varied in structure, activity, and shifting residents, and children move between them so often, that it is hard to talk of a major transition out of a narrow, fixed, or protected domestic sphere for children. Nor do youth and young adults leave their households at maturity (howsoever that is reached). Generally, men, and the many women who do not marry, build a house within a family compound in a village. If they build on a new lot elsewhere or live in rented housing or with others in a city, they maintain rights to stay in huts in their "home" compound (and often build one there too) and to keep cattle at a shared cattlepost. (Women who marry are supposed to relocate their primary residence to their husband's family's compound, but they tend to spend considerable time with their own families, a frequent cause of marital conflict.) Illness and continuing misfortune are often dealt with in a parent or senior uncle or aunt's compound, giving the sense that one's life, subjectivity, and identity continue to be bound up in these places.[11]

Nonetheless, there are significant differences between the social movements of youth and those of children, as the educational (or choral) tour of the Herero Youth Association and the march down the streets of Gaborone on Youth Day attest. This movement—and also the response some of it generated against the HYA—can best be understood by looking at some ideas of independence and dependence and effective sentiment and emotion.

Starting with the last, emotion in Botswana is something that grows in effectiveness throughout life, like wisdom (as opposed to knowledge). Children are messily emotional beings, crying and laughing and displaying anger readily. People respond to their emotions, but children's emotions are not thought to have profound, physical effects on other people in the same way that the emotions of older people do. Lambek and Solway (2001) have described the emotion known among Tswana as *dikgaba* (justified anger; the term also applies to the cooling treatments that allay the anger and its effects). Justified anger is effective when directed against juniors (adult or otherwise) by elders, as it manifests as illness in the bodies of others and as misfortune. Because of the power of such anger, older people ought to control their feelings or use them to correct and direct misbehaving juniors, though many are suspected of not doing so. Herero I knew in the village also tried to restrain sentiments of jealousy, either by controlling their own "hearts" or by not flaunting good fortune in front of others to provoke their jealousy, because jealousy, and especially that of older people, could take effect in the bodies and fortunes of its object or other people associated with its object. Sadness, manifested in crying, is another emotion that older people across Botswana attempt to control, because of its effects on others and the negative ways it binds one to its object (Durham and Klaits 2002; Klaits 2005). Children display all these emotions freely and without restraint; however, their emotions do not have the depth of effect on others that those of older people do. Older people who allow themselves to burst out in angry tirades (as they do), to laugh or smile when walking alone down a street, or to cry are behaving childishly—and sometimes dangerously.

Emotion binds people together in positive and desired ways, as well as in harmful, negative ways. Love and caring are sentiments that link people together (see Durham 2002a, 2005; Klaits n.d.; Livingston 2005). Love and caring create bodily, mental, and material well-being in others through the sheer force of these emotions and through the acts such emotions engender. Children are important recipients of love and caring, manifested in their "fatness" and overall well-being, even from absent caring parents and caring others or from parents and others who are present for the child. Children are encouraged to create connections with their relatives by working for their relatives' well-being as well—fetching wood for fires and water for baths, washing clothes and pots, cooking. Nonetheless, children are not thought to be either naturally "caring" or effective emotionally; they are more characterized by selfishness and a kind of willful independence. When not performing household tasks, they are said to be playing, which is accepted but also the cause for much scolding. As children grow older, developing positive and physically substantial relationships with household members through work and care has become more problematic in recent decades because they are now obliged to be at school or because the cash incomes and contributions that have become so important to households are difficult for the young to provide.

Children and youth, as well as people in a junior position, are praised for their ability to hear, understand, and obey—three meanings attached to the Setswana word *go utlwa* and also the Otjiherero term *oku zuva*. *Go utlwa* (or *oku zuva*) should not be thought of as passive, but as active modes through which people build relationships with others. Frederick Klaits describes how members of a church in Gaborone become "spiritual children" of the prophet by "hearing" her words, something they do insofar as they are motivated by love and care. Reciprocally, "hearing the word of God gives rise to sentiments of love and care, and to new forms of relatedness" (Klaits n.d.). Listening is also a quality shown by *bagolo* (Setswana: big people, adults). In the traditional setting of the kgotla, the oldest, and wisest, members speak last. They listen to the speeches of all the others, and then, when the time is right, they speak, referring to others' points, considering all the angles, and relating these to "our customs" before forming and presenting their own understanding. One cover of *The Youth Enquirer* (December 1999), a newsletter of the Botswana National Youth Council, showed an audience of young people sitting on benches, their heads resting on their hands, "listening attentively" and showing a "positive attitude" (as the caption said). It was an issue focusing on youth political empowerment. Although I initially was amused by this picture of obedient youth sitting and listening to the messages of the government, I realized the importance of recognizing that their listening, like the listening of children and senior men, is an important form of social action in Botswana and does not necessarily signal passivity or subordination.

A person's life is not organized around increasing independence and self-determination, but around increasing interdependencies and the kind of mutualities that come with effective sentiment, in which older people have more effective, powerful, and determining roles. Youth is a time when people are particularly active at building up a wide range of relationships, which they do through increasingly sentimental and effective practices (in the broad but connective sense that I use *sentiment* and *emotion* above). These practices include developing cooperative groups, such as the HYA or the less formal groups that practice songs together in evenings, pursuing love affairs, performing labor for a wider range of households, and singing for the community's joy and to represent it to others. All such practices are effective in building relationality through the combined effect of sentiment and work. Youth who do not do so are cause for anxiety. One of the leaders of the Herero Youth Association, approaching forty,[12] had a high-level government job. He was an enthusiast of Western consumer goods and had a dishwasher, a washing machine, and many other items in his house near his job. These were never mentioned by the people from the village who visited him. Instead, they talked about the fact that he seemed to have no girlfriends and no offspring, a concern compounded by his not having a girl from the home village or a distant relative or children to do laundry, cook, and clean. Although he was admired for his professional success, leadership skills, and strong interest in Herero history, people worried about his "oddness" in living alone. He was independent at a time of life when he should have been demonstrating increasing interdependencies, especially through girlfriends, and beginning to attract dependents.[13]

Having love affairs, joining singing practices and associations, beginning to hire people or attach dependents for house and agricultural work, and having children—the kinds of things that begin recognition of adulthood—do not serve to separate the young person from his or her household, as noted above. Eventually, the young man with the laborsaving devices did marry. The marriage took place after my last field visit, but if it proceeded like other marriages I observed, it did not result in separating husband and wife from their old households (although they probably continued to use his device-filled house and perhaps a house near her work site as well) as much as in connecting their two families with a set of complex, sentimentally dense ties realized in a variety of material, social, and emotional exchanges. These engagements, and building mutualities, are not necessarily all positive—they are fraught with the risks that come with increasingly effective anger, jealousies, and suspicions of diverted love or caring. The increased engagements with in-laws, wider circles of relatives, new dependents or laborers, or perhaps a patron or an employer do establish the individuality of people, not in terms of separation and independence, but by creating circles of mutualities unique to each person, allowing people to forge their adult, or eternally sub-adult, selves in different ways.

At the same time, however, Botswana hosts a powerful discourse of liberal democracy, sponsored largely by the government, both in the rhetoric of politicians and civil servants and in the development apparatus. Key to the discourse is the idea of liberal individualism. "Batswana must work hard to develop themselves" is a phrase endlessly repeated in speeches and in the media, suggesting that individuals are responsible for their own fate and should not rely on others (especially not the government). This ethos is embraced by many citizens and echoed in public forums. Examples that might sound surprising to Americans are kgotla discussions in which many people favored reintroducing school fees and proposals for new value-added taxes, saying that the latter would allow people too poor to pay income tax to contribute to the government. Many people thought it proper that they should pay school fees—currently being eradicated elsewhere around the world—and not expect handouts from the government. In one kgotla discussion of a youth economic empowerment initiative pressing young people to take out government business-development loans, a speaker noted that youth probably would not have the capital to qualify for the loans—taking for granted that people would approach these programs as individuals, relying exclusively on their own resources.[14] He did not refer to the actual webs of interdependency in which most people live; any project is inevitably supported by loans, work, and gifts from many people. Paydays and bill-paying dates see a flurry of activity as people seek to borrow and repay various debts. Similar tensions between interdependence and independence pervade Botswana society and are seen in uncertainties about citizenship, in which ideals of individual accomplishment and political identity provoke endless suspicion of nepotism, favoritisms, and tribal allegiances (see Durham 2002b).

BRINGING AGENCY HOME

What does all of this mean for a project that looks for youth agency in the several examples given here? It makes for a complicated and very contradictory picture, no doubt. The riotous youth of Mmankgodi, torching buildings and tormenting government officials, are significant to people in Botswana not so much because the young people are taking a heroic, independent position against an oppressive government, or against authority generally, but because they speak to effective activity, youth or otherwise, in Botswana society. These youth's actions express a sense of anger, found elsewhere in Africa, that young people are being thwarted in their search for opportunities and advancement by greedy elders holding on to wealth, jobs, and appropriate support (see Comaroff and Comaroff 1999). During the mid-1990s, when the riots took place, the private and government press carried on an extensive discussion about "deadwood"—old men sitting in government or other private sinecures rather than surrendering these to a better educated, eager generation. Much of the language, especially as the debates were picked up in the Internet discussion lists mentioned above, included elements of liberalist ideology, focusing on individual accomplishments, and of the language of interdependence, arguing about care, debts, and jealousy. Contributors to the botswanacf forum asked why young people were not on parastatal boards of directors or sitting as MPs in government—questions also asked by members of the BDP youth wing to Botswana's president at one of their meetings.[15]

It is interesting that when newspaper articles (like the one described in note 15) or studies by scholars such as Burke (2000) look for evidence of young people's capability in decision making and management, the examples given are in the home—where youth's effectiveness and "power" may lie more in their ability to build relationalities and interdependencies than in breaking out and becoming independent directors of boards. The anger of the rioters in Mmankgodi was effective, but not because it gave youth an independent voice in reforming education, policing, or government. Rather, it drew the attention of government to the community's needs for better policing, more accountability in government officials, and economic development, as well as the obligations of elders to care for their children and not afflict them with jealousy, anger, and selfish indifference. Otherwise, the rioters would be evaluated—as they were by some in Mahalapye—as being childish, exhibiting the uncontrolled and ineffective rage of children. In homes, childish rages are laughed at and ignored: if they are an expression of individual desire or will, they are ineffective in moving people.

In this way, as agentive youth, the rioters were much more akin than would seem at first glance to the cheerful marchers on the streets of Gaborone on Youth Day 2000 and, indeed, to all the choirs that perform at concerts and political events. As youth, their effectiveness is in how they facilitate the linking of different groups in the nation—the schools with their governing officials, families with the schools and the nation, villages with the cities and state. The choirs do this in a number of ways: by representing in the public sphere the communities and households they are from (or representing Botswana abroad, as some choirs do), by forming personal relationships with others and with other spheres, which they then link up with their households, and by emoting with growing force, which they are learning to control and use relationally. Young people's performances are intended to be "happy"—recall the woman telling the miserable children in scanty "traditional dance" costumes to smile and be happy. Choral performances are a source of great pleasure to singers and audience; everyone present is liable to smile, even staid elderly men. People often make eye contact during singing, some to share pleasure and build existing emotional connectivity, others to initiate it. When the Herero Youth Association began to press the smaller children in the community into singing (almost inaudibly) at concerts and later as a choir and nascent youth group at public events, it is no coincidence that the HYA named them "The Happy Choir." Although young people, even into their forties, rarely speak in the traditional public forums where community issues are debated, they contribute by forging mutuality through enjoyment. Relatively inarticulate with words, they articulate through joy.

This is how the Herero Youth Association started out—partly as a choir, a venue for youthful socializing as they practiced through the evenings, partly as a group performing community labor (cleaning the kgotla, taking care of chores at weddings and funerals), and partly as an initial entry into the work of community. It is clear, however, from the tensions surrounding the educational tour of Namibia, that whether they were continuing to do the work of communality—forging links between people, households, town, state, and world—had become disputable to some. The question raised was whether the group was beginning to exert some kind of agency over and against the values and ties that bound together a fragile Mahalapye Herero community. The elections, committees, chairs, and strict bureaucratic procedures by which the HYA governed itself were fascinating to me. Many of these procedures directly challenged the principles of authority that had dominated Herero life in Mahalapye. I could easily recognize that the Herero youth were very active cultural agents, in the sense enjoined by Bucholtz and others. So, too, were children, who brought home from school new ways of growing vegetables and of promoting hygiene and who guided aging grandparents through the monthly rituals of paying water bills. So, too, were adults, who started new forms of businesses, tried new educational schemes for their children, and brought car batteries and TVs into their homes. But insofar as the HYA activities were not integrated into the community (such as, initially, the trip to Namibia), insofar as they threatened not to readjust but actually to break relationships, Herero saw the HYA's actions as "just playing" (as one woman said to me) or as cause for anger. The HYA had many plans. It wanted to build a nursery school to help working mothers and to help grandmothers "properly" educate children, to build a community hall, to choose a dress style for its main associational uniform. These and many other projects that it failed to materialize or agree upon generated amusement or disdain among the community.

It is remarkable to other Africanists when I tell them that people from Botswana who are sent to school in Britain, the United States, and elsewhere almost always return to Botswana and do not attempt to stay overseas. Of course, one explanation is the Botswana economy. After expanding at one of the fastest rates in the world in the 1970s and 1980s, it slowed in the 1990s, and pessimism about opportunity and employment grew (see Hope 1996). Nonetheless, Botswana is a wealthy country compared with many in Africa. But this is not enough of an explanation. People in Botswana feel their agency—their ability to act effectively and to grow in their own power—primarily as it becomes manifest in ties of interdependence with other people. Youth is a particularly potent stage of life in which to develop the capacity for effective action—when people learn to use emotion and labor (conjoined practices) and "hearing" and mobility to build mutualities, interdependencies, and social linkages. People who married or studied overseas often found themselves cut off from developing those ties. The Herero youth were successful agents and were "given hands," not when their actions signaled growing independence, but when their acts recognizably situated them more tightly in the community and at the same time linked the community with other people and social spheres.

There are many kinds of agency, as recent anthropological work has shown (Asad 2000; Davies 1991; Mahmood 2001; Strathern 1988; Utas 2005). To state that youth have agency is not enough, especially if that agency is theorized as a function of an autonomous selfhood opposed to others or a social-cultural system. Youth in Botswana are and are not the kinds of agents of social and cultural change often envisioned in the West, where youth are popularly seen to be leaders in innovation and change. In Botswana, adults—recognized leaders with powerful oratorical and political repertoires or otherwise recognized for wisdom and resolution of contradictions and social tensions—are the people understood most typically to effect change. They are the people who "get things done," not on small, individual scales, but involving groups and relations between groups. Youth is not a period of liberation from a home society or cultural traditions, and the motif of development that youth engenders is not a linear move away from the past or from home. Youth do move, do make connections between different places, and do go "out" and bring things back home. But they do not become more independent—liberalized—and do not, as part of their "plot" of growing up, make something new. Although they bring new things home (new dress designs from Namibia or from the capital city, new ways of choosing leaders, new songs), their agency, or their ability to shape the culture and social relations around them, rests more in their ability to vest these things in relationalities, which they are only beginning to wield effectively in their later youth years. But other ideas about personhood—ideas that reject relationality as a moral position, ideas that privilege independence (based on knowledge, wealth, or personal hard work)—are also circulating in Botswana. Some young people flirt with these options: a Marxist university student, a wealthy entrepreneur benefiting from family wealth while discounting the importance of the relations in which he or she is embedded, overseas students on a listserv berating deadwood and demanding positions of leadership, and a young Herero enamored of Western laborsaving technology. But (as of 2000, at least) most "come home" again.

Acknowledgments

I have conducted fieldwork in Botswana since 1988, when I undertook a two-year research project on the Herero community of Mahalapye, Botswana, much of which focused on the Herero Youth Association. From 1994 to 2000, I made five return visits of four to eight weeks each, many of which focused on youth associations, youth choral activities, and youth programs in the country. This research was generously supported by Fulbright-Hays, NSF, NEH, Wenner-Gren, the American Philosophical Society, and Sweet Briar College Faculty Grants. My understanding of Botswana has been deepened and extended over the years by many conversations with Dick Werbner, Jackie Solway, Charlanne Burke, Fred Klaits, Julie Livingston, Rijk van Dijk, and Keith Adams, although we do not always agree. My ideas on youth have benefited from the lively discussions at the SAR advanced seminar and also with Misty Bastian, Adeline Masquelier, and, of course, Jennifer Cole.

Notes

1. Xenophobia in Botswana can be targeted nonracially at the many Africans from neighboring states who come to Botswana for security or opportunity. Many are Tswana, Herero, or Kalanga (some of the larger ethnic populations in Botswana), others from Nigeria or Ghana. But some racial elements do exist: South Asian citizens of Botswana, though much admired, are viewed suspiciously for their business success.

2. In the large urban village where I worked during much of the 1990s, twenty-two-year-olds still thought of themselves as children and would not vote.

3. On this general history and inequality, see Denbow and Thebe 2006; Edge and Lekorwe 1998; Good 1993; Nteta, Hermans, and Jeskova 1997.

4. June 16 was designated the African Day of the Child by the African Union soon after the Soweto massacre. In 1999 the United Nations designated August 12 as International Youth Day; the first international celebrations were in 2000. The internationalization of youth and children is significant and includes new demographic measures of who is a child (often those under twenty-one or under eighteen) or youth (defined by the United Nations as those between fifteen and twenty-four) and ideas about government programs to help youth, based on common Western youth "problems" such as school delinquency, teenage pregnancy, drugs, petty criminality and violence, and official unemployment. See Durham 2004.

5. The *cf* in the Internet address means "cyberforum." There has been a series of Botswana Internet discussion groups over the years, which I followed throughout the 1990s. I first joined a group in 1993: from then until mid-1995, it was run out of McGill University as botswana@cs.mcgill.ca. When the list owner returned to Botswana, the forum was relocated to Duquesne University at botswana@mathcs.duq.edu. The Duquesne list manager then graduated, and in late 1996 two lists were formed, botsnet@newton.ccs.tuns.ca and botswanacf@sheffield.ac.uk, which were up and running when I stopped following them at the end of the century.

6. This and other quotes from the article are taken from a copy of the article circulated on botswanacf@sheffield.ac.uk, April 16, 1997, the same date the *Botswana Gazette* published the article.

7. The significance of Segametsi Mogomotsi's murder and the events surrounding it has been discussed in various lights: Burke 2000, Durham 2004, Good 1996, Gulbrandsen 2002.

8. botswana@mathcs.duq.edu, posted March 4, 1996.

9. Otjiserandu groups, or "troops," are independent, but often join together for the annual celebration. Some years, other troops would come to Mahalapye; other years, the Mahalapye group would travel to other Herero locations. See Durham 2003.

10. A developing class structure means that the new elite of Botswana may be raising their children differently; research is needed on this group.

11. AIDS has dramatically affected children's lives. Botswana has one of the highest HIV infection rates in the world. Although retroviral drug treatments are now widely available, death rates remain high, and many children have lost their parents. Children are raised by other family members. Botswana's orphan policy expects that all children continue to have a family responsible for them after their parents' death and supports nonresidential orphanages and orphan programs. Bianca Dahl is completing doctoral work at the University of Chicago on Botswana's orphan programs; I thank her for this information.

12. The Herero community and association members usually considered "youth" to be people in their mid-twenties to forties; people in the early twenties or younger were children. Across Botswana, similar ideas about age groups contested with newer ones more in line with Western age ranges; see Durham 2004.

13. Those who have too many girlfriends, especially in short-term relationships, and who fail to acknowledge children from those relationships are often said to be "just playing" in the sense of being child-like, selfish, and not creating interdependencies through them. See Durham 1999 on such accusations against one man.

14. "Youth Participation in Development Negligible," *Botswana Daily News*, November 19, 2001; read online at http://www.gov.bw/cgi-bin, November 21, 2001.

15. The article "Youth Tired of Being Excluded from Decision Making" in the *Botswana Daily News*, June 6, 2001, reported, "They wanted to be MPs, ministers, members of parastatal boards," directly echoing comments made on the Botswana Internet discussion list in the later 1990s. The article was read online at http://www.gov.bw/cgi-bin, June 15, 2001.

8

Pocket Capitalism and Virtual Intimacy

Pokémon as Symptom of Postindustrial Youth Culture

Anne Allison

Children are inundated by Pokémon today. In the morning they eat Pokémon
seaweed on their rice; they exchange Pokémon cards with their friends at
school; they play the Pokémon Game Boy game after school; and they have
Pokémon chocolates for snacks. They eat Pokémon curry for dinner, watch
the Pokémon *anime* (cartoon) in the evening, and when they get into their
futons at night, they read the Pokémon comic book [in *Korokoro Komikku*].
We've had plenty of fads starting after the war with war games and plenty
of franchising crazes with, i.e., chocolates and cards. But there's never been
a boom in Japan like Pokémon before.—*Nikkei Entertainment*

Pokémon (also called Pocket Monsters) is a world of endless consumption and imaginary relations. In this media-mix complex—of electronic game, trading cards, cartoon (anime), comic books (*manga*), movies,
and tie-in merchandise—the basic premise is of a virtual universe inhabited
by wild monsters that players seek to capture and then domesticate as tools
in capturing more monsters. Inhabiting this playworld, with its magical
topography of towns, forests, and caves, are 151 pokémon (now, more than
300 with later Game Boy versions); the goal of the game is to capture them
all. This process, *getto suru* ("getting" or "gotta catch 'em all," in the US ad
campaign), is both repetitive and increasingly complex. With its quest for
continual accumulation, Pokémon mimics capitalism. But countering and
interwoven with this is an alternative agenda of interpersonal and cybor-
gian communication: building ties with others, both human and virtual, in
order to reach one's goal. Encouraging kids to make "friends" (with monsters and other players) and to endlessly expand their control (by getting

ever-more monsters and thereby becoming "the world's greatest Pokémon master"), Pokémon breeds compulsive acquisitiveness while fostering cooperation and intimacy.[1] This tension is at the heart of the game's logic, as well as its appeal.

Pokémon was created in Japan and released there in 1996. Within two years, it became a global craze and, as a media-mix empire, has generated billions of dollars and set global trends from Singapore to Brazil. With this and other successful kid hits, Japan has emerged in the new millennium as a competitive producer of cutting-edge "cool" goods in the tough market of global youth culture, a market long dominated by the United States. Designed to be at once technologically enticing and cutely cool, these products carry an aesthetic identified as both distinctly "Japanese" and globally cosmopolitan. As such, coolness forms a point of articulation for the dislocations of global capitalism and the flexible intimacies that can be built within it.

A sign of Japan's burgeoning "soft power," Pokémon is also a symptom of the anxious times that launched it. Japan's Bubble Economy, an era of runaway spending and skyrocketing investment, burst in 1991, triggering a deep sense of unease (*fuan*) across the nation. Hit by a severe recession that led to unprecedented layoffs, downsizing, rising unemployment, and mounting suicides, Japan has been gripped in a crisis about its national identity: an identity forged in the postwar era by a corporate capitalism ideologically built on deep-seated commitments to company, family, and school. After rising to the rank of global industrial power in the 1970s, Japan is now faced with new fears about the country's future.

In this context, the anxieties and doubts of the moment have crystallized around youth: the segment of the population that embodies, both literally and figuratively, the future (see also Flanagan, chapter 6, this volume). On the one hand, youth are pitied for having to endure the rigors of a social economy that pushes all its subjects to work intensely hard, perform continually at the highest level, and sacrifice personal desires and friendships in the process. In this society geared toward academic achievement (*gakureki shakai*), the pressure to study, succeed, and compete starts almost at birth. Concurrently, both the space and the time for play have diminished. Given that commuting time is also extensive, Japanese increasingly spend more time alone. In an environment where everyone moves fast to accomplish more and more every day, the human connectedness (*ningenkankei*) once held as fundamental to society is said to be eroding, if not out-and-out gone. Children are particularly affected by an "orphanism" (*kojinshugi*) characterizing contemporary times (Takeda 1998:38).

According to a 1997 study by Hakuhōdō advertising agency, most ten-to fourteen-year-olds return home after dark (the average time is 8 p.m.), eat dinner alone, and are involved in exam preparation (44 percent attend cram school). Members of today's generation are "*amenbo* kids," children who, like water spiders, attach easily, but superficially, to multiple things (Hakuhōdō Seikatsu Sōgō Kenkyūjo 1997). In a 2004 study on the post-Bubble generation (kids who grew up in the 1990s), Hakuhōdō reported that youth today lack dreams for the future. Instead, unsure that even hard work at school will guarantee job security as adults (as it once did for their parents), they (particularly girls) are absorbed in the immediacy of the present. The study calls teenage girls today the "sugar generation" for their attachment to immediate pleasures (Hakuhōdō Seikatsu Sōgō Kenkyūjo 2004).

On the other hand, Japanese youth are also blamed for the angst of the times. Throughout the 1990s, they have been the target of a moral panic fueled by the mass media. In what is said to be a rash of social pathologies (refusing to go to school, living solitary existences in their bedrooms, causing havoc in classrooms, committing violent crimes, preferring part-time to full-time jobs, and, as schoolgirls, engaging in "amateur prostitution" in order to buy brand-name goods), youth are seen to symbolize the collapse of Japan's collective culture and the excesses of materialist hedonism. Even more pointedly, they are decried for lacking the commitment to socially productive futures, such as studying hard to enter a high-ranking university or working toward a corporate career (Yamada 2004). Indeed, newspapers are filled daily with reports of how youth today are unwilling to embody (or are incapable of embodying) those very qualities of hard work and attachment to family, job, and school that have anchored Japan's corporate capitalism for more than a half century (see also Anagnost, chapter 3, this volume, for an example of how children in post-socialist China are seen as a sign of value, rendered in terms of their human capital for economic productivity).

Such a crisis of and for youth is hardly unique to Japan. Rather, it is symptomatic of the global mapping of neoliberalism, techno-informationalism, and migratory movements that mark the twenty-first century, what I call "millennial capitalism." In an economy that has shifted from according the central role and value to labor, to centering more around consumption, a speculative and presentist logic has replaced the modernist belief in progress organized by hard work and savings. Fortunes and futures are now pinned on what the Comaroffs (2001) call "occult economies"—get-rich schemes, lotteries, gambling, magic. Neoliberalism turns workers from investors in the future to spenders in the present (Rifkin 1995:20). In an era when, as Lawrence Grossberg has argued for American teens, deep anxiety about loneliness, isolation, and the inability to connect to others combines with ardent desire to belong, kids are in crisis, caught in the middle of a struggle over what it means to be a modern nation (Grossberg 2005). As their place and relations within the social order transform, youth become the "unintended consequence" (Grossberg 2005:106) of the radical change in the nature of modernity and its attachment to progress. Once the hope and embodiment of the future, kids are in peril under a neoliberal economy driven by speedup and risk (Giroux 2003).

Precisely because of such postindustrial conditions, which reorganize the conception of the future and therefore of youth itself, children are uniquely positioned to symbolize the very possibility of a new social and economic order (Grossberg 2005). It is this connection that lies behind the global fetishization of youth-identified trends and fads today that, repackaged into commodity form, sell wildly even to adults. This is certainly true of Pokémon, a stupendous moneymaker that has been praised for the way it mimics contemporary times: a playscape that both reflects and reimagines contemporary conditions of speculation, fragmentation, and digitalization. Fans of the game reiterate how it offers them a "space of their own" and a constellation of what I call flexible attachments, which give intimacy to connections formed with other kids, electronic pocket monsters, and digital play itself. Yet precisely because of the New Age–ness of Pokémon's play (also said to evoke an "older" Japan whose spirituality, communitarianism, and gift giving have now "vanished" [Ivy 1995]) and the multifarious bonds it forms around "getting," the game has been supremely successful on the market, spreading across ever-more venues for sale and becoming a model of and for Japanese capitalism in the twenty-first century.

In these play products—targeted at youth and constructed to appeal to the desires and anxieties stemming from their postindustrial living conditions—Japan has located a response to its anxiety over national identity and the post-Bubble economic crisis. That is, the industry of youth goods and "cool" techno-trends that has been booming since the early 1990s extends to the global marketplace, constituting what has been called Japan's "GNC"—gross national cool (McGray 2002). One of the few success stories in Japan's recessionary economy, kids' entertainment is earning the country much needed capital, both real (more than $15 billion by Pokémon alone in domestic and global sales between 1996 and 2003) and symbolic (an international reputation in pop-cultural goods that is historically unprecedented). Increasingly, corporate and government leaders have come to recognize the importance of its "GNC" and actively promote "Japanese cool" today as a source of national soft power that will, they hope, restore the country's economic security and global prestige.

Ironically, the state of flesh-and-blood youth is still the source of much hand-wringing in public discourse for some of the very qualities—flexible versus long-term attachments, presentist play versus future-oriented work— packaged so enticingly in "cool" entertainment goods. In this chapter, I examine the play structure and commercial property of Pokémon in these terms: as a fantasyscape that promises an alternative world of connective- ness but in which the logic of play also presumes, and socializes children into, a worldview of accumulation, competition, and consumption very much aligned with the problems of youth in millennial capitalism. Pokémon is a playscape full of complexities and contradictions. Evocative of something both old and new in Japan, it is this doubled nature—flexible intimacies and virtual "getting"—that accounts for the popular and globalized spread of Japan's millennial brand of cultural goods today.[2]

COMMUNICATION: SPEAKING MONSTERS AND THINGS

Pokémon (or *Poketto monstā* in its longer version)[3] was originally de- signed as a software game for Game Boy, the handheld digital game con- sole launched by Nintendo in 1989. Created by a young game designer, Tajiri Satoshi, and his staff at Game Freak for a Japanese consumer base of boys ages eight to fourteen, Pokémon was bought by Nintendo and released in February 1996. Predictions were initially modest because Game Boy's 8-bit technology was on the wane in an electronic gameworld becom- ing dominated by far more powerful machines. Sales were far better than expected, however, in part because the game is simple yet catchy and because the handheld Game Boy fit in with the time's portable (*keitai*) cul- ture. Sensing the start of a fad, its marketers sought to expand Pokémon across a mix of media venues. In summer 1996, Pokémon came out as a serialized comic in *Korokoro Kommiku*, read by half of all Japanese boys in fifth to eighth grades.[4] Playing cards, distributed by Media Factory, fol- lowed in the fall. The television anime (cartoon) produced by Terebi Tokyo debuted in April 1997. Toy merchandise by Tomy appeared in spring 1997. The first movie hit the screens in the summer of 1997. Besides these major media, there has been a concatenation of tie-in merchandise, such as the sheets and rice bowl used by the eight-year-old in the epigraph. Almost immediately, in 1997, Pokémon was exported. Beginning in East Asia with Taiwan, Hong Kong, and China, it entered the United States in 1998 and then Australia, Canada, Europe, Latin America, Israel, and the Middle East.

Months after its launching as a Game Boy game in February 1996, Pokémon gained fame in Japan not only as a commercial sensation but also as what some experts were calling a new form of play and a "social phenomenon." As described by Okada Toshio, a University of Tokyo professor and an expert on mass culture, Pokémon is play that goes beyond the world of the game itself (Yamato 1998:247), a description I heard often in the course of doing fieldwork. Its software is relatively simple, and the game can be played alone or with others. In this, Pokémon is somewhat different from the trend in electronic and video games, which have become increasingly complex since the late 1980s, demanding intense concentration and single-minded, often solitary, absorption. Its designer, Tajiri Satoshi, purposely crafted the game to feature not only matches (*taisen*), the competitive motif of trying to beat, eliminate, or kill an opponent, standard in action games today, but also exchanges (*kōkan*), cooperative negotiations with other players to trade monsters (Nintendo 1999:12). It was the latter concept, innovative in the world of gaming, that attracted Nintendo to sign on the project in 1991 and to support development for the five long years Tajiri took to complete it. Yet instructed not to remove matches altogether (on the grounds that a game without battles would be boring for kids and sell poorly for Nintendo), Tajiri built Pokémon with two strategies for getting pocket monsters. He further programmed the game so that 11 of the 151 monsters could be acquired *only* through exchanges (Hatakeyama and Kubo 2000:75–76).

In designing Pokémon, Tajiri said that he had two major motivations. One was to create a challenging yet playable game that would pique the imaginations of children. The other was to give kids a means of relieving the stresses of growing up in a postindustrial society (Nintendo 1999:13). Born in 1962, Tajiri shared the opinion of many in his generation that life for children at the millennial divide had become overly regimented, fast-paced, and solitary. Nostalgic for a world not yet dominated by industrial capitalism, he strove to create a kind of neotraditional environment in the imaginary playworld of Pokémon. To "tickle" memories of the past (Nintendo 1999:12), Tajiri drew from his own childhood experiences in a town where nature had not yet been overtaken by industrialization. As a boy, his favorite pastime had been insect collecting. Fascinated by the abundance and diversity of species in their natural environment, Tajiri spent long hours studying, raising, and collecting bugs. It was this activity, involving interactions both with nature (adventure, discovery, mastery) and culture (trading and sharing with others), that the game designer aimed to transmit to contemporary youth bereft of natural playgrounds and the age-mates that go along with them. For this postmodern insect collecting, Tajiri chose virtuality: a medium that conforms to children's mobile, industrial lifestyles and with which they are conversant. A game junkie (*otaku*) himself since the age of twelve when a video arcade with Space Invaders arrived in town, Tajiri became as hooked on these virtual worlds as he had once been on nature. In this electronic gameworld, he rediscovered the same type of adventure, exploration, and competition he had earlier enjoyed in bug collecting, with one major difference (Hiratsuka 1997:168–170). Whereas the latter opens up a child to horizons beyond the self, games enclose kids within their virtual constructions.

Disturbed by the tendency toward atomism visible in gaming and in society at large, Tajiri designed Pokémon to promote more interactivity. He did this by, first, making the game challenging but playable even by young children; the rules are easily grasped, and players can make progress as long as they persist. Given the surfeit of detail involved in Pokémon, however, kids are also encouraged to gather and share information with other children. This emphasis on information, making the gameworld something like a language whose acquisition and mastery promote communication, is an important part of Tajiri's design (see also Thorne, chapter 4, this volume, for another example of how commercialized children's culture operates as what she calls a "global lingua franca"). In his vision, *tsūshin* (communication) is further stimulated by the exchanges that constitute a central feature of playing Pokémon. His hope was that exchanges would be perpetuated outside the parameters of the game itself and into currencies of other kinds. One example given by Tajiri was that a child might exchange one of his pokémon for a bowl of ramen or a comic book, in a mixing of metaphors, economies, and pleasures (Nintendo 1999:12). As Tajiri intended, exchanges enmesh players in webs of social relationships. The ideal here is that communicating with Pokémon will build a community of friendship.

Interactivity was crafted into this playscape in yet a third way, by giving children a fantastic world of made-up monsters and virtual landscapes with which to commune, so to speak, with their imaginations. As I heard repeatedly from marketers, commentators, and child experts in the course of doing fieldwork, Pokémon provides youth a "space of their own" (Nakazawa 1997:22) that, even though make-believe, is emotionally real and cushions them from the daily grind of test taking, studying, and commuting. Typically, adults referred to it as a "fake" (Hori 1996:95) or "fictional" (Nakanishi 1998: 295) environment, but children were more prone to describe Pokémon as a mix of the real and the fantastic. The world is "like reality, only fake," with monsters that are "like animals but mutated and made up."[5] In creating the pokémon, Tajiri instructed his staff to draw on childhood memories of insects, animals, and the outdoors, with the aim of capturing the "fascination" these hold for a child. His own childhood memories shaped his design of, for example, Nyoromo, a roly-poly pokémon with a translucent body, plug legs, and a tummy stamped with a big twirl, modeled after a tadpole (Hatakeyama and Kubo 2000:106–107).

The world of Pokémon is constructed to be playful yet intricate. Superimposed onto digital grids, its landscape is an array of cute habitats: bountiful forests, chubby trees, simple villages. Linking these habitats is a series of pathways: the bridges, tunnels, and roads by which players seek out ever-more frontiers in search of wild pokémon. Typologized by the habitats they come from—sea, mountains, fields, sky—pokémon have particular powers and traits. Each is characterized by type, such as grass, fire, and water, which inform players' gaming strategy; in matches, water trumps fire, and fire trumps grass, for example. To acquire ever-more monsters, children must master the complex science of pokémon details. The complexities cannot be overstated, for not only do the pokémon have multiple traits, but also these change, mainly by strengthening, morphing, and evolving, as they win matches. A complicated and fluid life form, pocket monsters need to be known in order to be "gotten." This requirement also makes playing the game a pursuit of "pokémonology" (*pokémongaku*): mastery over a wealth of information, manipulating it into strategies for winning.

Of course, children also study at school for mastery of information, but school-based learning is pressurized and standardized and performance is intrinsically linked to future jobs, success, and social status. As Kubo Masakazu, a producer of the cartoons, comics, and movie versions, put it, kids today are beaten down by an educational system that enforces endless memorization of sterile facts to be disgorged during stressful exams.[6] In his opinion, youth who are overly regulated by this regime are rejuvenated by the playworld of Pokémon, which is imaginatively rich and comes with a game course that anyone can navigate and even customize to one's own preferences. Because the monsters are imaginary, the stakes here are different from those in school. Study is involved in both, but the facts in Pokémon are literally animated, producing a commitment and bond that feel intimate. A player becomes personally invested in her monsters: in knowing them, cultivating their strengths, and assuming ownership.

Such a socially utopic vision of Pokémon—unsurprising for this producer and marketer of the property—underplays its commercial and consumerist orientation. For if, as Kubo has argued, the school system fetishizes one kind of object, Pokémon certainly fetishizes another. Fans the world over have been described as compulsive in seeking to master what is an encyclopedic storehouse of data. Also, because this information is embodied in ever-more Pokémon goods, it feeds a desire to consume that, as parents have complained, is never ending. Even though the taxonomies in Pokémon are borrowed from nature, they can be transferred all too easily to the realm of commodity fetishism.

The practice of communicating through pokémania encourages a subjectivity akin to what Fredric Jameson has recently called the "addictive capitalism" of the millennial era.[7] Addiction to the rush of acquisition is part of the pleasure in Pokémon. The desire to consume, enforced by the game, echoes what Ōhira Ken has described as the emergent Japanese subject in contemporary times—people who, inept at human relationships, are compulsive consumers and taxonomers of brand-name goods in which they invest value and affection. Based on insights from his psychiatric practice, Ōhira calls them "people who speak things" (*mono no katari no hitobito*) and argues that attaching so much to acquisition does not correct the atomism of millennial times as much as extend it in a new (intimately consumerist) direction (Ōhira 1990).

CUTENESS: EXPANDING THE EMPIRE WITH IMAGINARY KINSHIP

Pokémon's success was totally unexpected. Never intended to be global, designed for only one audience in Japan (boys ages eight to fourteen), the Game Boy game's immediate success prompted marketers to expand their horizons. Developed first into the media of comic books, trading cards, and toy merchandise, later the cartoon series and movie versions held the most promise. Conventional wisdom in the children's entertainment business is that, to become a fad, even a successful toy or video game must be accompanied by a television show or film. In the case of Pokémon, telling the story of how three kids travel to discover, catch, and accumulate ever-more pokémon has widened and altered the scope of what started out as a mere Game Boy game. As the anime producer, Kubo Masakazu, explained to me, Pokémon, Inc. is built on three pillars: the electronic game, the trading cards, and the movies and television cartoon (serialized also as comics).[8] These embody a host of elements with diverse appeal to a variety of audiences; the overarching quality is what he called "cuteness" (*kawaisa* or *yasashisa*, "gentleness").

Speaking specifically of Pokémon and its success on the export market—such as becoming the top-ranked children's show on US television when it launched on Warner Bro. network in fall 1998—Kubo added that cuteness gave Japan "cultural power," something Japanese are "polishing" in order to accrue overseas capital and prestige. Cuteness, the Japanese cultural critic Okada Toshio has argued, is one thing that registers for all people. In his mind, Pokémon defines cuteness, a cuteness that may well be Japan's key to working foreign capital in the twenty-first century (Yamato 1998:244). Others have suggested that Japan's future in influencing, even leading, global culture will come through three industries central to the business of cuteness: video games, anime (animation), and manga (comic books). The market for these three industries has surpassed that of the nation's car industry in the past decade, leading some economists to hope that these will pull Japan out of the red. As one economist notes, what Japan has, instead of Silicon Valley, is the "*anime komikku* game industry," which will be the root of the new, twenty-first-century culture and recreation industry (*Nihon Keizai Shinbun* 1999:3).

What makes Japan newly successful in its marketing of games, comics, and cartoons is not simply technological or business prowess, but what has been called the "expressive strength" (*hyōgenryoku*) of Japanese creators (*Nihon Keizai Shinbun* 1999:3). Identified for its portable convenience, dataized flexibility, and fantastic spirituality, this postmodern play aesthetic is thought to borrow on the old and the new in Japan. For example, in an article on DoCoMo (a wireless Internet service), *Wired* magazine reports that Japan is "putting its stamp on the times" in consumer electronics (Rose 2001:129). The DoCoMo cell phone converts into a handheld computer and a wireless e-mail receiver and is sleekly designed, a fashionable accessory. It can also relieve stress with games that can be downloaded or images such as Hello Kitty that can be added as screen savers. "Gazing at Hello Kitty on their handsets, [users will] relax for a moment as they coo, 'Oh, I'm healed'" (Rose 2001:129). As the article states, the feat here was to design technology that is not only efficient and convenient but also cozy and fun. Healing in times of rupture and individuation, technology doubles as playtoy and communicator: a prosthesis with infinite and intimate possibilities, personal and social. The word used more than any other in Japan to label this quality of technology, play, and consumer culture is *cute* (-*ness*).

Yasashisa, or the gentle aspect of cuteness, is precisely the word Japanese producers used to characterize the marketing of Pokémon in Japan.[9] As they pointed out, however, this was not Pokémon's original sensibility when it started out as a role-playing action game targeted at boys. Cuteness came with the story versions, particularly the animated cartoon developed by Kubo and his staff. As Kubo told me in an interview, the overarching objective was to extend the audience of Pokémon to girls, younger children, and even mothers (who are vital in the marketing of children's entertainment in Japan). Giving narrative and characterization to what are only sketch lines on a Game Boy screen, the cartoon also foregrounds a central figure that, like Mario or Mickey Mouse, could serve as an icon for the entire phenomenon. Instead of a humanoid character with whom audiences could identify, a pocket monster was chosen, engendering a different imaginary bond of possession, companionship, and intimacy key to the construction of yasashisa. This character is Pikachu, the yellowy, cute, mouse-like pokémon. Merely one of 151 monsters in the original Game Boy game, Pikachu became the lead pokémon in the television cartoon and, subsequently, a global icon on the order of the Nike swish and McDonald's golden arches.

According to Kubo, a checklist was involved in making this selection. Criteria included a memorable but warm image (Pikachu has a squiggly tail, pointy ears, and sweet face), a noticeable but nonthreatening color (yellow), a catchy name (*Pikachu*), an unforgettable refrain (*pika pika chuuuu*, which is reproducible by even small kids and can be globalized without translation), and a face that could be inscribed with a range of emotions, including tears, for the cartoon and movie versions (Kubo 1999:344). Most important, the monster had to be cute, an ideal that Pikachu has realized in spades, serving as the epitome of cuteness according to practically everyone I interviewed about Pokémon.[10] As Kubo summed up, this character "grabs" people's emotions. Its huggable look delights children and makes mothers feel safe.[11] But equally important are the fierce powers Pikachu holds within its cute frame.

When asked to characterize Pikachu, or pocket monsters more generally, children invariably coupled cuteness with other features, namely strength, and spoke less of static traits than of relations they formed with their fantasy beasts. According to one ten-year-old boy in Tokyo, "Pokémon are imaginary partners, creatures that can be your loyal pet if you control them. They're companions until the end, sort of like animals that are real, except mutated." A seven-year-old girl in the United States declared, "Pokémon are like creatures that are made up. The creators got ideas from nature, but they turned nature around. People care a lot for their pokémon, but they also use them to fight other pokémon."

A relation of usefulness and intimacy is at the heart of the cute fetish promoted by Pokémon (see Cole, chapter 5, this volume, for a similar structure of utility and intimacy given to fashion by Malagasy *jeunes*). Serving as its icon, Pikachu is also the vehicle by which cuteness was expanded from a relatively minor role in the game version into a more complex web of affective and utilitarian value through the story-based media of manga, anime, and movie. Moving into media more reliant on storytelling, that is, Pokémon enveloped the matches and strategies of "getting" monsters in the game within dramatic subplots and elaborate adventures almost always involving pokémon and their multivalent relations with humans. As the iconic pocket monster, Pikachu figures heavily in these dramas, developing as a character largely in terms of the complex bond it shares with Satoshi, its human owner, master, and friend.

In the stories, Satoshi (Ash in the US version) is the lead human character who travels Poké-world in search of wild pocket monsters. This ten-year-old boy aims to become the "world's best pokémon master." Accompanying him in this mission are two pals—Kasumi, a ten-year-old girl, and Takeshi, a fifteen-year-old boy—and his most trusted pokémon, Pikachu. The boy and monster first meet in the initial episode (of the cartoon and also the graphic comics) when, mimicking the structure of the Game Boy game, Satoshi is given his lead-off pokémon by Dr. Oak. Seeing the yellowy cute monster, the boy is initially disappointed, assuming that this will be a weak tool for realizing his ambition of capturing all 151 pokémon. But Pikachu surprises him, first with a display of indomitable will. Ordered into the monster ball by which all pokémon are digitalized for travel, Pikachu refuses. By forcing Satoshi to carry it atop his shoulders (like a pet or young child), the monster acquires a badge of distinction. For, as the only pokémon to remain outside the ball—and therefore the currency of equivalence into which all the other pokémon are convertible—Pikachu never gets "pocketed" in the cartoon. Always appearing more monster than thing, it is forever visible and cute: the material sign of use value in what is (also) a generalizable medium—monsters that, like money, stand for and generate wealth.

Engaged in what Roland Barthes (1972[1957]:123) called a "constantly moving turnstile," pokémon continually oscillate between meaning and form, full on the one side and empty on the other. In this process, Pikachu serves as an alibi: the material sign of use value in what is simultaneously a system of exchange. It is the boy's property, possession, and tool, but also something much more in the cartoon: free agent, loyal pet, personal friend. This deeper relationship starts in the first episode of the cartoon. Having refused the monster ball, Pikachu is riding with Satoshi on his bicycle when the two are attacked by killer birds overhead. The boy is soon knocked unconscious. Pikachu, going into warrior mode, battles the birds on its own, thereby saving its master. Awakening seconds later, Satoshi is duly impressed by his pokémon's bravery and skills. In a trope recurrent in the series, next the monster gets injured, and Satoshi risks his own life to ride his bicycle through the birds and deliver Pikachu to the Pokémon Center (where it can be healed). In this drama of reciprocity, gifts of kindness are exchanged, establishing a social relationship.

The bond between Satoshi and Pikachu is referred to repeatedly as one of "friendship" in the text of the cartoon. For example, in one memorable episode when Satoshi is competing against the whiz kid at a cram school for Pokémon trainers, he refers to his monster as a "friend" (*tomadachi*). Criticized for treating this underling as a pal, Satoshi nevertheless wins the match by using Pikachu. Taking note, his competitor concedes that he has learned something new: displaying kindness toward one's pokémon actually strengthens its fighting abilities. This message recurs throughout the cartoon series: humans must act not only as masters but also as trainers, tending kindly to their pokémon for reasons both moral (maintaining an interpersonal relationship) and practical (maximizing monster utility, hence value).

As morality and practicality merge, pokémon become both relations and things, gifts and commodities. Within this mergence is something feudal and futuristic. On the one hand, the monster–human bond resembles that between vassal and lord; the pokémon serve and sacrifice for their masters and, in return, are tended to, fed, and trained. On the other hand, monsters are commodities that fetishize the power of personal accumulation and interpersonal intimacy, even kinship, between human and nonhuman. Monsters are a flexible, fluctuating, and interchangeable currency, shifting between means and end, capital and companion, property and pal. Fluctuating between use value and exchange value, as exchange value they also fluctuate between an economic value ("getting" leading to mastery and wealth) and a value of relationality—what, following Weber (1987), we could call the spirit of (pokémon) capitalism.

Cuteness thus is expanded and rearticulated in the process of narrativization and brings together, in narrative formats, millennial alienation and a new, flexible intimacy. As it does so, the game's capitalist logic of getting merges with other, more communitarian, altruistic sensibilities. In one exemplary cartoon episode, the story starts as usual; the triumvirate arrives in a new place looking to discover and catch new monsters. The scene is a natural wonderland whose eco-balance has been recently disturbed by the invasion by one species of beetle into the habitat of another. Asked by a worried naturalist to put aside their desire to "get" pokémon for the moment and help him restore order, the children selflessly set to work. In time, they discover the root of the problem and return the forest to eco-logical harmony. This task has been time-consuming, however, and their scheduled stop is almost up. Preparing to leave without a single catch, Satoshi is approached by one of the rescued beetles, which indicates that it wants to join his traveling band. The boy orders it to stay put with its "own kind," but the beetle persists. Shrugging his shoulders, Satoshi throws his monster ball and, upon crawling inside, the beetle becomes, as the narra-tor announces, the boy's latest "acquisition." The objective of getting has not been displaced as much as contained within the loftier agenda of help-ing others. As a reward for his kindness, the boy receives another monster, part of his personal stock but also what will become a kind of (interspecies, human/virtual) kin relation.

In this way, nature collapses into capital (wildness into acquisitions) and capital into culture (a relation of things into interpersonal relations). Such a ploy occurs often in the cartoons. Touched by the altruism of humans, pokémon leave behind their "own kind" to join the worldly human mission to discover and pocket more monsters. Needless to say, this is a gentler, cuter method of acquisition than attacking wild monsters with balls or winning them in battle after they have been whiplashed, pummeled, or stung. It also reimagines the bond(age) formed by freely entering into a system that will reduce them to balls. Here the representation mimics that of capitalist ideology: people who are "free" laborers willingly contract work for a wage in an economic system built on exploitation and reifica-tion. Implicitly, the monsters making this choice exchange the "wildness" of natural habitats for something not only enticing—worldly travel, nomadic adventures—but also moral, in the Maussian sense (Mauss 1967). Exchanging a gift (human kindness) for a gift (the monster itself) results in a storehouse of goods, but also New-Age intimacies and attachments. Cuteness makes this whole operation appear childlike and sweet, with pokémon such as Pikachu cutifying the relationship of "getting" and simul-taneously doubling as pets and pals.

CONCLUSION: THE PLAY LOGIC GOES GLOBAL

On a sunny day in March 2000, I interviewed a group of Pokémon fans in Greeley, Colorado—children ages seven to twelve, girls and boys, all white and middle-class. Although their tastes and passions varied widely—some played the Game Boy game, others only watched the cartoon, some loved the cute pokémon, others concentrated on strong monsters alone—what the group shared was a tendency to view this playworld in terms of both affection and utility, warmth and instrumentality. One seven-year-old girl put it this way: "I love the pokémon. They're my friends, and they help me win more pokémon." A nine-year-old boy added, "A pokémon is loyal and your servant. I mean, it's mine, but I take care of it too." Only one child, a girl age seven, thought it odd that players had to continually put their pokémon into battle, where they were injured and maimed. "Uh, why did the designers make it that way? Aren't pokémon supposed to be our friends?" But even this girl admitted to being an avid player of the Game Boy game. She was also, as were almost all the kids, an impassioned card collector who kept all her prized cards in a binder used to collect and trade with other kids. The ones she liked best she eagerly displayed to me, listing all their key traits. For this group of fans, value was calibrated in various ways: affection for the way a pokémon looked, utility based on how a poké-mon could be played in the card game, and "market value" based on prices listed in unofficial card collector guides (which practically all the kids owned). Her brother shouted, when opening his pack of Pokémon cards I had brought from Japan, "Hey, Dad, I got a $25 card!"

Similarly, news coverage of this fad in the United States tended to fluc-tuate between its friendly and acquisitive aspects. At one end were the reports of the "buy and sell bazaar" (Healy 1999:27) atmosphere it fos-tered, in which kids, who went into trades with friends or at malls on Saturday mornings with Pokémon collector albums tucked firmly under their arms, were turned into miniature salespeople, investing in their own form of stock. Indeed, for its arousal of a market sensibility in kids, Pokémon was considered a new kind of collector play by some commenta-tors: a kid craze different from marbles, yo-yos, and even Beanie Babies (Healy 1999). Certainly, this market sensibility is what led to acts of vio-lence—incidents of theft, stabbings, and punch-outs mainly over cards—and also lawsuits. Parents sued Nintendo for inciting kids to buy endless packs of cards, expending hundreds, even thousands, of their parents' dol-lars (Halbfinger 1999). Yet despite some concerns about the addictiveness, acquisitiveness, and commercialism it generated, the overall attitude toward this Japanese import was approval. Significantly, adults often praised the connections and friendships inspired by Pokémon, sometimes seeing "some-thing notably Japanese here…values that are admired but not always hand-somely rewarded in American society" (Strom 1999:4).

To my mind, the cultural logic of inter-relationality attributed by some to a Japanese "past" does not, in itself, account for the global appeal of Japanese entertainment products today. What does, rather, is the intermix-ture of a market economy (trading, gambling, accumulating wealth) with fantastic monsters that double as portable property and pals. This sense of collapsibility, or reversibility—between gifts and things, relations and acquisitions—defines, for me, the essence of Pokémon. Does this represent a new playmode and a form of global capitalism? Perhaps the distinction here is more of degree than of kind. I do agree, however, with Michael Hardt and Antonio Negri (2000) in their depiction of a world today (which they call "empire") that is decentered from such modernist brokers and institutions of power as the family and the nation-state and is increasingly less organized in terms of clear-cut distinctions. I see such a world(view) reflected in Pokémon: a space populated by endless entities that break down into endless parts (of powers, strengths, attacks, values) that can also be "gotten" by players and variously (re)connected (offering various and flexible attachments for players as well).

Such a play of getting and connecting can be comforting to kids, giving them something that feels personal and invites interpersonal relationships. But it also is part and parcel of a market economy, of a playscape that is bought and sold on the marketplace and of a play logic that, itself, mimics a marketplace of continually transacting and accumulating things. This is both the underside and the future of a play that doubles so closely with capitalism, a play in which "alternative space" to postindustrial life at the millennium is simply another version ever-more intoxicating and compelling to kids. It is with such a logic that Japanese playgoods are making their mark in the global youth market, yielding vast profits and "soft power" in shaping the world, both virtual and lived, of postindustrial kids today. I urge those who criticize the presentism of youth, their disinvestment in futurist goals, the loneliness and rage that often accompany their addiction to consumerism, to focus instead on the conditions of empire and millennial capitalism that are so productive of, and that find so profitable, such youth behaviors of today.

Notes

1. I use *kids, youth,* and *children* interchangeably in this chapter to refer to the audience of Pokémon players who, in Japan and elsewhere, have a broad age range: from about age two (as watchers of the cartoon) to mid-twenties and above (as players of the video and Game Boy games and collectible card games). This elastic age range also pertains to global youth culture more broadly these days as the category "youth" has become something of a floating signifier, standing for and stretching to a wide body of behaviors, practices, and goods used or appropriated by an increasingly large

segment of the population. One example of this is hip-hop. Its fans range across the entire age spectrum even though it still gets identified as youth based.

2. The height of the Pokémon fad occurred in 1998 and 1999. The fad is currently over. Yet in Japan and other marketplaces, such as the United States, the cartoon is still broadcast on TV, new movies are still being made (the most recent one was released in summer 2005), and new Game Boy games, as well as other electronic products, are still hitting the market. In this chapter, I therefore use both the past and present tenses to refer to the Pokémon phenomenon.

3. I write capitalized *Pokémon* to indicate the game and lowercase *pokémon* to refer to the monsters in the game.

4. This figure was given me by Kubo Masakazu, executive producer in the Character Business Planning section of Shōgakukan Inc., the publishers of *Korokoro Kommiku*. Kubo has been one of the most important figures in the Pokémon business in Japan. Masterminding the original comic book version, he has also been one of the main producers for the cartoon and movie series.

5. From interviews with Japanese children, November 1999.

6. In a personal interview, December 1999.

7. In a talk titled "Utopia and Actually Existing Being" given at a conference (The Future of Utopia: Is Innovation Still Possible in Politics, Culture, and Theory?) held at Duke University, Durham, North Carolina, April 24, 2003.

8. Personal interview, December 1999.

9. Personal interviews with executives at Tōkyō Terebi, Shōgakukan Production, ShoPro, and Tomy Company.

10. During my fieldwork on Pokémon, conducted in Japan and the United States (1999–2000), I interviewed producers, designers, marketing executives, teachers, parents, children, child psychologists, educational experts, scholars, reporters, and cultural critics.

11. Personal interview, December 1999.

9

Chronic Mobb Asks a Blessing

Apocalyptic Hip-Hop and the Global Crisis

Brad Weiss

In the summer of 2000, I returned to Arusha in northern Tanzania armed with a copy of *The Source*, the self-described "magazine of hip-hop music, culture and politics," which I expected would be a hit with many of the young men I knew in town. Indeed, this large glossy issue quickly circulated through the streets of the city center, and many of the young men—and a few young women—who combed through it valued it especially as a source of stylistic inspiration. The magazine was lauded as *katalogi* ("catalogue"; see also Cole, chapter 5, this volume, on the use of this term in Madagascar). In contemporary street Kiswahili, *katalogi* refers primarily to a way of dressing in contemporary, youth-oriented clothing and accessories, as well as to the multiple media through which such fashions are displayed. One afternoon, a month after my arrival, I sat down to peruse *The Source* with a few guys who were hanging out in front of a kiosk. As one of them flipped through its pages, he made comments typical of other such browsers: "I don't like those pants," "Those shoes are fierce," "That Eminem is crazy!" But he slowed down to read an interview with the artist Q-tip, MC for the crew Tribe Called Quest.[1] Tapping the accompanying picture with his knuckle, he noted, "*Huyu, anapiga swala tano* [This guy hits five prayers]." That is, he prays five times a day. This remark points to ways in which participation in the stylistic possibilities of hip-hop—its music, culture, and politics—also provides a great many youth in Arusha with a means of defining and affirming their religious affiliations.

Such stylistic possibilities are especially significant—perhaps even pressing—concerns in contemporary Arusha. At the turn of the twenty-first century, Tanzania, particularly the Aru-Meru region in which Arusha is situated, has been engaged in highly public and often turbulent deliberations over the nature and meaning of religious association and spiritual practice. In the early 1990s, fractious and openly violent conflicts within the dominant Lutheran diocese across Mount Meru and Mount Kilimanjaro attracted the attention of national church and state authorities (Baroin 1996). By the end of the decade, contentions had been further fueled by Pentecostal fervor, which today attracts an interest across the region that goes far beyond internecine Lutheran conflicts. Moreover, religious affiliation has had an abiding significance in the historical transformation of Arusha's social and spatial organization. Colonial policies promoted the presence of Muslim "Swahili" traders as proper urbanites in the residential areas of Arusha town. Inhabitants of mountain communities from Kilimanjaro and Meru were assumed to be rural peoples and therefore outsiders and migrants in town (Peligal 1999).

Today, however, many descendants of the long-standing urban Muslim residents (as well as Muslims who come from areas all across northern and central Tanzania to work and live in Arusha) frequently see themselves as besieged by what they understand to be powerful, privileged, external forces—in particular, Chagga and Asian entrepreneurs. Indeed, turmoil surrounding national electoral processes in 1995 and 2000 prompted many of Arusha's Muslims to insist that their very citizenship is at risk. "This is becoming a Christian nation" is how many young Muslim men in Arusha assessed the contemporary political climate. Just for good measure, as well as ecumenical scope, I would also note a broad, if not consuming, concern within contemporary Arusha for the resurgence of malevolent spiritual forces of various forms. Meruhani spirits from the Indian Ocean threaten the fertility of newly betrothed women in town. Even the *Arusha Times* reported that "(t)en female pupils [ages nine to thirteen, both Christians and Muslims] of the Naura primary school in Arusha municipality, recently collapsed in fits of hysteria after allegedly being strangled by what they believed to be 'demons'" (Nkwame 2002; see also Smith 2001 for similar events in southeastern Kenya).

My purpose in citing these tensions is not to introduce a wider discussion of the nature of sectarian conflict in Arusha. Still less do I hope to characterize a range of specific positions—Lutheran, Pentecostal, Muslim—

as they emerge in these interactions.[2] Rather, I want to emphasize a repeated observation about contemporary Tanzania (Baroin 1996; Kelsall n.d.; Stambach 2000): in a period of rather densely articulated and rapid social, political, economic, and cultural transformations, discourses emphasizing problems of religious affiliation and identity have come to the fore in the Tanzanian public sphere. I argue that these religious discourses, as well as their current predominance, are best understood not as responses to the shifting Tanzanian landscape but as implicated in the changes the discourses themselves articulate. My central concern, therefore, is an understanding of how religiosity is (re-)created within dynamic sociocultural fields such as those prevailing in Arusha today.

Consider, for example, the range of social processes that greatly accelerated in Tanzania during the 1990s: the proliferation of print and electronic media across the nation; the collapse of what were already tenuous public services as a condition of Structural Adjustment; the official rejection of African Socialism (Ujamaa) and the consequent meager, but nonetheless powerful, influx of capital into formal sectors of the economy; the institution of multiparty democracy and the attendant crises of both presidential electoral cycles; the continuing spread of the HIV/AIDS epidemic throughout the nation. This litany at once locates a specific history of contemporary Tanzanian society and politics and also gives evidence of the effects and implications of globalization. Indeed, the intersection of popular cultural practices with contentious religious affiliation is a prominent site on this local–global terrain—perhaps especially so for youth, who feature both as targets and agents of these powerful social projects. My contention is that, by situating current spiritual concerns within these simultaneously local and global processes as intrinsic, constitutive dimensions of diverse and extensive transformations—in Tanzania and elsewhere—it becomes possible to problematize the prominence of these religious discourses and, further, to draw attention to the ways that spirituality has been reconceived by these recent historical shifts.

POP CULTURE, POST-SOCIALISM, OR YOUTH IN TANZANIA

By now, a host of critical studies on the African production of modernity (Barber 1997; Burke 1996; Comaroff and Comaroff 1993; Geschiere 1997; Larkin 1997; Masquelier 2001; Meyer 1998; Piot 1999; Weiss 1996) has made it impossible to assert that the kind of religious claims made in Tanzania today are vestiges of recalcitrant tradition that provide a moral compass in a sea of global change. Further, when we talk about popular culture in its globalized forms, it is important to recognize that these modes of cultural production include not only FuBu sweatshirts and Fila sneakers, Destiny's Child and the Disney empire, but also circulating cassettes of eminent Maalams and stadium-filled revival services. It is especially interesting to note that, within this multitude of disparate forms, current popular practices in urban Tanzania reveal important *convergences* of what are routinely seen as oppositional discourses, such as morality and desire, piety and pleasure, or devotional practices and katalogi clothing as represented through *The Source*. Because my argument concerns the reformulation of religiosity in urban Tanzania, I am especially interested in the confluence of these seemingly contradictory discourses and practices, which hip-hop performance often embodies. A close examination of this confluence reveals how themes of piety and moral caution structure the possibilities of the hip-hop world and, reciprocally, how global hip-hop reformulates religious commitments.

Recognizing and articulating the conjunction between religiosity and rap within urban Tanzanian popular culture is hardly a narrowly circumscribed endeavor. Hip-hop incorporates a wide array of activities including modes of dress, dance, visual arts such as graffiti and tattooing, and sonic forms such as DJ mixing and scratching. All are present to some degree in Arusha. As diffuse as hip-hop is, the field of religion (if such a discrete entity exists) is even more expansive, amorphous, and intensely debated. I do not presume that hip-hop and religion are distinct forms brought together in a specific time and place, but I do describe how their themes create each other in concrete social practice. I recognize the risk that this convergence of concerns articulated (often quite explicitly, as I will indicate) on the scene in Arusha, when scrutinized, simply dissolves as a phenomenon or dissipates into the broad context of culture. I cannot hope to offer a definitive take on hip-hop and religion that will demonstrate their mutual construction in Tanzania. Still, I argue that there are certain core themes and dynamics in the practices I describe and that these serve to define and create the character of "living the life" in its religious and hip-hop senses.

The hip-hop/religion convergence also points to some important issues for the more general study of youth within prevailing globalized conditions. A number of scholars have recognized that the circumstances faced by young people around the world today have been profoundly shaped by widespread neoliberal, political-economic reforms. "The cumulative impact" of these reforms, writes Cole (2004:573), "has been to create contradictions for youth by simultaneously targeting them as consumers and making them particularly vulnerable to socioeconomic exclusion" (Comaroff and Comaroff 2000b; Weiss 2004; see also Cole, chapter 5, this volume). My argument here addresses one of the broader problems posed throughout this work—why youth now?—by situating it within the general tension between exclusion and inclusion, a tension exacerbated and specified in the recent history of Tanzanian economy and society. I would note, along these lines, that the young men whom I interviewed (more than women),[3] who work and hang out in the "informal sector"—the barbershops, "saloons," bars, and bus stands—constitute a large audience for the consumption of hip-hop media and commodities *and* are among the most deeply interested in the current maelstrom of urban Tanzanian religious discourses. Indeed, groups of young barbers took me to the rap shows in Arusha, where verses about religious righteousness and moral caution were enthusiastically performed and received.

This coupling of moralism with consumerism indicates, as we shall see, that a profound ambivalence accompanies the neoliberal production of "value as self-fashioning" (a theme reiterated in many of these chapters; see especially Thorne, Cole, and Allison, chapters 4, 5, and 8, respectively). A contradictory consciousness that shapes the experience of youth is manifest at several levels. In part, those who most fully endorse the prospects of global cultural production exemplified by hip-hop are also most acutely aware of how severely limited their access to that world is. This leads to a sense of frustration, and occasionally despair, that is palpable in most social milieus in Arusha. Moreover, a simultaneous embrace and mistrust of such social projects as education, the media, political reform, the market, and commodity forms is apparent in this ambivalence. The most prevalent and celebrated forms of social engagement—to wit, those that promote such consumerist self-fashioning—are also subject to widespread *critique* as unsatisfying, illusory, and (as we shall see) unreal sources of value. In other words, youth often sense that they are confronting a crisis and, further, that the very resources that might permit them to overcome that crisis may be inaccessible—or worse, *illegitimate.*

THEORIZING THE GLOBAL HIP-HOP NATION

Only in recent years have the scholars of hip-hop begun seriously to examine the global dissemination and production of its musical and cultural forms. This is not simply because hip-hop went global well after it had already gained a tremendous following in the United States (in Tanzania, there has been a flourishing hip-hop scene since the early 1990s). Rather, it reflects a core concern of hip-hop artists and aficionados, one that many of its analysts have taken up as a theoretical principle. This concern is what might be called a relentless commitment to locality, a notion that what is probably *the* critical feature of hip-hop performance, crucial to its aesthetic and even moral value, is its authenticity. In particular, a great many devotees of rap most appreciate what they call the "realness" of its performance. As Krims (2000) indicates, the qualities of authenticity and realness are characteristically expressed in judgments that are firmly tied to time and especially to place. Krims observes: "It is not at all an obscurity, among listeners, to refer to someone as having an 'old school flow,' or even an 'early 90s West Coast flow,' or a 'new-style Queens flow.' Such terms are fodder for record company ads, artist interviews, song lyrics, and discussions among fans" (Krims 2000:44; see also Forman 2002:passim). Even a figure such as Eminem, often vilified as a crass, commercial misappropriator of African American practices, can be lauded for his authenticity:

> Three kinds of authenticity are initially evident [in hip-hop].
> First, there's a concern with being true to oneself. Rap illustrates
> self-creation and individuality as a value. Next, there's the question of location or place. Rap prioritizes artists' local allegiances
> and territorial identities. Finally, the question becomes whether
> a performer has the requisite relation and proximity to an original source of rap. Eminem is firmly grounded in these three
> kinds of authenticity. [Armstrong 2004:340]

Although such essentially aesthetic categories are indispensable to an understanding of hip-hop's cultural productions (in everything from the self-identification of performers and audiences to the international marketing of a potent commodity), a concern with bona fide origins is central to many analytical assessments of worldwide hip-hop. Russell Potter writes: "As [hip-hop] gains audiences around the world, there is always the danger that it will be appropriated in such a way that its histories will be obscured, and its messages replaced with others" (Potter 1995:146). It is as though global rap music were an imitation (notably pale) of the Ur sounds created in the South Bronx of the 1970s.

Recent scholarly works have challenged the assumption of African American origins as a critical feature of hip-hop's authentic character, a character that is at risk of being diluted and misrepresented through hip-hop's mass mediation. The works of Krims and the comprehensive collection *That's the Joint!* (Forman and Neal 2004), as well as the essays collected in Tony Mitchell's volume *Global Noise* (2001), for example, argue that a concern with the putatively essential and original qualities of hip-hop disables our understanding of its truly global realizations. In general, these critiques of authenticity follow from what are now pervasive anthropological perspectives on globalization more generally. Global hip-hop is shown to participate in the worldwide production of locality through a process of "indigenization," which involves the assertive appropriation of rap music and hip-hop forms by performers who incorporate local linguistic and musical idioms, as well as wider popular (especially) political concerns, in the creation of a hybrid art form (see Mitchell 2001:passim). In Urla's eloquent discussion of one Basque group, she writes: "Negu Gorriak's performances of a hybrid Basque rap may [best be] understood not as an Americaniza-tion or imitation but as a strategic deployment of signifiers that affords youth a window into their own situation and what it shares with that of racialized minorities" (Urla 2001:181). Concerns with authenticity in the transnational context of hip-hop performance may be less relevant to its productive possibilities than are the dynamics of rap as a kind of global idiom through which profoundly local conflicts can be reimagined and acted upon.

These critiques of appropriation as inauthenticity are crucial. Indeed, related critiques have a long and important, if frequently overlooked, history in the social-scientific understanding of African social practice in particular (Mitchell 1956; Ranger 1975). Yet I am reluctant to dismiss altogether the relevance of authenticity as a principle of cultural production. A number of critics have recognized the ways that images, like pastiche, when used as interpretive categories, have the effect of dehistoricizing the material they are intended to address (Gilroy 1994; Mitchell 2001:10). Arguments emphasizing the capacity of performers to select among an array of idioms, vernaculars, styles, and sounds tend to extract these processes of recombination from the contexts—both meaningful and material—in which they are possible. This runs the risk of celebrating what are highly specific notions of freedom and value embedded in consumerist models of choice. Further, it is not entirely clear that hybridity and ludic indeterminacy are the terms through which practice is made meaningful in the lives of those engaged in these activities. In Friedman's characteristically polemical discussion, he asks:

> If the city landscapes in Stockholm now combine ethnically and
> linguistically mixed populations and store signs in American
> English, if we observe (at the airport) the Nigerian, Congolese
> or Papua New Guinean sporting a can of Coke and a ham-
> burger...is this to be interpreted as creolization in the sense of

cultural mixture? Is it to be interpreted as hybridity in the sense of the liminal sphere between the modern Western and the pre-modern, non-Western.... What is really going on in such referred-to realities? Does anyone have to ask or is the observation enough? What about other peoples' experiences, intentionalities and lives? Are not such hybrids defined as such because they seem to be betwixt and between our own "modern Western" categories, i.e., hybrids for us? [Friedman 2000:640–641]

This critique of the hybrid as an unexamined premise of our own social and analytical categories is crucial, not simply as a corrective to over-theorized and underinvestigated models of globalization, but also because this critique makes it possible to address the ways in which these apparently plural realities are experienced and increasingly valued in much of the world. The notion of authenticity as an *analytical* category that establishes a kind of genealogical distinction between the original and the imitation, or the pure and the contaminated, is certainly not valuable. However, it seems equally crucial to recognize that some understanding of authenticity as a category of *interpretive* judgment is central—especially in popular cultural circles—to contemporary notions of taste, experience, and, more broadly, social being. Affirmations of authenticity—expressed in hip-hop circles in Arusha, and elsewhere, as a concern for realness—have flourished rather than dissipated with the ready availability of a global and manifold set of styles and images. These values, this concern for allegiance to an unmediated, "true" reality, increasingly dominate the lived experience of those caught up in transnational processes such as global hip-hop, as well as reformist Islam and evangelical Christianity. The commitment to realness and the anxieties about its beleaguered condition in the world today therefore offer a means for exploring the conjuncture of these diverse moral discourses across a range of popular cultural practices in contemporary urban Tanzania.

THE ONE TRUE RELIGION AND REALITY RAP

Many contemporary religious inclinations in Arusha, as in much of (especially urban) Africa, emphasize the importance of specific, fixed attributes of identity—authenticity, in effect—as foundational dimensions of social and personal being. Put more succinctly, participants in popular Muslim and Christian practices insist that their way of life is more "true" and more accurately reflects reality than do other sectarian and secular positions. In the summer of 2000, I regularly engaged in conversations with groups of young men deeply committed to securing my personal salvation by persuading me that Islam is, as they put it, "the only true religion." These discussions generally focused on what I would characterize as hyper-rationalist critiques of Christian dogma (as these Muslims understood it): for example, rejections of the Trinity as counter to the doctrine of mono-theism; dismissals of Christ's divinity as a violation of the fundamental dis-tinction between human materiality and God's transcendence; assertions that Christians elevate their clergy to the status of divinity. These rational-ist critiques were paired with an insistence on the absolute veracity of the Koran, not just as a sacred text but also as an encyclopedic source of all human knowledge. As I have indicated elsewhere (Weiss 2004), these young men described the Koran as a guide for living but also as a source of empirically verifiable knowledge. "*Kila kitu kimeshaandikwa ndani* [Every-thing has already been written in it]" is how many put it. Indeed, they framed the Koran as a guide for proper scientific investigation, its fore-known truths awaiting demonstration by research. Many of the Muslims I know demonstrated this experimental attitude with Internet reports about scientific practice in the West inspired by readings of the Koran.

Claims like the ones made to me in Arusha indicate that many con-temporary young Muslims, as Swedenburg (2001:70) suggests in his dis-cussion of French Muslim rap, increasingly understand Islam as "an attitude that [is] very rational and scientific, but most importantly, mysti-cal." In effect, the mystical character of Islam is revealed and confirmed by the rational and empirical truths that a true understanding of Islam dis-closes. The irrefutable truths revealed in the Koran and already proven through human historical observation also provide evidence, for many of the young Muslims I know, of the certainty of Koranic revelations yet to come. At the turn of the twentieth century, it was not surprising to find that these same young men asserting the *scientific* proof of Koranic authority also were offering predictions about the "End of Days" (*Nusu Kyama* in Kiswahili), citing obvious contemporary evidence that portends the appear-ance of a false God and world destroyer who will reign over humanity before the righteous are granted celestial immortality. Apocalyptic asser-tions such as these have a long history throughout the Muslim and Christian worlds; they are by no means novel in this context. What is com-pelling, though, are the ways that such mystical and transhistorical asser-tions are explicitly tied to the empirical and rational validity of the Koranic text. Such apocalyptic visions, in other words, are embedded in pro-nouncements about the *broader* integrity and authority of the Koran. This textual absolutism—in urban Tanzania and elsewhere (Masquelier 1999)—

becomes critical grounds on which adherence to Islam as a true and invariant practice, that is, as the authentic religious identity, is proclaimed.[4]

Supreme truth and authenticity are often posited as critical features of what Tillich calls the "ultimate concerns" of religion. In the world of hiphop, notions of truth and authenticity are equally crucial analytics. Forman notes: "The boundaries between real or authentic cultural identities and those deemed inauthentic are carefully policed from within the hip-hop culture, and the delineations that define 'the real' are taken with deadly seriousness by those who ascribe to hip-hop's cultural influences" (Forman 2002:xviii). Fans of widely divergent hip-hop styles and rap music genres recognize this pronounced identification of authenticity with the real (Krims 2000:54–61). Yet all such stylistic variations and virtues are said to constitute ways of "keeping it real" and thus assert the preeminence of authenticity—in the guise of realness—as a shared symbolic value.

In urban Tanzania, these concerns and commitments are equally important to hip-hop. One young man, Rahim, told me why he thought rap was so popular in Arusha and why he himself had composed rap verses: "It's a voice [*sauti*]. Youth have no voice. You cannot get a minister or a businessman in an office to hear your complaints, so you need a loud voice. You need to 'represent' the youth." In keeping with this construction of truth and its symbolic assertion, Rahim added, "We need to speak about REALITY as it is for youth, and rap is the music that has this voice." Rahim's assertions depend upon an understanding of an unassailable truth, a "reality," as he puts it in English, or *hali halisi* in Kiswahili, using terms and claims lifted directly from a widespread hip-hop vernacular. More specifically, and somewhat paradoxically, I would argue, Rahim insists that this raw, unmediated reality actually requires some means of demonstrating its truth in order to realize its implications. That is, it requires a "voice" to give expression to this truth. Further, this voice is characterized not as a style, as interpretation, or even as a *way* of knowing and speaking, but simply as an embodiment of the fundamental reality it expresses. Voice here is evidence of the authenticity with which it speaks. Voice is unassailable because it is a true expression of lived reality as it actually is.

To give voice in this way is—to use Rahim's language, a vernacular (in English) plucked from the global hip-hop order he extols—to "represent." This term in such usages is understood *not* as a means of speaking on behalf of some under-represented, voiceless constituency, but as a way of expressing a commitment to the truth of the reality that the constituency lives. Krims describes American hip-hop sounds: "If one of the principal validating strategies of rap music involves 'representing' and 'keeping it real'—in other words, deploying authenticity symbolically—then that ethos is formed (and reflected) differently in each [rap] genre" (Krims 2000:48). Further, modes of hip-hop performance that emphasize the immediate and unmediated character of reality are equally concerned with the importance of giving voice to that (otherwise unvoiced and under-represented) reality through rap music. This is exemplified in such claims as Chuck D's celebrated celebration of rap as "the black CNN we never had" (Forman 2002:251) and MC Eiht's statement "I just talk about the 'hood. That's just spittin' the real" (Forman 2002:93). Here is a characteristic tension in hip-hop cultural production, plainly evident in urban Tanzanian accounts as well. On one hand, representing, or giving voice, is a direct embodied expression ("a loud voice," "spittin' the real") that partakes of a given and incontrovertibly true reality. On the other hand, it is a means of confirming and establishing—literally creating—the specific qualities and character of the real itself (Dinwoodie 1998). Indeed, the realness of the voices that represent are constantly subject to scrutiny and critique by those they would claim to represent. This tension is rather different from the much ballyhooed crisis of representation, for it is the real itself that is explicitly embraced as an authentic truth and is also the subject of perpetual challenge and (as Forman puts it) policing by those who participate in hip-hop's performances. For these participants, reality seems uncertain and therefore at risk.

KNOWING REALITY

The sense of reality being at risk—an apocalyptic contention intrinsic in the perpetual efforts of hip-hop participants to assure that reality is acknowledged, that voices are representing, keeping it real—both transcends and connects global and local orders of meaning and practice. Such a shared *and* differentiated perspective clearly posits some notion of authenticity as a central symbolic quality, even as the paramount value. Yet I would also insist that this notion of authenticity is not concerned with adhering to the foundational tenets of some originary source of meaning, or an essential way of being, that is either incompatible with other modalities or in danger of being diluted or corrupted by those who would appropriate it. Shiite Muslims in Arusha, for example, can embrace the Koran as the unvarnished truth without feeling the need to immerse themselves in Arabic *or* to renounce the significance of other social-cultural products— hip-hop clothing, rap music, the popular press—as inauthentic scourges of meaning. In fact, the Koran is grasped by these young Muslims as an immediate expression of their own concrete existence—a body of knowledge that is confirmed in their own sensible world of experience—giving this text its "sacred" character and also its ultimate reality. The Koran, to use a familiar vocabulary, "represents" their "reality."

The thematic of authenticity is as evident in hip-hop's commitment to keeping it real as it is in the fascination (on the part of many of those also in the hip-hop world) with apocalyptic pronouncements. An understanding of the real as a phenomenon that is in danger of displacement or even disappearance plays a prominent part in reconfiguring social worlds in Arusha and in reconstituting religiosity as well. What this perceived assault on reality indicates is a broadly shared ontology. In turn, this implies that there is actual ontological work to be done by popular practice, as an audience and as a congregation. Participation goes beyond upholding abstract, even sacred, principles, or maintaining moral strictures, or accurately reflecting the circumstances of one's peers. It requires engaging in these practices as a means of sustaining reality. This ontological crisis demands, in particular, that you make your voice an expression of your being-in-the-world so that your identity, or self-representation, partakes of the reality it upholds.

For many youth in Arusha today, this specific dynamic is a feature of both hip-hop performance and religious devotion. To describe this dynamic, I first sketch out certain features of participation in popular culture in Arusha more generally. I then show how these modes of participation serve as important means of demonstrating and concretizing the sociocultural process of establishing authenticity and the real. I also show how the themes of realness and its fugitive character are given a voice that is realized in certain performances of popular culture, embodying specific qualities of this "real" world. To illustrate the process, I show how voice is explicitly realized in the verses of the Tanzania rap music—both mass-mediated and less widely distributed—that I heard in Arusha in the summer of 2000. A number of English- and Kiswahili-language tabloids are readily available in Arusha. Some of these are published in Tanzania, and many of the most popular come from Kenya. I found that many young men and women kept scrapbooks made up of materials culled from these media. Occasionally, these scrapbooks—simply called *daftari*, or notebooks—were highly intertextual, consisting of notes received from friends, headlines pulled from multiple papers, and photos of the celebrities, which were often subsequently removed to decorate a family sitting room or a workplace. The most consistent feature in the dozen or so notebooks that people shared with me was the page after page of carefully handwritten copies of the lyrics published in these Sunday papers.

This kind of writing practice, which has a long history among school goers in East Africa (see Fugelsang 1994; R. Thornton, personal communication, November 2000), provides a glimpse into convergences in contemporary urban Tanzanian popular culture. The youth who keep these notebooks regard them with a telling significance. Most people I asked told me that they wrote out the lyrics because such exercises are "educational" (*yanafundisha*). This notion of the educational value of participating in popular culture resonates with the meanings that audiences, for a variety of popular practices in Arusha, give to their actions. As I have discussed elsewhere (Weiss in press), audiences for radio and videos, especially internationally distributed soap operas, routinely describe the experience of reception as one that is "educational." When I asked people what a soap opera or rap lyrics taught them, they invariably answered that they learn about their "surroundings" or "environment" (*mazingira*) through forms like these. Some participants said that they learned of disparities between the surroundings of Arusha and the ones represented in popular media. Others said that they learned of parallels between changing circumstances in urban African life and the life depicted in these mediated products. In both cases, education cultivates an awareness of interconnections among circumstances and the possibilities (and impossibilities) of establishing and sustaining those interconnections. More than just identifying with or desiring the celebrated world represented in popular media, audiences such as those in Arusha seek to understand their own experience as a part of that powerful reality and, in many respects, to make *their* world one specific circumstance *within* that overarching context.

The concern with an awareness of one's transforming surroundings, with the claim that participation in popular culture constitutes a critical means of developing such acumen, is a prominent theme in hip-hop globally and in Arusha. Groups of performers who fashion themselves as practitioners of reality-based rap often emphasize the role of consciousness-raising in their performances, seeing hip-hop as an educational vehicle. Such consciousness-raising is often linked to the Nation of Islam, which has a significant following in American hip-hop. Consider the "5 percent nation," which "refers to the idea...that at any given time, only 5 percent of any population are politically aware enough to be influential" (Krims 2000:96–97). In keeping with this claim, many hip-hop performers self-consciously seek to constitute this 5 percent nation in order to shape a wider politics. The extent to which these specific ideas inform the global development of hip-hop, even among explicitly Muslim rappers and audiences, is open to considerable debate (Swedenburg 2001). In Arusha, as indicated above, many Muslim youth are aware of the religious affiliations of hip-hop celebrities and embrace the Muslim identity of those (such as Wu-Tang Clan, Nas, and Mike Tyson) who identify with the Nation of Islam.

The theological particulars of the Nation of Islam are, to my knowledge, irrelevant in the Tanzanian case. What is absolutely crucial to hip-hop in this context is its concern with consciousness-raising as a political project. In Arusha, the notion of awareness is captured in a self-descriptive term used by many who follow hip-hop: *MaMental*. *MaMental* is a Kiswahili neologism derived from the English word *mental* and has currency in some hip-hop circles as a term that refers to intellectual activity and indicates understanding or insight.[5] This autonym might be approximated as "The Knowing Ones" or "The Thinkers." Those who take part in hip-hop performance in urban Tanzania clearly understand themselves to be working to develop a form of consciousness, a theme that resonates with wider understandings of popular culture practice in Arusha. This stance is condensed and objectified in the "mental" condition of these youth.

The critical self-awareness embraced by hip-hop participants illuminates a more general concern with authenticity, the real, and the proper modes of expressing or representing it. These urban youth characterize the relevance of their own actions in terms of "knowing" qualities. Their acts are valid and legitimate so long as they seek to achieve and communicate an awareness of the world. In this way, reality and its representation go hand in hand. Popular expressions, or voices, are real insofar as they articulate an awareness of and insight into changing circumstances; the real is defined as the object of thinking and knowing as valued actions. The concerns with tireless thinking as a means of "keeping it real" further suggest a crucial aspect of authenticity as it is understood and acted upon in Arusha. If thinking and being conscious are vital to sustaining a commitment to reality, then this implies that reality is threatened by a pervasive lack of awareness, a vast unknowing. In urban Tanzania, the threat to the real from ignorance and unthinking action is a deeply felt problematic, one that characterizes a great many contemporary lives.

LOSING YOUR WAY, KEEPING IT REAL

To demonstrate the force of this concern with the fugitive character of reality, the threat of ignorance, and the value of the authentic, let me return to my initial discussion about the prominence of religious interests and practices in Arusha. Pentecostalism in Aru-Meru has attracted the most scholarly attention (Baroin 1996; Stambach 2000), but there is also a renewed interest in Islam, motivated and structured in broadly similar ways. Let me offer the brief testimony of two young men I know—one affiliated with the Assemblies of God and the other a Sunni Muslim. Each confronted a spiritual crisis in order to indicate how the real and ways of knowing it are grasped as part of contemporary religiosity. The first man, Michael, in his late twenties, worked as a security guard in town and had become a preacher in his church. He came to the Assemblies of God, he said, after leading a wayward life. He had been a trader in the black market all across Tanzania for many years and lived, in his own words, a life of "debauchery and nonsense [*usherati, na maisha ya ovyo*]." His life changed when his father became very ill and Michael was called home by his family. Back at home in Aru-Meru, Michael began to hear about the activities of the Assemblies of God, which, as he put it, "had answers to all the questions about what to *do* in life." This was in contrast to the Lutheran faith, which never offered any concrete solutions. "They don't care!" he told me. "If you come with questions, they just tell you to pray, but they won't help." Pentecostals, however, showed him that the Bible has answers to everything that can happen "as you live your life." Even a young woman in his village had been instantly cured of demonic possession by the utterance "*Yesu ni Bwana* [Jesus is Lord]" at an Assemblies of God prayer meeting. "Today," said Michael, "this woman has become a success and has given birth to many children."

The next account comes from a younger man, Ibrahim, who at age eighteen was just beyond secondary school age. Ibra came from the oldest Muslim residential zone in Arusha, from a family with more financial means than many but of wildly shifting economic fortunes. He lived in a matrifocal compound presided over by his mother's mother, along with his mother, her sisters, and their children. Ibra attended classes in tourism at one of the numerous "technical colleges" that offer such classes in the area. But he had also had the opportunity to attend secondary schools in Kenya, an opportunity that he lost, by his own account, because of his bad behavior. His mother, however, told me that he was unable to continue because the family could no longer provide the school fees.[6] I had known Ibra to be a dedicated "thug" (*muhuni*), in his own words, a denizen of one of the numerous barbershops that have sprung up all around town, places of informal gathering and meager economic prospects for thousands of young men. But I also found in the summer of 2000 that he had become a devout Muslim, attending prayers at his neighborhood mosque five times a day. When I asked Ibra why he had taken up his faith, he told me that he had returned to Islam after getting kicked out of school for the last time the preceding year. He told me that he had "lost his way" (*nimepotea njia*) and he was returning to what he had known since he was a child. All the trouble he had gotten into at school and especially the "sins" of smoking *bhangi* (pot) had not improved his life at all. "Life changes [*Maisha yan-abadilika*]," he told me, "and these changes make you search for the right way [*njia ya kweli*]." On a subsequent occasion, Ibra took me to his mother's sitting room, where he showed me texts, published in Kuwait, on how to pray and the proper meanings of Islam. He told me that he had known the proper rites since he was a child but he enjoyed seeing them published in an imported text and written in English.

These brief accounts recapitulate a number of themes I have described. The centrality of the Bible, for example, as a text in which all of experience is found exemplifies the textual absolutism also attributed to the Koran. The way that a Kuwaiti text written in English situates Ibra's direct, bodily praxis in a global context also recalls the significance of education as a mode of forging connections between disparate circumstances. In each account, the truth of an authentic reality is held to be incontestable. Undoubtedly, there are important dimensions of these men's histories that should be distinguished; these men's religious experiences are not identical, nor simply tokens of a common type. But they do point to a shared set of concerns, a way of characterizing existential crises and their practical resolution that informs each of these perspectives. Both Michael and Ibra determine what is "the real" through a specific way of knowing, one that confirms the truth of what they know and the authenticity of their expression of this knowledge (in the form of Michael's preaching and Ibra's daily prayers, each a mode of voicing faith). Each man describes coming to an awareness of the truth through his encounter with falsehood and nonsense. Each lost his way and became aware of that deviation by "coming back," returning to the proper condition to which he had access all along. Michael returns home only to be "born again," and Ibra rediscovers a Muslim practice he had known since childhood. Michael self-consciously rejects his past Lutheranism as inadequate, and Ibra embraces a familiar faith.

In both instances, "the real" is an entity that has always been present and that they had only to recognize in order to acquire. At the same time, what *allows* this recognition to take place is the aberration—the debauchery, the bhangi, the nonsense—through which they come to a clearer understanding. Losing one's way validates and authenticates the value of "the real" to which one returns. Moreover, the themes of aimlessness and nonsense as dimensions of knowledge confirm, yet again, the apocalyptic premise that "the real" is at risk. Therefore, such experiences of deviation are *routinely* incorporated into renewed understanding of the truth and frequently characterize the authenticity of the voice. Such voices speak with greater authority—that is, are more real—because of how they came to their insights into that reality, the hali halisi, as it is lived today. Again, the real and ways of representing it are mutually constituted.

These concerns are paramount in a revitalized spirituality and in the popular music of Arusha. Consider the song that probably received the most airplay across Tanzania in the summer of 2000, "Chemsha Bongo" (literally, "Boil Your Brain," or "Think Hard") by Hard Blasterz Crew. The very title of the song immediately denotes the value of thinking and knowing. It also connotes ties to place through its association with *bongo* (brain), a colloquial term for Dar es Salaam, an appellation that further indicates the centrality of thinking to popular cultural practice. This song was the first track from the album *Funga Kazi* (Finish the Job), which plainly implies the qualities of "hardness" and "toughness" predominant in this kind of reality rap. The song begins with the chorus:[7]

> Savior, I offer my soul. Free me from this chaos.
> If I fool with this life today, I'll go to bed hungry.
> Think hard before you are trapped. You'll be amazed.
> Think hard before you are trapped. You'll be astonished.

The chorus neatly encapsulates the crisis (a world of chaos and foolishness), which might be resolved by thinking through one's predicament in the hopes of salvation. The lyrics of "Chemsha Bongo" elaborate on this process, describing in detail the world of chaos and a failure to properly think about the consequences of such nonsense. The song describes the life of a young man, J, who comes from a loving and modestly well-to-do home and is drawn through his desire for "the sweetness of life" (*utamu wa maisha*) to forget his respect for his parents and elders. Instead, he pursues a life of beautiful women, crates of beer, and a posse of followers (*wapambe*, literally, "those who decorate"). Eventually, these infinite desires lead him to the pursuit of crime, a life on the run in Zanzibar, and the accumulation of debts. His friends, who once celebrated his arrival at the bars and clubs, now say, "*Cheki J arosto amesha zeeka* [Check out J. He's already grown old]."

In the concluding verse, J's parents are killed in a bad accident, and J's first thought is one that actually cheers him up (*Nikajipa moyo*): "I knew I'd inherit wealth because of this disaster [*Nikajua nitarithi mali kutokana na hayo maafa*]." Suddenly, J is overcome with astonishment at his relatives. In an act akin to divine intervention ("*Vilianza kutokea vizingiti na sielewi vilipo ibuka* [They started to break through the floodgates. I don't understand where they popped up]"), all his remaining family begin fighting over money, and he realizes, too late, that he is as good as dead. Horrified by this epiphany, J addresses his listeners and reminds them of the importance of religious devotion:

> Rich people, pray to God before you depart.
> Man is like a flower. He sprouts and he dies.
> And money is like a devil.
> If you have it, you can never be found worthy.

The song concludes with a horrifying vision of corporeal damnation:

> Friends, I cry. I've already been undone.
> Right here I smell of sweat. I'm entirely spoiled.
> My body is like a piece of cassava that's been scraped down.

and an ecumenical call for renewed spiritual commitment in order to avoid the disasters that J faced:

> It's true what they say about the Prodigal Son.
> The Bible and Qur-aan, they say the remorseful are forgiven.
> Angry citizens still want to take me for a thrashing.
> They wanted to burn me. They've soaked me in oil.
> Say your prayers, and search every hour and every minute.
> Don't hope to find, my brother, what I found.

The poetic structure, as well as central textual features of "Chemsha Bongo," produce a narrative through which an authentic voice is created. The narrator, J (many listeners will recognize J is the actual nom de guerre— Nigga J—of the rapper), recounts his own experience. He starts by reporting that he will condense his entire life in these verses ("*Kwa kifupi* [In short]"), beginning with the way he was raised. J's childhood is focused especially on education and is clearly situated in a social world of "parents" and "wise elders." Yet the very comforts of his life plant the seeds of his ultimate undoing: "*Maisha yalikuwa matamu nilisahau yote haramu* [Life was sweet. I forgot all that was forbidden]." This statement, early in the song, establishes the central tension in the overall narrative; in effect, J's life is shaped by his forgetting. The significance of "forgetting" is concretized in a series of contrasts: his parents and elders, present in the initial and concluding verses, are replaced by the "chicks" (*mademu*) and "posse" (*wapambe*) with whom J runs in the body of the song. Poetically, J's life is motivated by sweetness, in contrast to the foul stench of those who would restrain or impede him. This sweetness is literally embodied in the foods J enjoys and provides for his crew—especially roast pork and beer (*kiti moto na bia*)—foods that are specifically forbidden (*haramu*), directly exemplifying what he has forgotten. Ultimately, these same poetic devices are inverted. J's very body and blood emit the odor of death, and his body, which had enjoyed the expensive foods of the sweet life, becomes "like a piece of cassava that's been scraped away" (the cheapest, most common and flavorless of foods).

Underlying these contrasts, and in many respects at the root of J's forgetting, is the fate of J's "intelligence" (*akili*). J begins his life showing his intelligence, heading straight to school. His intelligence, though, soon gives way to the power of money. When elders cleverly advise him, he hears them as "speaking in riddles." His money "was like a hammer [*fedha kwangu ni kama nyundo*]" used to destroy all in his way. Facing a life of crime to maintain the lifestyle he has pursued, J is cut off from the wealth of his parents. The parents try to shift the focus of his ambitions:

Only my parents tried to show me that my inheritance is education.
I decided that you study in order to get money.

From this moment forward, J's life is in rapid decline as he "eats" his wealth. Women who once fell all over him now laugh at how he has aged. "Poverty comes knocking [*Umasikini umepiga hodi*]." In the end, J's fatal transformation is revealed as his "head starts to spin [*Akili ilianza kuniruka*]," (literally, "My intelligence passed over me") and his relatives bitterly fight over the money of their dead kin. "*Kwa kifupihl*": in short, as J would have it, love of money destroys the possibility of learning. Only after he has been destroyed by this monetary pursuit, literally undone, is he able to offer a lesson for others, one that reaffirms, in the "name of truth," the power of prayer, the need for repentance and perpetual devotion to God. In so doing, J also reaffirms the centrality of education and intelligence to acquiring the real, by rendering his own life as an illustration, indeed, an embodiment of this process. A further illustration of this point is that J has now gone solo with a hit release, "Machozi, Jasho, Na Damu [Tears, Sweat, and Blood]," with the new moniker Professor J. Moreover, the voice through which he articulates these changes exemplifies the total process of education, one that has forgotten the truth, lost its way, and is fully achieved upon its return to an ever-present and authentic reality.

"Chemsha Bongo" was (and remains) one of the most popular rap songs in Tanzania, but it is by no means unique in its explicit and strikingly apocalyptic message. All the informal crews in Arusha told me that they liked to listen to and create verses about *dini* (religion). One duo with whom I worked for several weeks called itself Chronic Mobb. The two young men were eighteen years old, Nesto Dogg and Spidah Killa. When I first met Nesto, he was living with his mother and grandmother in a small pair of rented rooms in one of the most notoriously dangerous areas of town, near the open-air market. Nesto was still finishing primary school, working intermittently at a barbershop near his home, and hoping to find a way to get to secondary school. His father, who lived in Dar, had taken a second wife, leaving the members of Nesto's house to scramble for resources where they could. The following year, I met up with Nesto when he performed with Spidah at a local weekly rap competition. He told me that he had not been able to continue with school but that he and Spidah, who had long been friends, were still barbering—and regularly going to the Tanzanite mines at Mererani, *kutafuta mkwanja* (looking for cash). Spidah and Nesto were quite taken with stories about those who had struck it rich in the mines. They were equally amused by reports of how easily these fortunes were blown. Nesto's mother was also working "in the bush" (*porini*), vernacular for working at the mines, in her case not as a miner but as an aspiring gem trader.

Chronic Mobb, like many crews in Arusha, generally describe the "message" (*ujumbe*) of their verses in terms of the "lessons" (*mafundisho*) and "intelligence" (akili) through which they hope the audience will "become aware" (*watakuwa*, "mental"). A number of groups further linked these concerns with religion and concretized this connection, as did Chronic Mobb, by beginning their performance with widely recognized Christian hymns. The following song by Chronic Mobb takes its title from such a hymn, "Katika Viumbe Vyote Vilivyo Umbwa [Of All Creatures Created]." The first two lines are from the hymn:

> In all of God's creation,
> Man was created above all others.

Chronic Mobb sings these lines several times before launching into its own verses. Nesto told me that they like to use the hymn in order to "stir up" and "enliven" (*kuchangamka*) the audience, a technique that had the effect of generating audience participation on most of the occasions I saw Chronic Mobb perform (figure 9.1). This performative quality is plainly the "message" of their verses as well. "Katika Viumbe Vyote" is not presented as a narrative, and Nesto and Spidah do not describe their own conditions as object lessons in the way J does. Still, there are clear parallels between this rap and "Chemsha Bongo" in the immediacy of experience as this is represented in the verses. In each of the two verses, performed by Nesto and Spidah in sequence, the rappers address their audience through reference to their own bodily condition. In turn, these bodily conditions are grasped as generic human conditions, presented as indisputable evidence of our "created" condition. Nesto begins by lamenting how "sad" and "tired" he is and warns: "Let's not be stupid [*Tusiwe akili fyatu*]," but instead recognize that we were actually created. Like J, who forgets his initial condition of intelligence, Nesto asserts that "we don't remember" who created us and what that requires of us. Creation is confirmed as both real and orderly, with Man above all others and God above Man. The initial lines of Spidah's verse reiterate these claims, urging people to remember their created condition and directly describing the hierarchy of the human body ("With a head to think with and eyes to see/A nose for smelling, ears to hear") as self-evident proof of this creation.

Having established the forgotten fact of creation, Nesto and Spidah go on to detail the ways in which this creation is directly subverted in contemporary life.

> But even though the Lord created us,
> I see the disgrace of men lying with men
> Until chicks are barren
> And even little girls have abortions.

Nesto further denounces the inversion of age hierarchies, decrying "kids beating their mothers" and "old folks tripped up." Spidah's verses follow the same pattern of inversion of the proper order:

> We have ears, but we don't hear.
> Prophets guide us, but we don't follow.

In both verses, the persuasive force of the claims lies in the reality of our own "created" bodies. Nesto "sees" and "meets" the corporeal disgraces he describes, and Spidah's lament is the subversion of the body itself ("We have ears, but we don't hear"). In turn, Nesto and Spidah each call for a renewed bodily connection to divinity, "speaking from the heart" so that we will "put his will in our hearts." Whereas J offers his own life course as exemplary evidence of his spiritual claims, Nesto and Spidah (who would seem to exempt *themselves* from the horrors they decry) validate the realness of their assertions through the body, showing how the body is tangible proof of God's creation, how the presence of evil is manifest in the deviant condition of the contemporary body, and how the body also offers us a means to address these failures and remember our created condition.

FIGURE 9.1
Popular rap crew Chronic Mobb at a concert in Arusha, Tanzania.

CONCLUSIONS

In verses like those of "Chemsha Bongo" and "Katika Viumbe Vyote," the themes of religious devotion and spiritual crisis are hard-hitting and direct. There is no mistaking the call for an immediate return to divine guidance in a troubled world. Indeed, both Hard Blasterz Crew and Chronic Mobb make ecumenical pleas for the necessity of faith, extolling the Bible and Koran, churches and mosques, acting in "the name of Jesus," and asking for a Muslim blessing (*omba dua*). Not all of Tanzanian hip-hop is so manifestly concerned with religious matters, but these are clearly dominant themes in popular urban music. As the work of Remes (1999), Perullo (2005), and Stroeken (2005) reveals, rap music has become immensely popular across Tanzania, and rap produced in Tanzania has even been seen as a distinctively local product, known as Bongo Flava. Rap is widely seen as "an important means for marginalized Tanzanian youth to address mass audiences" (Perullo 2005:77). The theme of corruption is popular today, one of the many *ujumbe mkali* (strong, or fierce, messages) of Bongo Flava. Here, too, corruption is seen as hali halisi, as Mr. II raps in his composition of the same name (cited in Perullo 2005:81):

Siasa ni mchezo mchafu.	Politics is a dirty game.
Wanataka umaarufu.	They just want to be famous.

Wanasiasa wa Bongo wengi waongo. Lots of Tanzanian politicians
are liars.

Here, the theme of corruption is described as both an unvarnished examination of the harsh truth of "reality" (hali halisi) and a facade that distorts
reality. I would argue, therefore, that the power of rap performances such
as "Hali Halisi," "Chemsha Bongo," and "Katika Viumbe Vyote" illustrates
the extent to which religiosity itself has been rendered meaningful and per-
tinent through its mutual constitution with hip-hop and, undoubtedly,
other globalized modes of cultural production. The themes of losing your
way in a world of nonsense and returning to or remembering a more complete truth are certainly long-standing narratives in both Islam and
Christianity. Navigating these movements by the use of "intelligence" and
"education," through which you become "conscious" of your life's condition, is now a standardized strategy exemplified in spiritual chronicles,
soap opera fans' self-accounts, and rap lyrics. All these motifs strongly resonate with the fundamental purpose of keeping it real that pervades hip-
hop sensibilities wherever they are found.

Equally important is that these broadly shared, categorical understandings are concretized in the actual performance; these are not merely
semantic parallels, for they are underpinned by distinctive pragmatics. The
"realness" of these accounts is more than a conceptual assertion or even an
avowal of faith. It is embedded in the forms of articulation through which
the *voices* making these claims are created, so as to partake of the "realness"
they bespeak. That is, the authentic character of their ontological positions
is plainly exhibited in the representation of that reality. This wedding of
representation to reality is illustrated, as I have indicated, by J's account of
his own forgetting and consequent physical destruction and in Chronic
Mobb's equally embodied poetics, which demonstrates facts of divine creation in the forms of human suffering, experience, and evil. These features
of the voices deployed in these raps are further grounded in the musical
poetics of their performances. Of notable concern are "hardness," "toughness," and "endurance"—qualities especially beloved by young, un(der)-
employed men—which are exemplified in the names *Hard Blasterz* and
Chronic Mobb (*chronic*, according to Nesto and Spidah, signifying tireless
effort and diligence). The musical features of these rapper performances—rapid delivery or "flow" of the verses, dense clustering of note values driving a percussive rhythm forward, and layering of heavy beats with
light, dissonant electronic sounds (the keyboard accompaniment to Hard
Blasterz)—all generate "hardness" (Krims 2000:71–75). This hardness is

further contrasted with other popular musical genres in Tanzania, especially *taarab*, which rappers and their fans claim is "weak" and "soft." This hardness indicates the commitment of the performers and is intended to suggest, as do the textual features of their lyrical forms, a directness of expression and the unmediated character of experience. The truth of the reality these verses describe is meant to be intrinsic to its very utterance.

The global proliferation of popular cultural products such as hip-hop, evangelical Christianity, and Muslim reform are characterized not by a celebratory embrace of pluralistic choices, but by a firm attachment to an ontological truth, an assertion of the presence of authentic forces at work in human experience. In this sense, these cultural forces are akin to what Geschiere and Nyamnjoh (2000:423) describe as "a general obsession with autochthony," a quest to secure a vague, unspecified access to an originary force that establishes clear lines of political inclusion and exclusion. This obsession, like the workings of hip-hop and popular religiosity I have described in Arusha, is seen as "the flip side of globalization" (Geschiere and Nyamnjoh 2000:424) as mobility and dispersal are paired to the formation of new and more impermeable boundaries. The claims of urban Tanzanian religiosity expressed in hip-hop as I have described them are more profound and, in some ways, more troubling than the identity politics of autochthony. These Tanzanian claims insist not simply on difference at the levels of identity (indeed, they sometimes call for a certain ecumenicism, uniting all who follow God), but on a new grounding in a truer reality. They call, as well, for distinctive ways of knowing that reality, ways of using one's intelligence under conditions as they actually are.

What is troubling about this pronounced affirmation, this attachment to the real as an authentic way of being and doing, is the precarious nature of reality as it is defined. In a discourse that makes the very commitment to keeping it real the only legitimate mode of action, challenges to sell-outs, selfishness, and insincerity abound. But the crisis decried in Arusha is not simply a failure to toe the line of a doctrine; it is rather the threat—or perhaps the promise—that reality itself is under siege. Hard Blasterz Crew and Chronic Mobb offer explicitly apocalyptic accounts of the world as they find it. This message is part of their hardness, their directness, their realism. Moreover, this apocalyptic prospect is tied to the way of knowing reality (using one's intelligence and being educated) that this mode of reality rap defends. Indeed, in the case of Chronic Mobb, the truth that the singers put forth for MaMental (The Knowing Ones) to embrace is the consciousness of our pending obliteration. We must confront reality as it is: "the end of the world is near," but those who ask forgiveness for their sins will go to heaven. Although Hard Blasterz seems somewhat less worried about the end of the world, the critical act the crew calls for is "asking forgiveness." In either case, a final judgment looms.

How can we account for the tenuous nature of reality? Why is the apocalypse so potent and present a force in the lives of these young Tanzanian men? Apocalyptic pronouncements are nothing new in the worlds of either Christendom or Islam, yet simply assimilating these current dynamics to that recurrent legacy tells us little that is particular either to this specific historical moment or to the concrete terms in which the End of Days is understood and expressed. At the same time, it would be reductionist in the extreme to appeal to globalization, late capitalism, neoliberalism, or any of the other social scientific rubrics through which contemporary political economies are decried, as the underlying *source* of these profoundly spiritual and ontological claims. These verses may lament economic and social marginalization, but they are most concerned with educating humanity about its pending doom. Most important, if we want to read these popular movements as veiled critiques of shifting structures of political economy, then we must also recognize that these movements are captivated by the possibilities of these shifts. Hard Blasterz Crew plainly shows the considerable allure of mademu and wapambe (chicks and a posse), crates of beer, and gold-trimmed Benzs, even as it fears their influence. Spidah Killah and Nesto Dogg declaim the importance of asking a blessing and begging forgiveness for our sins, yet they gear up each month to dig in the local Tanzanite mines, hoping for that huge score, which they fully expect will evaporate as soon as they grab it.

Perhaps it is this latter dynamic that reveals something of the apocalyptic force of the present moment and manifests its contradictory characteristics in the experience of youth. More than simply the material constraints and abjection of global economic reforms, it is the nature of the possibilities these offer—the impossible dreams, the concreteness of excess, the massive jackpot—that seems exquisitely and uniquely *real* yet simultaneously evanescent, indeed, *necessarily* evanescent. This is value meant for destruction, a windfall intended for obliteration. More than economic limitations, the current moment institutes a mode of materializing and signifying value that is all-consuming and always consumed. I am hesitant to offer such tidy explanations for the apocalypse. Still, I would suggest that such a perspective alerts us to particular ways of being and doing that are increasingly commonplace in our world, modes of knowing the truth and acting on it, of representing the world and keeping it real.

Notes

1. Crews consist of young men who compose lyrics or perform at rap concerts and competitions in town. Rap competitions for local crews are held in a number of venues in Arusha. A few nightclubs and hotels with performance venues occasionally host local hip-hop artists. The rap competitions I attended took place in a small club associated with the downtown movie theater. Local groups performed on consecutive weekends for a small cash prize sponsored by the club owners. Some rappers from Arusha—most notably, X Plastaz (whose members were barbers in town)—signed with producers from the Netherlands and have received international recognition.

2. Indeed, as we shall see for some in Arusha, the distinction between these positions is paramount, whereas for others the lines of delineation are much more fluid and contextual.

3. I have written elsewhere about the masculinist ethos that pervades barbershops (Weiss 2004, in press). Here I would note that the exaggerated masculinity of barbershops—in which their interest in hip-hop is a central theme—bespeaks an attempt to give purpose to male bodies and relations in a neoliberal world where the men's productive capacity is extremely tenuous (see also Buford 1993; Cole, chapter 5, this volume).

4. I would add that I had remarkably similar discussions with Pentecostal Christians in Arusha about the scientific and mystical character of the Bible.

5. See, for example, the UK group Fun-Da-Mental. In Arusha, *MaMental* is also incorporated into the names of local rap groups and appears in rap lyrics.

6. Primary education is fully funded in Tanzania, but secondary school—especially secondary school in Kenya—requires fees.

7. See the appendix for English translations of the full Swahili texts.

10

Globalization from Way Below

Brazilian Streets, a Youth, and World Society

Tobias Hecht

Street children probably lead lives more like modern-day hunters and gatherers—substituting the fruits of nature with a precarious economy of scavenging, theft, the oldest profession, and the largess of passersby—than like denizens of a supposedly globalized and postfordist world. What, then, is the relevance of globalization to the lives of such children, children who do not travel in airplanes, use computers, enter shopping malls, work in foreign-owned factories, or produce any goods for the international market?

Based on research conducted at various times between 1992 and 2002, this chapter examines how one individual—Bruna Veríssimo, who grew up in the streets of the Brazilian city of Recife—lives this era of globalization and how she seems to imagine a place for herself in world society. The chapter also discusses experimental methods of research as tools for understanding the individual within processes of global change; it makes the analytical link between the individual and the global by means of the notion of commodity chains. Through an examination of Bruna's life story and the decade-long process of getting at that story, I argue that concern over, talk about, and advocacy in behalf of street children are related to much larger economic and cultural processes.

In the countries south of the Rio Grande, one cannot really conceive of globalization as a new force; the very name for the region—*Latin America*

—would make little sense if the place it described had not been born of something like a global process. In other parts of the world, similar problems arise with the concept.

In considering the place of globalization in the study of Africa, Frederick Cooper (2001:189) argues that there are two problems with the concept, "first the 'global' and second the 'ization.'" The first problem, Cooper argues, is that what passes for global is often just wishful thinking on the part of neoliberal economists or else the alarmism of those who fear market tyranny. Capital does not go everywhere, markets are not as open as advocates of free trade would like, and the nation-state is hardly irrelevant. The suffix *ization* suggests a phenomenon that is not only new but also arrant, a force that is reconfiguring our social and economic lives at this particular moment in history.

Like any scholar of empires, Cooper has seen it all before: Southeast Asians enslaved by Dutchmen and sent to the southern tip of Africa; West Africans kidnapped by Portuguese, British, and French traders and made to work plantations in the Americas that, in turn, enriched Europe; mass migrations; intercontinental plagues; transoceanic mercantile conglomerates. "For all the growth in international trade in recent decades, as a percentage of world GDP it has only barely regained levels found before the First World War" (Cooper 2001:194). Cooper's larger point is not that nothing is changing but that globalization may not be a useful analytical tool for understanding what is.

Is the new buzzword *globalization* merely déjà vu all over again? In *The Anthropology of Globalization*, Ted Lewellen summarizes other reasons why scholars have dismissed the putative newness and challenged the reach of globalization:

> Long-term migration—often considered a key element of globalization—affects only about 1% or 2% of the world's population and...earlier mass movements, say of the Irish, Italian, and Chinese to the New World in the 19th century, proportionately exceeded anything that is going on today when Western countries have imposed tight restrictions on immigration. The formation of political, economic, and military alliances, such as the European Community, NATO, and the ASEAN, represent more a regionalization than a globalization.... If homogenization of culture is a criterion of globalization, as many in the media claim, then how do we explain the explosive increase in ethnic politics, religious fundamentalism, and local organizing? In

> most larger countries, 80% or more of production is still for
> domestic consumption. [Lewellen 2002:9]

Lewellen suggests that a globalized economy has been emerging gradually over the past five or so centuries and that advances in communications have long been making the planet feel smaller. Yet, he argues, and here I agree, that something qualitatively new was born at the opening of the twentieth century's final decade: with the demise of the Soviet Union, large parts of the third world came to embrace neoliberalism. Even where this was not the case, the International Monetary Fund and the World Bank could virtually dictate the economic policies of poor countries (Lewellen 2002:16).

Although I would agree with Cooper that globalization is ineffectual as a tool of analysis, I do consider it useful as a name for something that is qualitatively different about the world since about 1990. Moreover, I suggest that some of the economic changes implied by globalization are linked to international concern about the plight of children, including street children. Globalization brings to mind the macro-effects of liberal trade policies, the communications revolution, capital flows, and the mass movement of people and ideas, but it is also about that now familiar idea of an imagined community. Benedict Anderson (1983) wrote of imagined communities mostly with reference to nationalism, but the idea could easily be applied to the notion of a global community. To see ourselves as part of a global system is not simply a matter of acknowledging the extent of economic integration around the world; it is also a matter of imagination. Talk of the "world's children" and of the collective and custodial responsibility of adults to protect them is one manifestation of that imagination, an assertion of our common humanity.

If globalization is about enormous and rapidly increasing flows of goods, information, and labor across international borders, the lowering of trade barriers, and a revolution in communications, then Latin American street children may have become involved in an analogous and, as I will argue, not entirely unrelated process at about the time the Berlin Wall fell.

Consider the international flow of information about Latin American street children. By the late 1980s, they had become the subjects of films (most notably, Hector Babenco's 1980 feature *Pixote*, until recently the third most commercially successful Brazilian film [Levine 1997]) and numerous television documentaries. They were featured in women's home magazines, in-flight publications, tabloids, and broadsheets. Just as children can be a sign of value, a font of "latent potential" (Anagnost, chapter 3, this volume), their mistreatment can be taken as a reflection of the ill health of the nation. Latin American politicians campaigned on promises to improve the conditions of street children, whose plight was even the subject of hearings in the European Parliament and the US Congress. Meanwhile, UNICEF identified street children as an important priority, and Amnesty International (1990a, 1990b) and Human Rights Watch (1994) released damning reports about their treatment, accusing governments of tolerating death squad killings of youth. At the same time that a number of international and multilateral institutions declared street children to be of great concern and a new focus of their work, specialist nongovernmental organizations burgeoned, with the appearance of such first-world organizations as Childhope and Covenant House and a rapidly growing and changing array of NGOs based in developing countries and dedicated to helping street children. Brazil became host to a vibrant array of nongovernmental activist organizations and service providers. In Rio, one study counted thirty-nine institutions that catered exclusively to street children in that city (Valladares and Impelizieri 1991:9). The survey noted that all these programs had been created around or after the mid-1980s and that their numbers changed rapidly: in the course of the five months it took to complete the study, four new programs were created. In Recife, the setting for my research, a gamut of projects had emerged, with government, civil, and religious organizations all vying for a role. Elsewhere (Hecht 1998), I have suggested that in Recife there was approximately one adult working full-time in behalf of street children for every child living and sleeping in the street.

GLIMPSES OF THE GLOBAL: THE VIEW FROM A BLIND ALLEY

The first time I saw Bruna Veríssimo was at one of the weekly meetings of the National Movement of Street Children. At the time, 1992, the organization was perhaps Brazil's most spirited social movement, the focus of much local and international attention. The Movimento, as activists referred to it, had championed Brazil's new Statute on Children and Adolescents and, through a well-organized media and human rights campaign, helped to make the murders of poor urban youth a national bane. I began attending the meetings in June of that year in Recife, a port city of some two million in Brazil's northeast.

Boisterous affairs, the meetings brought together representatives from neighborhood base cells (*núcleos de base*) who reported on violence and other matters of concern in their respective areas and discussed the movement's municipal, regional, and national activities. The young activists, invariably from very poor families, were not street children in any strict sense; nearly all resided with their families, and most did not work in the street either. Rather, like most urban children in Brazil, they led lives of quiet hardship in crowded shantytowns and slums. But some homeless children from the city center did belong to the movement.

A few minutes into the second or third meeting I attended, a tall adolescent in a miniskirt and skimpy halter top sashayed across the room and sat on a table. Bruna Veríssimo's bare feet, unexpectedly large, were rough with calluses and poorly healed wounds and hung from the edge of the table, above the heads of the other children, mostly younger and smaller, who sat on the floor. Her feet were so weathered because she was one of the rare members of the movement who actually lived in the street. Biologically male, Bruna cross-dressed and used female adjectives when speaking of herself.

Discussed that day were a police operation to round up children in the street, the contents of a newsletter, an upcoming regional meeting, and a report about violence against street children. Bruna spoke her mind a number of times, demanding to know at one point what difference the report about violence would actually make.

Several months later, I came across Bruna sitting on the warm pavement of a blind alley behind a church in central Recife, embroidering. By then, I had seen her a number of times, but we had never spoken. She sat concentrating on the movements of the needle, her long hair containing her gaze. I greeted her, introduced myself, and was offered a muffled hello in return.

By that point in my research, I had devised a semistructured survey, a loose set of questions I put to the children in the form of a conversation, each question leading to a series of other subjects, which I would ask about in a more or less unpredictable fashion. With the church bells peeling four-thirty, it was that pre-dusk hour when Recife's mangrove mosquitoes (*maruins*) are especially active. Resolved to interview Bruna at some other time, perhaps once we got to know each other better, I sat there in awkward silence, scratching at my legs. Then Bruna, without looking up, told me, "Go ahead. Ask the questions. I know how to answer."

Unsettled, I took out my tape recorder, inserted a blank cassette, and before the bell tolled five, heard her recite how she had been raped by her stepfather at the age of nine, gone to live in the street with other children, stolen, sold her body, longed for her mother's love, known hunger, slashed her wrists, ridden on the back bumpers of buses, sniffed glue, swallowed pills, eaten from the trash, witnessed murders, and come to hate those

FIGURE 10.1
Bruna's self-portrait and cityscape.

passersby too afraid not to steer a wide berth. In the same tone of restive ennui, she told of how she had been featured on the radio, in the newspapers, even in a video about street children. "In a place like Italy, a film about street children is worth more than a porn flick," she concluded, looking up for the first time.

STREET CHILDREN IN THE GLOBAL COMMODITY CHAIN

What Bruna had realized, of course, is that street children were of interest to people thousands of miles beyond the narrowly circumscribed tangle of streets where she and other youths spend their days and nights and also that many researchers, journalists, and international advocates were speaking about them, even mentioning their names. Their plight, it seemed to Bruna, was something that could be packaged (say, in the form of a video) and easily transported to places like Italy (by plane) and might benefit the purveyor far more than the subjects. She might not have called street children a commodity, but this seems to have been the general thrust of her quiet accusation.

Anthropologists have used commodity chain analysis to study the social relations that accompany the voyage of exchangeable goods from producer to consumer, say, of diamonds collected in Angola, cut in Antwerp, and sold in Tokyo. Of importance is not the long-distance travel itself but the economic relations and their reverberations at each stage of production, distribution, and consumption. To use the example of diamonds, one might ask how, in Japan, the demand for diamond engagement rings was created in the absence of such a tradition. Might the use of diamond engagement rings be suggestive of changing notions of status, social class, and even love? At the other extreme in the commodity chain, in Angola, one might ask who is collecting the diamonds, how, and who is profiting. What is happening with the money? Not long ago, the profits were fueling a war. How many land mines can be purchased with the money earned from the sale of a single diamond? How many limbs are lost during the lifespan of a dozen mines?[1]

Can such a form of analysis, commodity chains, be applied to Latin American street children, and, if so, would it tell us anything useful? For a number of reasons, the analogy is murky. First, street children are, of course, not being exported, and they likewise produce nothing that is traded internationally. Second, a commodity such as diamonds has existed, to all intents and purposes, forever, but what of street children? Might talk about street children in the early 1990s not have reflected the emergence of a new or at least suddenly acute problem, one that warranted swift attention? Third, although money is moved in the name of street children, it would be cynical to say that the organizations helping them form anything like an industry. Yet as the vignette in the preceding section suggests, street children themselves realize that their image and ideas about them do cross borders and have an exchange value; representations of street children can, in short, be commodified. As these images travel, much information and a certain amount of money are being moved.

Historical records suggest that there is nothing new about children living on their own in urban Latin America. Already in colonial times, many Latin American cities, such as Bogotá, had street urchins (Röggenbuck 1996). The early 1990s was likewise not the first time that children had been a subject of international debate and action in Latin America. By the second decade of the twentieth century, experts in the fields of medicine, education, and criminology gathered at the Pan American Child Congresses to examine the situation of abandoned, destitute, and ill children and to reform laws and institutions with an eye to helping children and infants (Guy 1998). What was new by the last decade of the twentieth century was the degree of prominence children had attained in the international imagination about Latin America, particularly Brazil and Colombia. Street children and their violent deaths came to be two of the most widely known features of these countries.

If diamonds are transported by plane, then how did the images of Latin American street children reach Europe and North America? The simple answer is that these children travel through the advocacy of nongovernmental organizations and multilateral institutions such as UNICEF and the writing and images produced by journalists, filmmakers, researchers, and advocates. For Southern African diamonds to be purchased by consumers in Japan or anywhere else, however, it is not enough for the diamonds to exist and for their transport to be possible. There must, of course, be a demand for their consumption. Demand can be invented where it did not once exist, as with diamonds.

The idea of a commodity chain, and globalization more generally, may have useful applications when it comes to understanding the sudden attention to street children in the late 1980s and early 1990s. First, the idea of the chain draws attention to the myriad players and mediators between the diamond and the consumer, between the child who lives in the street and the middle-class individual in the first world who might, say, make a donation to a charity based on a direct-mail appeal (in one year, the US-based Covenant House raised more than $28 million in this way [Walton 1991: 25]). Second, just as the mine worker may benefit less than all others involved in the process of moving diamonds from mine to consumer, the consultants for UNICEF doubtless live much better than, say, the adult facilitators of Brazil's National Movement of Street Children, people work-ing on the front lines of an effort to help impoverished children.

The northern interest in Latin American street children required a sort of breaking down of barriers, a kind of universalism that advocates minimum standards in the treatment of children. If the UN Convention on the Rights of the Child, adopted in 1989 and ratified subsequently by all countries except the United States and Somalia, was the world's most important expression that such standards exist, then street children were held up as one of the most obvious signs that the conditions of third-world children were indeed dismal. In Brazil, the National Movement of Street Children campaigned in behalf of poor children generally; the organiza-tion's name and the centrality of street children to its identity, however, served as a way of galvanizing local and international support for a far larger problem. One adult activist suggested to me in an interview, "If we were called the National Movement of Children, no one would listen."[2]

Cultural relativism was of no use in explaining away the problem of street children, and this worked to the advantage of advocates: a practice such as female circumcision, widely condemned in most of the world, tends to be defended by some on the grounds of respecting different, competing cultural norms. When it came to street children, however, public opinion in Latin America may have been divided on just how to contend with them—from calls to help them and their families, to suggestions that they should all be rounded up and incarcerated, or worse—but no one could be heard advocating that the street is a suitable place for children to grow up. Street children became one of the only publicly acknowledged points of worldwide consensus about children. People everywhere are apt to be against children dying of malaria, but no prominent social movements have taken up this cause—which is surprising, given that the number of children killed daily by malaria is roughly the number of adults who died in the 2001 terrorist attack on the Twin Towers.

Just as globalization is about a single world of linked producers and consumers, attention to street children raises questions and facilitates con-sensus about the treatment that children deserve regardless of borders, national traditions, and regional ideologies. If globalization is introducing any degree of homogeneity into patterns of popular culture, nowhere is this happening in a more dramatic way than in relation to children and youth. Today, Mickey Mouse doubtless has better name recognition among ten-year-olds across the planet than does any single living human being. Meanwhile, movies, television programming, computer software, and the marketing and distribution of toys and children's literature are mostly controlled by a handful of companies; with minor adaptations, multinational corporations can now peddle the same products to children anywhere in the world. For this to be possible, children must be seen as legitimate consumers in the market economy. And it is hard to argue that this is not the case. According to an undated letter sent in 2002 as part of a direct-mail campaign by *Harper's Magazine*, consumers across the planet—children and their obliging parents—have spent four and a half billion dollars on licensed Star Wars merchandise since 1977. Even street children have taken consumer fads to extremes: one anthropologist argues that boys in Caracas are more likely to murder for a pair of Nikes than for food to fill their empty stomachs (Márquez 1998).

Despite some of their consumerist practices, street children turn notions about youth and globalization on their head. They violate most every aspect of increasingly global notions about how childhood should be lived: in the protective realm of school and home, in training as future workers and citizens. Street children live independently of adults, they are visible and often violent, and most of them, in the harshest of cities, do not survive to adulthood. Street children offend a modern awareness of the vulnerability and rights of children while also raising alarm over public safety.

BACK TO THE ALLEY

Seven years after carrying out my initial research, I returned to Northeast Brazil and, following a chance reencounter with Bruna, decided to see whether we might work together to write a book about her life and about her generation of street children, so many of whom, in just a fraction of a generation, had died.

Her life story, as she tells it, begins not so much with her birth but at the age of nine, when her stepfather sexually abused her: the day the street became home and her body a means of livelihood, the day he decided to be she. From that point, her descriptions move both backward, to vague memories of life as a boy in a violent home, and forward, to numbing years of fear, prostitution, drug use, and unrelenting discrimination in the streets, years that defy narration as the discrete incidents typical of biographies.

For a number of reasons, Bruna Veríssimo's life might seem an unlikely point of departure for attempting to understand social groups in Brazil, much less global society. For a start, even the modern consumer choices offered by globalization are inaccessible. But more to the point, Bruna hardly fits easily into any recognizable unit of anthropological analysis. As a young child at home, she was amid the legions of Recife's destitute families. Her mother, a sometimes prostitute, would also beg and worked for a time in a motel, cleaning rooms. The family lived at first in a shack perched along the banks of the Beberibe River, but in a slum clearance scheme, they were resettled to a new community in the Atlantic rain forest, far from the center of Recife. Initially, there was no running water or electricity. None of the hardships Bruna, then known as José Edson, endured were unusual for Recife's underclass. At the age of six or seven, she would hitchhike with her mother to the city's wholesale produce market, where they scavenged for discarded vegetables or offered to carry around crates of produce. Soon, she discovered a more lucrative means of earning money for the family: men would pay her to go off into the forest with them to be fondled and kissed. She became a sex worker at a time when other children were learning the alphabet. She (he)—the pronouns are a matter of confusion here—began to favor playing with dolls and dressing in her older sister's clothing. These feminine tendencies ("My mother's sperm was stronger than my father's," as Bruna explained it) did not go unnoticed by her step-father, a violent binge drinker.

Raped at the age of nine, Bruna ran away to the streets of the city center. There she joined up with a group of girls who had formed a sort of informal gang. Together, the Pá da Galega,[3] or Blond Girl's Band, roamed, slept, sniffed glue, and stole under the tutelage of Safira, who was a bit older and more experienced than the others. Yet not only was Bruna the sole member who was biologically male, but also she soon rejected her age-mates' means of subsistence:

> With a boy on one side and a girl on the other, whoever passed
> between us had no way out, old ladies, pregnant women, crip-
> pled people. With crippled people, I had this way of kicking away
> the crutch to stick my hand in the person's bag, which made me
> feel very sorry later. I never wanted to do it again. That was when
> I started to be different. I was different from the rest of them, not
> only from the boys but also from the girls. Like my friend Safira,
> who thought I was going soft because I no longer wanted to rob
> pregnant women. I didn't want to mess with crippled people. I
> was afraid to rob old ladies because they might have a heart
> attack and I'd feel guilty.... So I started to distance myself from
> theft.

Eventually making a promise to a saint never to steal again, Bruna moved formally into the sex trade at the age of about eleven. Never a typical street child, she was likewise not a typical transvestite prostitute. For one thing, there was her age:

> Twenty-four hours a day, I was in the middle of the street dressed up in drag like a woman. I showed up so many times in the newspapers…. Sometimes the photographers would stop me in the middle of the street to take my picture. I thought it was because I was sniffing glue in the street, but no, it was because I was so young at that time, cross-dressing as a woman and not hiding my homosexuality.

Bruna was an anomaly as such a young transvestite, and in other regards as well. Transvestites, not an uncommon sight in the poor neighborhoods of Recife, generally say that they are accepted in their communities. "People see us every day, and they are used to us," I was told by a number of them. In the city center, however, transvestites—who probably make up the majority of sex workers in that area—are plentiful at night but can almost never be seen in the street during the day, and certainly not living in the street. The fact that Bruna slept in the street resulted in rejection from the transvestite community as well, who look down on such people. Also, whereas transvestite prostitutes usually claim that they enjoy having sex with clients (see Kulick 1998), Bruna is impotent and speaks of her encounters with johns as a dreaded means of survival. A sense of great loneliness emerges from her narrative, a sort of economy of the emotions in which she says that she has never and will never fall in love, that she loves, only the mother who stood by and did nothing to protect her from an abusive stepfather.

Despite never having attended school, Bruna had learned to read and write by studying street signs and sometimes culled the garbage for newspapers, magazines, and books. I taught her to keep an ethnographic journal, in which she wrote about her daily activities, her encounters with people in the street—housewives who would give her food, fellow homeless people, rag pickers, people walking their dogs in the park. I also lent her a tape recorder so that she could begin conducting interviews on her own.

Our work together consisted of recording our conversations, discussing her journal entries, speaking with people who had known her at different times during her life—friends from childhood, her mother, social workers, and others. We held group interviews with other transvestite sex workers, and Bruna did many interviews on her own, sometimes with questions I gave her but always complemented by her own questions and informed by her peculiar way of interviewing. In addition, Bruna was provided with pastels, watercolors, sequins, glue, drafting paper, and other art supplies. Her pictures represented idealized versions of herself, goddesses, life on the streets, and more abstract representations. In one pastel drawing, a scantily clad prostitute walks along a street. In the background figure a policeman—tiny in proportion—and his car. The self would seem to be large, but the threat of authority is pervasive. In another drawing, a mother and child lie on the pavement outside a department store. As if Bruna had been studying the theories of Philippe Ariès, she depicted the child as at once a pacifier-sucking toddler and a miniature adult, complete with a halter top and makeup.

In exchange for meeting with me a couple times a week, writing in her journal, and conducting interviews, Bruna received a salary, the minimum monthly wage in Brazil. She was also given emergency payments when necessary and various sorts of assistance in kind. My hope was to forge a different sort of research relationship this time, one in which the "trade barriers" between researcher and subject were lowered, where ethnography need not be likened to pornography. Later, during a final period of research and writing in 2002 and 2003, Bruna was paid a regular salary under a grant from the H. F. Guggenheim Foundation. I was also able to sell her drawings and paintings, remitting a sum that was to have paid for a house. What I had not counted on was just how Bruna wanted to organize her relationship, through this collaboration, to a wider global society beyond the streets of Recife.

IMAGINING THE GLOBAL

The anecdote about my first interview with Bruna suggests a troubling nexus between globalization and street children. Street children can come to feel that their image and their intensely private anguish are sought by people from near and far who go to extraordinary lengths to get at them—and with practically nothing to offer in return. Yet my own subsequent ideas of what might constitute fairer and more collaborative research strategies failed to take into account how my co-researcher would interpret and act on these strategies. Here is an example of what I mean.

In late September 1999, Bruna began to conduct interviews on her own for our research about her life story. On the first of October, we met on the grounds of the Law Faculty in the center of Recife.

We took a seat on one of the ornate benches in the garden. I handed her a set of three bottles of nail polish and a copy of *Marie Claire* (she is fond of women's magazines). Bruna examined the nail polish and then picked up the magazine and began to leaf through the pages. The pictures were what captured her attention: advertisements for makeup, soap, jewelry, lingerie.

"Were you able to do any interviews?"

"Yes," she said, without looking up.

"Can we listen to them?"

"All right."

Bruna pressed the play button. There was a lot of white noise on the tape. Wind? Breathing? A muffled conversation in the background. Bruna turned the page and looked at an advertisement for eye shadow. Every imaginable hue from peach to lime green.

"What is this?"

"Mascara."

"I mean, on the tape."

"An encounter, last night."

"With whom?"

"Last night, I was out on Mário Melo, walking around, looking at the city, when a man came up to me. He said, 'Someone wants to talk to you.' It was Mônica, a transvestite who is new to Mário Melo, who was looking for me. She said, 'Bruna, this man wants a *suruba a três*...a ménage à trois. Do you want to participate?' I didn't have any money and I was hungry, so I said all right. The man said he would pay me ten and pay Mônica fifteen. I said I wanted fifteen too, but Mônica said she was the one who had found the man. The man said that he was going to pay us twenty-five because that was all that he had, we could divide it up however we wanted. Since he didn't have any money for a motel, we went down to the edge of the river. I had the tape recorder in my bag and turned it on."

There was an elderly lady on the next bench, straining in our direction. I wanted to lower the volume so that she would not hear, but also to raise it to know whether I was actually hearing what Bruna claimed was on the tape. I raised it. The old lady scooted slightly toward the end of her bench nearer us.

"You taped a session with a client?"

"I had the machine in my bag. This is the sort of thing you want to know about, isn't it?"

The man on the tape was muttering a plea.

"He wanted to have sex without a condom," Bruna intoned. "So I said, 'If you are going to penetrate me, put this on.'"

"You taped this?"

"Yes."

"Did he know you were taping him?"

"Of course not."

"You didn't ask for permission?"

"No." She looked up, suddenly impatient. "I wanted it to be very spontaneous. Isn't that what you want?"

"That's dangerous. You can't do that."

"I know. I never have sex without a condom."

"I mean, you can't just record people without telling them."

"Who would guess they were being taped at a time like that?"

It was difficult to disagree with that point, but I still said, "If he had found out, he might have hurt you."

"He didn't find out."

"All right, he didn't. But he could have. Besides, you didn't have his permission. It isn't right."

"Did I give permission to the men who took me inside their cars when I was eleven?"

Other problems surfaced too. Bruna began complaining about rejection by other transvestites on the avenue where she worked. Believing that Bruna was about to publish a book, they protested her presence there. I cringed at this, knowing that if the book was ever to be published, it would be unlikely to make her much money. In any case, the rejection was coming from people who were a part of her everyday life. Still, Bruna suggested that we begin working (to use her words) "like paparazzi," secretly photographing prostitutes at night as they solicited clients.

Something had changed in the research dynamic and within Bruna's life on the street. Although she was sensitive to and hurt by the verbal abuse she regularly received from strangers in the city center, it was something she had lived with most of her life, and it did not happen all the time. In fact, it seemed to occur more when we were together than when she was a short distance away, on her own. I began to notice that, when she would go off alone, say, to a nearby kiosk to buy cigarettes, her presence hardly attracted any attention. When people stared, it was generally when the two of us were together. The combination of the foreigner and the local transvestite attracted attention more than either of us by ourselves. On my own, I was merely a visiting foreigner; on her own, from a distance, Bruna would generally be taken for a woman, and her provocative style of dress was nothing unusual to women in Recife. Yet I drew attention to her, and she to me.

My presence in Bruna's life doubtless changed the life we were studying, altering her relationship with her peers and eventually making both of us the subject of vague threats from transvestite sex workers apparently jealous over Bruna's prospects of being the subject of a book. In Bruna's interviews with her peers, the same questions were asked of her that had been put to me years before when I had done my dissertation research, questions I had hoped, in vain, would not arise in a collaborative project such as this. Those interviewed by Bruna wanted to know how she stood to benefit by collecting their stories and how she might profit by, in effect, peddling their image. What was different this time around was that, instead of being perceived as the perpetrator of this sort of work, I had become a mere accomplice, delegating the most difficult questions about ethnographic authority to Bruna. Seven years after my first maladroit interview with her, Bruna was being asked what she had once—through her guarded gaze, her studied indifference—asked me: what do you stand to gain by trading in my image?

A final period of research on this project was undertaken during three months in 2002. By that time, Bruna and I had interviews spanning a decade. That was when something became disquietingly evident: though much of what Bruna had been telling me could be verified, a good amount was patently untrue. In one of her recorded interviews, she spoke with a young prostitute named Michele. Michele talked about why she had decided to leave home to live in the street, what led her to become a prostitute, what it was like to go out with johns she did not know, and what she did with the money. At one point in the exchange between Bruna and Michele, the improbably high voice of this "girl" suddenly became Bruna's. The interviewer and the interviewed were one and the same. Other characters and events in Michele's life were likewise invented—a "sister" who died of dengue fever never existed, and a murder that had taken the life of a fellow sex worker in 1999 was in every detail the same murder that took the life of a sex worker in 2002. Bruna, despite always maintaining that what she most wanted in life was to leave the street, spurned real opportunities to do so. I had become a client—not the sort she normally dealt with, to be sure, but someone to second-guess, someone with a fantasy to satisfy. Despite my hopes to carry out collaborative research in an egalitarian fashion, a series of imprecise patron–client ties seemed to guide everything. I was a patron in the sense that I was sponsoring the research and offering a measure of economic security. But I was also a client who was seeking something from her and depending on her collaboration.

In telling her life story, in telling stories about her life, Bruna was constantly trying to situate her subjective experience in relation to what she saw as an audience, not only to what she believed I wanted to hear but also to what an imagined readership might want to read. When I asked her why avowedly heterosexual men made up the bulk of the transvestite sex workers' clientele, she would say that those men were looking for what they could not get at home, what ordinary women could not give them. The telling of her own life story was something analogous: the imagined readers were after what contrasted most starkly with the routine events in their own lives. As she seemed to see it, what people wanted to know about, what she had to offer a readership, were tales of sex and violence. And who could say that she had miscalculated?

THE INDIVIDUAL AND THE IMAGINATION OF GLOBAL SOCIETY

The individual is generally seen as an idiosyncratic, unpredictable point of departure for grasping the collective. For Durkheim, individualism was merely indicative of failed social integration. But some have championed the study of the individual as a means of understanding social systems; biographies by Oscar Lewis (1961), Sidney Mintz (1960), and Paul Radin (1926), among others, pushed anthropology in new and contested directions. In this era of great movement of labor, capital, and cultural experience, the notion of a bounded community holds little sway. Michael Herzfeld suggests in his *Portrait of a Greek Imagination* (1997) that the ethnographic biography, an apparent oxymoron, may provide a way of delving into the interlocking social worlds all members of humanity have to negotiate. I believe that the approach is a fruitful one for understanding a life that does not fit easily into any community but that is lived somewhere on the periphery of many different worlds.

It would be difficult to find a more certain target of discrimination in Brazil than a dark-skinned, destitute, homosexual transvestite who practices prostitution and sleeps in the street. But Bruna Veríssimo also associates with concerned housewives, human rights lawyers, artists, proselytizers, and fellow homeless people and prostitutes. Day in and day out, she observes Recife's police, petty merchants, and politicians (she sleeps outside an important government building). Yet she maintains that her only friends are the stray dogs she adopts and that she would not feel comfortable sleeping in a home so long as there are children who must sleep in the street.

Bruna Veríssimo's life offers vistas onto Brazilian urban existence and raises questions about world society. Her lived experience has taken her through *favelas* (shantytowns) and into the street, to reformatories and jails, but also into boyhood and the life of a transgendered prostitute. She has lived as a child, as an adult, and as a black Brazilian. As one of Recife's few surviving members of her generation in the street, Bruna's short but frighteningly eventful life is our only source of knowledge about the scores of murdered children she has known. Her life also intersects with a far wider world in which children and childhood are vital to any consensus that has emerged or might emerge about the nature, terms, and limits of global society. If globalization is anything more than an abstract idea, it can be understood only through subjective experience. Through Bruna's sense of herself as a sort of commodity—one that is photographed and written about, in whose name money is raised and social movements galvanized— she seems to have come to imagine herself into a far larger picture, one in which she rightfully belongs. In 1999, the government of Fernando Henrique Cardoso was actively selling off state assets, often to foreign interests. This irked public opinion because the enterprises were frequently being sold on the cheap, workers were being laid off, and ownership of the companies was shifting to foreign investors. This was the side of globalization most discussed in Recife at the time. A man in the park where Bruna and I would meet joked, "The next thing you know, we're all going to be foreigners," by which he meant that Brazilians themselves would soon be foreign owned. In the second half of the 1990s, the Brazilian press was awash with stories about foreigners coming to Brazil for inexpensive illicit sex, often with minors. Notwithstanding that there was no lack of Brazilian clients for sex workers and that in a city like Recife there are few foreign tourists at all, let alone sex tourists, transactional sex functions as a sort of metaphorical link in the commodity chain between the Brazilian local and the global.

In *Modernity at Large: Cultural Dimensions of Globalization*, Arjun Appadurai distinguishes between fantasy and imagination:

> The idea of fantasy carries with it the inescapable connotation of thought divorced from projects and actions, and it also has a private, even individualistic sound to it. The imagination, on the other hand, has a projective sense about it, the sense of being a prelude to some sort of expression.... Fantasy can dissipate (because its logic is so often autotelic), but the imagination, especially when collective, can become fuel for action. [Appadurai 1996:7]

Bruna was in the business of guessing the very private fantasies of her clients and bringing those fantasies to life. Gender was one realm in which she had already reinvented herself, in this case, as a putative woman—through dress, demeanor, the pitch of her voice, her peculiar sashay, the use of feminine adjectives in self-reference, and the assumption of what Brazilians call the "passive," or receptive, role in sex.[4] She was inventing not only her gender but also her nature, as if she herself were a character in multiple and concurrent scripts, accommodating the fantasies of others. On one hand, for concerned housewives who served her meals or gave her food for her dogs, Bruna was the tame object of charity: a representative of the deserving poor, a Catholic (who never mentioned her devotion to the saints of the Afro-Brazilian pantheon), someone who did not steal, drink, or use drugs. On the other hand, when I first met her in 1992 and she belonged to the National Movement of Street Children, Bruna was a member of an excluded underclass whose lot could be improved only through political organizing.

Bruna maneuvered through, observed, and reflected on several layers of Brazilian society. Although her life had been lived within a narrowly circumscribed mesh of city streets, her imagination—or, to follow the distinction made by Appadurai, her fantasies—had a far wider spatial dimension, taking her to what she referred to as "the other world," by which she meant somewhere beyond Brazil, somewhere richer, where her image (in a film, in a book) could be sold. She was not what you would call "future oriented." The fantasies that she occasionally spoke of formed no part of a project. She was not saving money to travel to Italy, where so many Brazilian transvestites who do manage to leave the country go. There was little to save. In any case, she always found an immediate reason to spend whatever money she had. Bruna was haunted by the fact of still being alive, always aware that she was one of the few survivors from her generation of street children. "I never imagined I would be celebrating my twenty-fourth birthday," she said on that occasion. Her fantasies seemed to be rooted more in the spatial than in any relationship to the future, as if the better life were a parallel existence that would be hers if only she could find it. "Bruna, slave of reality, freed by her dreams," she announced one afternoon as we walked across the city center. She asked me to write it down for my book.

Being hopeful implies imagining beyond the here and now. But there is a painful side to hope because it evidences precisely what is lacking in the present. In Bruna's case, knowing more about the "other world"—be it San Francisco, where she believed that homosexuals could marry (this was before any time when they could), or Rome, where transvestite sex workers like her make much more money—made her immediate reality appear all the more dismal.

In the end, Bruna's autonomy, ironically, depended on her success in marketing herself. Whereas contemporary childhood can rightly be seen as representing a reprieve from the market (Fass, chapter 2, this volume), Bruna bet on the benefits a global market might offer her. Reluctantly, she sold her body, a local enterprise that brought her tremendous suffering, but she was eager to sell her story, a prospect she hoped would allow her to transcend her status quo. As a plane flew overhead one day, she lamented the fact that she would probably never be able to travel in that way. Yet she clearly imagined herself as a protagonist on something like a global stage, an individual with a story to tell or to invent, yearning to satisfy the imagined expectations of a readership not yet extant. We were standing not far from the mangrove swamp where she took her clients who were too poor to pay for a motel room.

Notes

1. For a detailed example of the use of commodity chains in anthropology, see Collins 2000.

2. In a similar way, AIDS orphans and mother-to-child transmission of HIV have been at the heart of a much larger debate about the use of anti-retrovirals in Southern Africa. See Bray 2003.

3. In Brazil, the word *galega* (*galego* in the masculine; literally, "Galician") refers to people who have light-colored hair or skin. *Pá* is a shortened version of the word

patota, a band or informal grouping. The galega here was Safira, whose hair was bleached from the sun and the salt air.

4. Unlike the case of Madagascar (see Cole, chapter 5, this volume), clothing in itself does not have such transformative powers. It is not the clothing that makes the man womanly in Brazil. Heterosexual men dress up as women during carnival, for instance. The most important feminizing activity is receptive sexual intercourse. In Brazil, men who practice only the penetrative role in sex with other men are not necessarily considered homosexuals. But taking the receptive role is said to make a man into a woman. For two points of departure on this subject, see Kulick 1998 and Parker 1991.

Appendix

"Chemsha Bongo"

Lyrics by Moses E. R. C., Esq.

Chorus

Mwokozi nitoe roho niepuke hili balaa

Maisha nilichezea leo hii nalala njaa

Chemsha Bongo kabla ujapagaa ukashanga

Chemsha Bongo kabla ujashangaa ukaduwaa

Verse 1

Kwa kifupi nimekulia kwenye maisha ya kitajiri

Wazazi wangu walinipenda walinipa lile na hili

Na tangu nikiwa mdogo nilionyesha kwamba

nina akili

Sio siri nilikimbia umande kusoma sikuona dili

Maisha yalikuwa matamu nilisahau yote haramu

Ilitakiwa uwe na hadhi fulani upate japo salamu

Washkaji niliwapita maskani kama vijisanamu

Wazee wenye busara walisema kijana hana nidhamu

Hawakuniumiza kichwa niliamini hawata nilisha

Hawata nivisha

Na hawajui utamu wa maisha

Mimi ndio mimi mwendo mdundo

Wengine niliona uvundo

Niliamini naweza kula muwa pasipo kukuta fundo

Walisema mafumbo

"Think Hard"

Chorus

Savior, I offer my soul, free me from this chaos

If I fool with this life today, I'll go to bed hungry

Think hard before you are trapped, you'll be amazed

Think hard before you are trapped, you'll be astonished

Verse 1

In brief, I was raised with a comfortable life

My parents loved me, gave me this and that

And since I was little, I showed my smarts

It's no secret I ran off early, saw no point in school

Life was sweet, I forgot all that was forbidden

You had to have some respect even to be greeted

I passed by friends' homes like they were pictures

The wise elders said, "That boy has no manners"

They didn't hurt my head, I decided they wouldn't stop me

They won't stunt my growth

And they don't know the sweetness of life

I indeed am the beat of the drum

Others stunk to me

I decided I could eat sugarcane without finding the knot

They spoke in riddles

Fedha kwangu ni kama nyundo

Na kila aliyenighasi sikusita kumjibu utumbo

Nilibadili mikoko mbali mbali ya kifahari

Nilikuwa napanga crate za beer wapambe waoshee gari

Mademu walijigonga mashangingi walinipenda

Nilikuwa na toto mbili kila kiwanja nilichokwenda

Niliitwa Billionaire Bill Gates mzee wa kuku

Wapambe walipembelea wewe mambo iko huku

Na kila aliye nighasi sikusita kumpatia buku

Aliye jifanya kiburi hakutafuna japo ruzuku

Tulikuwa tukihamahama leo Oíbey kesho mikocheni

Nilikuwa nabadilisha bar leo Sleepway kesho kwa macheni

Wazee walinishauri nikasema wanga niacheni

Na kama hamna shughuli kasukumeni mikokoteni

(Chorus)

Verse 2

Kila club niliyoingia wapambe walishangilia

Kwa kuwa walipata hakika kula kiti moto na beer

Mademu walinigombania kila mmoja kunikumbatia

Wengine walikuja kwa nyuma "J tunakuzimia"

Nilikuwa na desturi kila kiwanja nafunga bar

Nilipo sema wote kunyweni bure hakuna aliye shangaa

Siku moja nilikuwa nikiishi na demu mmoja ukipenda Zuwena

Asikwambie mtu jibaba nilikuwa na hela

Niliku nimepark Mercedes Benz Convertible ebo

Ilikuwa nyeusi rim za gold si ya hela kidogo

Wapambe walikuwa wametanda na Range Rover nne nyekundu

Nilikuwa naongea kwa nyodo huku nikicheka kizungu

Nilifanya vurugu za mwaka na ushenzi tulivyotaka

Hadi tunatoa team waungwana walibaki nyaka nyaka

My money was like a hammer

And if anyone bugged me, I'd answer 'em in the guts

I took down the tough guys

I loaded crates of beer while my posse would wash the car

Chicks went crazy for me, fat ladies liked me

I had two young babes wherever I went

I was known as Billionaire Bill Gates, the chicken eater

Crews called for me, "Hey you, here's the party"

And if anyone bugged me, I'd give 'em a buck

Whoever boasted wouldn't be getting fed

We went where we liked, today Oyster Bay, tomorrow Mikocheni

I'd change bars, today the Sleepway, tomorrow Macheni

Elders would advise me, but I said forget that

And if there's nothing to do, go push a cart!

(Chorus)

Verse 2

Every club I went into, the posse had already arrived

'Cause they were sure to get some roast pig and beer

Chicks threw themselves at me, each one trying to grab me

Others came behind, saying, "J, we feel faint"

I had a custom every time I left a bar

When I said, "Everyone, drinks free," no one was surprised

One day I was living with a chick, Zuwena

Don't let 'em say otherwise, this player had cash

I was parking my Mercedes Benz Convertible, yeah

It was black with gold rims and not too cheap

The posse was chillin' in four red Range Rovers

I had a bad attitude, laughing like a white man

I created havoc, and any bullshit we wanted

We took on "gentlemen" and left them as pickpockets

Nilivunja sheria za barabarani na traffic alichekelea

Alijua akizuia msafara boss wake atamfokea; fedha iliongea

Hakuna aliye nisogelea na kila aliye nighasi aliozea segerea

Ila wazazi walinihusia kwamba urithi wangu ni elimu

Niliamini unasoma ili upate fedha

Hivyo sikuona umuhimu kwa kuwa nilikuwa

kiburi ndugu zangu hawakunipenda

Mtukutu jeuri familia yangu ilinitenga

Nilianza kula mtaji nionekane bado natesa

Niliuza gari zangu tatu na nyumba nikabaki na chaser

Maisha yalianza ku-change madeni yakawa mengi

Hivyo kuna wakati nilikimbia na kwenda kujificha zenj

Viwanja nilivyozoea hivi sasa nikawa siendi

Wale mademu na wapambe wote wakaanza kuniona mshenzi

Wote walinikimbia na mbaya zaidi walinicheka walisema

"cheki J arosto amesha zeeka"

Nikaanza kuweka bond mpaka vitu vyangu vya ndani

Niliishi kama digidigi sikuonekana mtaani

Umasikini umepiga hodi kuishi sasa sikutamani

Sijui nilie na nani jamani nipo mashakani

(Chorus)

Verse 3

Ilitokea ajali mbaya wazazi wangu wote wakafa

Nikajua nitarithi mali kutokana na hayo maafa

Nikajipa moyo mimi ni mzuka niliye fufuka

Ingawa nilikuwa na macho kumbe nilikuwa nimepofuka

Vilianza kutokea vizingiti na sielewi vilipo ibuka

I broke the rules of the road, and the traffic cop laughed it off

He knew if he stopped the traffic, the boss would be on him,
Money talks

No one pushed me around, and anyone who bugged me would
rot in Segerea [notorious Dar prison]

But then my folks tried to show me my inheritance is education

I decided that you study in order to get money

So I didn't see the point, 'cause I was prideful, and my brothers
hated me

Me, the big shot, and my family rejected me

Now I start to eat my wealth until I was cryin'

I sold my three cars and was left with just the chaser

Life started to change, my debts grew

So there came a time I had to run and hide in Zenj [Zanzibar]

All the places I went before, I could no longer go

All those chicks and posses started to treat me like a brute [liter-
ally, "pagan"]

They all ran me off and, worse, laughed at me, saying

"Check out J. That loser's already grown old"

I started pawning my stuff, even my furniture

I lived like a groundhog, I didn't show on the streets

Poverty came knocking, I'm living without hope

I don't know who'll feed me, people, I've got troubles

(Chorus)

Verse 3

There was a bad accident, and my parents were killed

I knew I would inherit wealth from this disaster

I took heart, I was the ghost who rose from the dead

Although I had eyes, whoa, I was blinded

They started to break through the floodgates, I don't know
where they popped up

Watoto wa nje na mama wa kambo walipandisha hulka

Wajomba na mashangazi wote wakawa wamecharuka

Akili ilianza kuniruka

Hharufu ya damu ilianza kunuka

Waligombea mali nikaona ni kheri kufa

Matajiri ombeni kwa Mungu kabla ya kuondoka

Binaadamu ni kama maua kwani huchanua na kunyauka

Na fedha ni kama shetani ukiwa nayo huwezi tukuka

Dunia kizingiti yataka mkono wa Mungu kuvuka nenda kwa mapoz

Mwenzio nalia nimesha umbuka

Hapa nilipo nanuka kikwapa siwezi mchafu kunuka

Mwili wangu ni kama kipande cha muhogo jinsi nilivyo pauka

"hutakiwi kucheka" walimwengu kweli najuta

mbele ya Mungu na hii dunia naamini milango itafunguka

Jina la kweli mwana mpotevu nanuka Bible na

Qur-aan vinasema msamehe anayejuta

Wananchi wenye ghadhabu bado wananipeleka puta

Walitaka kunichoma moto walisha niloweka kwenye mafuta

Fanya sala na kutafuta kila saa na kila dakika

Usitake yakukute ndugu yangu yaliyo nikuta.

Stepchildren and stepmothers were claiming high status

Uncles and aunts all started up too

My head started to spin

The stench of blood became rotten

They were fighting over money, I saw it was better to die

Rich people, pray to God before you depart

Man is like a flower, he sprouts and he dies

And money is like a devil, If you have it, you can never be found
worthy

To cross the earthly threshold takes the comforting hand of God

"Friends," I cry, "I've already been undone"

Right here I smell of sweat, I'm entirely spoiled

My body is like a piece of cassava that's been scraped down

You ain't supposed to laugh, people of the world, truly I am
remorseful

In front of God and this world, I believe the doors will open

It's true what they say about the Prodigal Son, the Bible

and Qur-aan say the remorseful are forgiven

Angry citizens still thrash me

They wanted to burn me, they've doused me with oil

Say your prayers and search every hour and every minute

Don't hope to find, my brother, what I found

"Katika viumbe vyote"

Lyrics by Nesto Dogg and Spidah Killa

Chorus

Katika viumbe vyote vilivyo umbwa

Binadamu kaumbika kuliko vyote

Verse La Kwanza (Nesto)

Nasikitika napo kumbuka

Mpaka machozi yananitoka

Kama kuishi tumechoka!

Basi, tuache kuropoka

Tusiwe akili fyatu ka Kaboka

We, binadamu, kweli umeumbika

Lakini wengi hatukumbuki

Ni nani aliyetuumba

Ardhi hata na mbingu

Ni yeye pekee Mungu

Nakulani we Shetani

Nitolee kiwingu nyuma yangu

Napata kizungu zungu

Kwa machungu, na omba dua kwa uchungu

Ee mwenyezi mungu

Nisamehe dhambi zangu

Nije kwako siku kufa kwangu

Lakini pamoja na mola katuumba

Naona norma madume kuwa wachumbe

"In All of God's Creation"

Chorus

> In all of God's creation
>
> Man was created above all others[1]

Verse 1 (Nesto)

> I'm sad when I remember
>
> 'Til tears fall from my eyes
>
> How tired we are of this life!
>
> Okay, enough of this nonsense
>
> Let's not be stupid like Kaboka [a cartoon character]

> People! Really, you *were* created
>
> But too many of us don't remember
>
> Who it was that created us
>
> Along with Earth and Heaven
>
> It is only God himself
>
> Who cursed the Devil
>
> And put darkness behind us
>
> I get so dizzy
>
> From the pain, I pray for a blessing for this pain

> Oh! Almighty God,
>
> Forgive me for my sins
>
> That I may rest in peace the day I die
>
> But even though the Lord created us
>
> I see the disgrace of men lying with men

Mpaka mademu kuwa magumba

Hata kitoto kutoa mimba

Tumechoka kuyumba yumba

Kulogana tu kwa ndumba

Hii safari inatisha

Bora maovu kujakatisha

Nasi tuswali 'swala isha'

Kwani dunia ni nusu kyama

Kutanana kitoto cha mpiga mama

Katafunua mtama

Ni norma hakuna woga wala huruma

Roho mbaya kama Osama

Mpaka mbuzi kupigwa para

Kizee kupigwa ngwara

Ooh! kila kona

Mabalaa yamezagaa

Usionee dagaa

Onea kambale

Ita: Mamental! Eee! *Jibu:* Eee!

Ita: Msujudie mola wako, Eee! *Jibu:* Eee!

Ita: Usamehe dhambi zako! Eee!! *Jibu:* Eee!

Ita: Siku ya kifo kwako, Eee! *Jibu:* Eee!

Ita: Uende pea peponi, Eee! *Jibu:* Eee!

Chorus

Katika viumbe vyote vilivyo umbwa Binadamu kaumbika kuliko vyote

Until chicks are barren
And even little girls have abortions
We are tired of complaining
Bewitching each other like evil sorcerers

This trip is scary
Better give up these evil ways
And say our evening prayers
Cause the end of the world is near
Meeting a kid that beats their mother
Slamming her to the ground
It's a shame! There's no fear or pity
There's evil souls, like Osama
So even goats are screwed for kicks
And old folks are tripped up

Ooh! On every corner
Shattered dreams spread all around
Don't chase after those little kids
Go for someone more mature

Call: Conscious ones! Eee! *Response:* Eee!
Call: Respect your Lord, Eee! *Response:* Eee!
Call: Ask forgiveness for your sins! *Response:* Eee!
Call: On the day you die, you! *Response:* Eee!
Call: You'll get to heaven, Eee! *Response:* Eee!

Versela Pili (Spidah)

Binadamu kiumbuka ulipo toka

Katika viumbe vyote vilivyoumba

Binadamu kaumbika kuliko vyote

Kichwa kufikiria hata na macho kuona

Puwa kunusia, masikio kusikia

Mdomo wa kulia

Mikono kushika

Miguu kutembelea

Tunamasikio lakini hatusikii

Manabi waliusia lakini hakuwafuati

Kufurahia tukazani msikitini

Kuinigia kanisani kuzamia

Nahata mola kumsujudia

Na moyoni tuweke nia

Tuache cheza na vitabu vya dini

Haya yote ni mambo ya dunia yatakwisha

Tufuate na mafundisho ya dini

Tuisome dini ni undani

Spida nazama kunywefani

Sitaki utani

Natoa yote moyoni ili sote twende peponi

Tumfunge kamba shetani tumlani

Awudhu bilah mina shaitwani rajim

Tumfunge kuzimwi kifo kuwe adimu

pamoja na adimu

Ushinde katika jina la Yesu

Verse 2 (Spidah)

People! Remember where you come from

In all of God's creation

Man was created above all others

With a head to think with, and eyes to see

A nose for smelling, ears to hear

Mouth for eating

Hands to grasp

Feet for walking

We have ears, but we don't hear

Prophets guide us, but we don't follow

Be happy to hold to the mosque

To dive into your church

And even to respect the Lord

Let's put his will in our hearts

Let's quit playing with these sacred texts

All of them tell of the end of the world

Let's follow the lessons of religion

And prayer will be our shelter

Spidah, I'm telling you for real

I don't like joking

I'm speaking from my heart, so we can all get to heaven

Tie up the devil and curse him!

Awudhu bilah mina shaitwani rajim[2]

Snuff out death til it's hardly there

You'll succeed in the name of Jesus

Sote ni wamoja hata na dini ndiyo moja

Tunamtegemea mungu mmoja

Lakini wengine watunga hoja

Kupingana ndiyo maana tunagombana

We're all the same, and religion is all one

We all depend on one God

But some are opposed

This conflict is why we fight

Notes

1. This chorus is from a widely known Christian hymn that Chronic Mobb sings to get the crowd into the rhymes.

2. This is a Koranic verse for casting out demons.

References

Addams, Jane

1907   Democracy and Social Ethics. New York: Macmillan.

1972[1909] The Spirit of Youth in the City's Streets. Champaign-Urbana: University of Illinois.

Adler, Felix

1915[1905] Child Labor in the United States and Its Great Attendant Evils. Annals of the American Academy, vol. 25 (May 19). *In* Selected Articles on Child Labor. Edna D. Bullock, comp. Pp. 417–418. Debater's Handbook Series. New York: H. W. Wilson Co.

Ahearn, Laura

2001   Language and Agency. Annual Review of Anthropology 30:109–137.

Amit-Talai, Vered, and Helena Wulff, eds.

1995   Youth Cultures: A Cross-cultural Perspective. London: Routledge.

Amnesty International

1990a   Brazil: Torture and Extrajudicial Execution in Urban Brazil. London: Amnesty International.

1990b   Child Victims of Killing and Cruelty. Focus (September):3–6.

Anagnost, Ann

1997   The Child and National Transcendence in China. *In* Constructing China: The Interaction of Culture and Economics. Kenneth G. Liberthal, Shuen-fu Lin, and Ernest P. Young, eds. Ann Arbor: University of Michigan Center for Chinese Studies Publications.

In press Embodiments of Value in China's Reform. Durham, NC: Duke University Press.

Anderson, Benedict

1972   Java in a Time of Revolution: Occupation and Resistance, 1944–1946. Ithaca, NY: Cornell University Press.

1983   Imagined Communities: Reflections on the Origin and Spread of Nationalism. London: Verso.

Anderson, Marston
1990   The Limits of Realism: Chinese Fiction in the Revolutionary Period.
         Berkeley: University of California Press.

Andersson, Frederick, Harry J. Holzer, and Julia I. Lane
2005   Moving Up or Moving On: Who Advances in the Low-Wage Labor Market?
         New York: Sage.

Appadurai, Arjun
1991   Global Ethnoscapes: Notes and Queries for a Transnational Anthropology.
         In Recapturing Anthropology: Working in the Present. Richard G. Fox, ed.
         Pp. 191–210. School of American Research. Santa Fe, NM: SAR Press.
1996   Modernity at Large: Cultural Dimensions of Globalization. Minneapolis:
         University of Minnesota Press.

Arai, Andrea
2005   The Neo-Liberal Subject of Lack and Potential: Developing "The Frontier
         Within" and Creating a Reserve Army of Labor in 21st Century Japan.
         Rhizomes 10 (Spring). http://www.rhizomes.net/issue10/arai.htm,
         accessed December 2007.

Ariès, Philippe
1962[1960] Centuries of Childhood: A Social History of Family Life. Robert Baldick,
         trans. New York: Vintage Books, Random House.

Armstrong, Edward G.
2004   Eminem's Construction of Authenticity. Popular Music and Society
         27(3):335–355.

Arnett, Jeffrey Jensen
2004   Emerging Adulthood: The Winding Road from the Late Teens through the
         Twenties. New York: Oxford University Press.

Asad, Talal
2000   Agency and Pain: An Exploration. Culture and Religion 1(1):29–60.

Babenco, Hector
1980   Pixote: A lei do mais fraco. Directed by Hector Babenco. Brazil: Unifilm.

Bailey, Paul
1990   Reform the People: Changing Attitudes towards Popular Education in Early
         Twentieth-Century China. Edinburgh: Edinburgh University Press.

Ballinger, Jeff
2006   United Students Against Sweatshops. *In* Youth Activism: An International
         Encyclopedia. Lonnie R. Sherrod, Constance A. Flanagan, Ron Kassimir,
         and Amy K. Syvertsen, eds. Pp. 663–667. Westport, CT: Greenwood
         Publishing Company.

Barber, Karin, ed.
1997   Readings in African Popular Culture. Bloomington: Indiana University Press.

Barlow, Tani
1994   Theorizing Woman: Funu, Guojia, Jiating (Chinese Woman, Chinese State,
         Chinese Family). *In* Body, Subject and Power in China. Angela Zito and

Tani E. Barlow, eds. Pp. 253–289. Durham, NC: Duke University Press.

2001   Spheres of Debt and Feminist Ghosts in Area Studies of Women of China. Traces 1(1):195–226.

Baroin, Catherine

1996   Religious Conflict in 1990–1993 among the Rwa: Secession in a Lutheran Diocese in Northern Tanzania. African Affairs 95(381):529–554.

Barth, Fredrik

1969   Introduction. *In* Ethnic Groups and Boundaries. Fredrik Barth, ed. Pp. 9–38. Boston: Little, Brown.

Barthes, Roland

1972[1957] Mythologies. Annette Lavers, trans. New York: Hill and Wang.

Bayly, C. A.

1986   The Origins of Swadeshi (Home Industry): Cloth and Indian Society, 1700–1930. *In* The Social Life of Things: Commodities in Cultural Perspective. Arjun Appadurai, ed. Pp. 285–321. Cambridge: Cambridge University Press.

Beatty, Barbara

1995   Preschool Education in America: The Culture of Young Children from the Colonial Era to the Present. New Haven, CT: Yale University Press.

Beck, Ulrich

1992   Risk Society: Towards a New Modernity (Risikogesellschaf). London: Sage.

Bennett, W. Lance

1998   The Uncivic Culture: Communication, Identity, and the Rise of Lifestyle Politics. PS: Political Science & Politics 31(4):740–761.

Berg, Ellen

2004   Citizens in the Republic of Childhood: Immigrants and the Free Kindergarten, 1880–1920. Unpublished Ph.D. dissertation, University of California, Berkeley.

Bettie, Julie

2003   Women without Class: Girls, Race, and Identity. Berkeley: University of California Press.

Bing Xin (Xie Wanying)

1949   Ji xiao duzhe [Letters to Young Readers]. Shanghai: Kaiming shudian.
[1923–1926]

Bluestone, Barry, and Stephen Rose

1997   Overworked and Underemployed. American Prospect 31(1):58–69.

Botswana, Republic of

1996   National Youth Policy. Gaborone, Botswana: Department of Culture and Social Welfare, Ministry of Labour and Home Affairs.

Bourdieu, Pierre

1977   Outline of a Theory of Practice. Cambridge: Cambridge University Press.

1984[1979] Distinction: A Social Critique of the Judgment of Taste. Richard Nice, trans. Cambridge, MA: Harvard University Press.

REFERENCES

Bray, Rachel
2003   Predicting the Social Consequences of Orphanhood in South Africa. CSSR Working Paper no. 29. Cape Town: Centre for Social Science Research, University of Cape Town.

Bremner, Robert, John Barnard, Tamara K. Hareven, and Robert M. Mennel
1971   Children and Youth in America: A Documentary History, vol. II, part V. Cambridge, MA: Harvard University Press.

Briggs, Jean
1998   Inuit Morality Play: The Emotional Education of a Three-Year-Old. New Haven, CT: Yale University Press.

Brown, Marilyn
2004   Images of Childhood. *In* Encyclopedia of Children and Childhood in History and Society, vol. 2. Paula S. Fass, ed. Pp. 449–463. New York: Macmillan Reference.

Bucholtz, Mary
2002   Youth and Cultural Practice. Annual Review of Anthropology 31:525–552.

Buckley, Jerome Hamilton
1974   Season of Youth: The Bildungsroman from Dickens to Golding. Cambridge, MA: Harvard University Press.

Buford, Bill
1993   Among the Thugs. London: Vintage.

Burke, Charlanne
2000   They Cut Segametsi into Parts: Ritual Murder, Youth and the Politics of Knowledge in Botswana. Anthropological Quarterly 73(4):204–214.

Burke, Timothy
1996   Lifebuoy Men, Lux Women: Commodification, Consumption, and Cleanliness in Modern Zimbabwe. Durham, NC: Duke University Press.

Butler, Judith
1999   Gender Trouble: Feminism and the Subversion of Identity. New York and London: Routledge.

Camino, Linda A.
2000   Youth–Adult Partnerships: Entering New Territory in Community Work and Research. Applied Developmental Science 4(1):11–20.

Camino, Linda A., and Shepherd Zeldin
2002   Everyday Lives in Communities: Discovering Citizenship through Youth–Adult Partnerships. Applied Developmental Science 6(4):213–220.

Carnavale, Anthony P.
1995   Introduction. *In* Declining Job Security and the Professionalization of Opportunity, by Stephen J. Rose. Research Report 95-04 (May). Washington DC: National Commission for Employment Policy.

Castells, Manuel
1996   The Rise of the Network Society. Oxford: Blackwell Publishers.

Chaplin, Joyce E.
2003   Expansion and Exceptionalism in Early American History. Journal of
            American History 89(4):1431–1455.

Chin, Elizabeth
1999   Ethnically Correct Dolls: Toying with the Race Industry. American
            Anthropologist 101(2):305–321.

Chow, Rey
1995   Primitive Passions: Visuality, Sexuality, Ethnography, and Contemporary
            Chinese Cinema. New York: Columbia University Press.

Chow, Tse-tsung
1967   The May Fourth Movement: Intellectual Revolution in Modern China.
            Cambridge, MA: Harvard University Press.

Christiansen, Catrine, Mats Utas, and Henrik E. Vigh
2006   Navigating Youth, Generating Adulthood: Social Becoming in an African
            Context. Uppsala, Sweden: Nordiska Afrikainstitutet.

Chudacoff, Howard
1989   How Old Are You? Age Consciousness in American Culture. Princeton, NJ:
            Princeton University Press.

Cleves, Rachel Hope
2005   Mortal Eloquence: Violence, Slavery, and Anti-Jacobinism in the Early
            American Republic. Unpublished Ph.D. dissertation, University of California,
            Berkeley.

Clough, Patricia Ticineto, with Jean O'Malley Halley
2007   The Affective Turn: Theorizing the Social. Durham, NC: Duke University
            Press.

Cohn, Bernard
1989   Cloth, Clothes, Colonialism: India in the Nineteenth Century. *In* Cloth and
            Human Experience. Annette Weiner and Jane Schneider, eds. Pp. 304–345.
            Washington DC: Smithsonian Institution Press.

Cole, Jennifer
2001   Forget Colonialism? Sacrifice and the Art of Memory in Madagascar.
            Berkeley: University of California Press.

2004   Fresh Contact in Tamatave, Madagascar: Sex, Money and Intergenerational
            Transformation. American Ethnologist 31(4):573–588.

2005   The Jaombilo of Tamatave (Madagascar), 1992–2004: Reflections on Youth
            and Globalization. Journal of Social History 38(4):891–914.

Cole, Jennifer, and Deborah Durham
2007   Introduction: Age, Regeneration and the Intimate Politics of Globalization.
            In Generations and Globalization: Youth, Age and Family in the New World
            Economy. Jennifer Cole and Deborah Durham, eds. Pp. 1–28. Bloomington:
            Indiana University Press.

Collins, Jane
2000   Tracing Social Relations in Commodity Chains: The Case of Grapes in
            Brazil. *In* Commodities and Globalization: Anthropological Perspectives.
            Angelique Haugerud, M. Priscilla Stone, and Peter D. Little, eds. Pp.
            97–109. New York: Rowman & Littlefield.

Comaroff, Jean, and John L. Comaroff
1999   Occult Economies and the Violence of Abstraction: Notes from the South
            African Postcolony. American Ethnologist 26(2):279–303.
2000a   Millennial Capitalism: First Thoughts on a Second Coming. Public Culture
            12(2):291–343.

Comaroff, Jean, and John L. Comaroff, eds.
2001   Millennial Capitalism and the Culture of Neoliberalism. Durham, NC: Duke
            University Press.

Comaroff, John L., and Jean Comaroff
1993   Modernity and Its Malcontents: Ritual and Power in Postcolonial Africa.
            Chicago: University of Chicago Press.
1997   Of Revelation and Revolution, vol. 2: The Dialectics of Modernity on a
            South African Frontier. Chicago: University of Chicago Press.
2000b   Millennial Capitalism: First Thoughts on a Second Coming. *In* Millennial
            Capitalism and the Culture of Neoliberalism. Jean Comaroff and John L.
            Comaroff, eds. Pp. 1–56. Durham, NC: Duke University Press.

Connell, Patricia
1997   Understanding Victimization and Agency: Considerations of Race, Class and
            Gender. PoLAR 20(2):115–143.

Constantino, Roselyn
2006   Zapatista Rebellion. *In* Youth Activism: An International Encyclopedia.
            Lonnie R. Sherrod, Constance A. Flanagan, Ron Kassimir, and Amy K.
            Syvertsen, eds. Pp. 704–710. Westport, CT: Greenwood Publishing Company.

Cook, Dan
2004   The Commodification of Childhood. Durham, NC: Duke University Press.

Cooper, Frederick
2001   What Is the Concept of Globalization Good For? An African Historian's
            Perspective. African Affairs 100(399):189–213.

Côté, James E.
2000   Arrested Adulthood: The Changing Nature of Maturity and Identity. New
            York: New York University Press.

Côté, James E., and Charles G. Levine
2002   Identity Formation, Agency, and Culture: A Social Psychological Synthesis.
            Mahwah, NJ: Lawrence Erlbaum.

Covell, Maureen
1987   Madagascar: Politics, Economics, and Society. New York: Frances Pinter.

Crapanzano, Vincent
1985   Waiting: The Whites of South Africa. New York: Random House.

2003   Reflections on Hope as a Category of Social and Psychological Analysis.
            Cultural Anthropology 18(1):3–32.

Crocker, Jennifer, Brenda Major, and Claude Steele
1998   Social Stigma. *In* The Handbook of Social Psychology, vol. 2. 4th edition.
            Daniel T. Gilbert, Susan T. Fiske, and Gardner Lindzey, eds. Pp. 504–553.
            New York: McGraw Hill.

Crosby, Danielle A., and Rashmita S. Mistry
2004   Children's Perceptions of Wealth and Poverty: Do Child, Family, and School
            Characteristics Relate to Their Experiences in Socioeconomic
            Environments? Poster presented at the Biennial Meeting of the
            International Society for the Study of Behavioral Development, Ghent,
            Belgium, July 11–14.

Cross, Gary
2000   An All-Consuming Century: Why Commercialism Won in Modern America.
            New York: Columbia University Press.
2004   The Cute and the Cool. New York: Scribner.

Cunningham, Hugh
1995   Children and Childhood in Western Society since 1500. London: Longman.
1998   Histories of Childhood. American Historical Review 103(4):1195–1208.

Dalbert, Claudia
2001   The Justice Motive as a Personal Resource: Dealing with Challenges and
            Critical Life Events. New York: Plenum Press.

Danziger, Sheldon H., and Peter T. Gottschalk
2005   Diverging Fortunes: Trends in Poverty and Inequality. *In* The American
            People: Census 2000 Series. Reynolds Farley and John Haaga, eds. Pp.
            48–79. New York: Russell Sage Foundation and Population Reference
            Bureau.

Davies, Bronwyn
1991   The Concept of Agency: A Feminist Poststructuralist Analysis. Social Analysis
            30:42–53.

Davies, David J.
2002   Remembering Red: Memory and Nostalgia for the Cultural Revolution in
            Late 1990s China. Unpublished Ph.D. dissertation, University of Washington.

de Bary, Brett
1993   Introduction. *In* Origins of Modern Japanese Literature, by Kojin Karatani.
            Durham, NC: Duke University Press.

De Coninck-Smith, Ning, Bengt Sandin, and Ellen Schrumpf, eds.
1997   Industrious Children: Work and Childhood in the Nordic Countries,
            1850–1990. Odense, Denmark: Odense University Press.

de Tocqueville, Alexis
1990 [1832] Democracy in America, Henry Reeve Text. Phillips Bradley, ed. New York:
            Vintage Books.

Deaux, Kay
2006   To Be an Immigrant. New York: Sage.

Denbow, James, and Phenyo C. Thebe
2006   Culture and Customs of Botswana. Westport, CT: Greenwood Press.

Dinwoodie, David
1998   Authorizing Voices: Going Public in an Indigenous Language. Cultural
            Anthropology 13(2):193–223.

Donzelot, Jacques
1997[1979] The Policing of Families. Baltimore, MD: Johns Hopkins University Press.

Dryfoos, Joy G.
1990   Adolescents at Risk: Prevalence and Prevention. New York: Oxford
            University Press.

Duara, Prasenjit
1995   Rescuing History from the Nation: Questioning the Narratives of Modern
            China. Chicago: University of Chicago Press.

Dublin, Thomas
1979   Women and Work: The Transformation of Work and Community in Lowell,
            Massachusetts, 1826–1860. New York: Columbia University Press.

Durham, Deborah
1999   Civil Lives: Leadership and Accomplishment in Botswana. *In* Civil Society
            and the Political Imagination in Africa. John L. and Jean Comaroff, eds.
            Pp. 192–218. Chicago: University of Chicago Press.

2002a   Love and Jealousy in the Space of Death. Ethnos 67(2):155–180.

2002b   Uncertain Citizens: The New Intercalary Subject in Postcolonial Botswana.
            In Postcolonial Subjectivities in Africa. Richard Werbner, ed. Pp. 139–170.
            London: Zed Books.

2003   Passports and Persons: The Insurrection of Subjugated Knowledges in
            Southern Africa. *In* The Culture of Power in Southern Africa: Essays on
            State Formation and the Political Imagination. Clifton Crais, ed. Pp.
            151–181. Portsmouth, NH: Heinemann.

2004   Disappearing Youth: Youth as a Social Shifter in Botswana. American
            Ethnologist 31(4):589–605.

2005   "Did You Bathe This Morning?": Baths and Morality in Botswana. *In* Dirt,
            Undress and Difference: Critical Perspectives on the Body's Surface.
            Adeline Masquelier, ed. Pp. 190–212. Bloomington: Indiana University
            Press.

2007   Making Youth Citizens: Empowerment Programs and Youth Agency in
            Botswana. *In* Generations and Globalization: Family, Youth and Age in the
            New World Economy. Jennifer Cole and Deborah Durham, eds. Pp.
            102–131. Bloomington: Indiana University Press.

N.d.   An Anthropology of Disgust. Unpublished manuscript.

Durham, Deborah, and Frederick Klaits
2002   Funerals and the Public Space of Mutuality in Botswana. Journal of
            Southern African Studies 28(4):777–795.

Edge, W. A., and M. H. Lekorwe, eds.
1998   Botswana: Politics and Society. Pretoria, South Africa: J. L. Van Shaik.

Ehrenreich, Barbara
2005   Bait and Switch: The (Futile) Pursuit of the American Dream. New York:
            Holt and Company.

Ehrenreich, Barbara, and Arlie Russell Hochschild, eds.
2003   Global Woman: Nannies, Maids, and Sex Workers in the New Economy. New
            York: Metropolitan Books.

Eisenstadt, Shmuel Noah
1956   From Generation to Generation: Age Groups and Social Structure. Glencoe,
            IL: Free Press.

Ellis, William
1867   Madagascar Revisited. London: John Murray.

Eltis, David
2002   Free and Coerced Migrations from the Old World to the New. *In* Coerced
            and Free Migration: Global Perspectives. David Eltis, ed. Pp. 33–74.
            Stanford, CA: Stanford University Press.

Erikson, Erik
1950   Childhood and Society. New York: W. W. Norton.
1963   Childhood and Society. 2nd edition. New York: W. W. Norton.
1965   Youth: Fidelity and Diversity. *In* The Challenge of Youth. Erik Erikson, ed.
            Pp. 1–23. Garden City, NY: Anchor Books.
1968   Identity, Youth and Crisis. New York: Norton.

Ewing, Katherine
2006   Between Cinema and Social Work: Diasporic Turkish Women and the
            (Dis)Pleasures of Hybridity. Cultural Anthropology 21(2):265–294.

Fabian, Johannes
1983   Time and the Other: How Anthropology Makes Its Object. New York:
            Columbia University Press.

Farquhar, Judith
2002   Appetites: Food and Sex in Post-Socialist China. Durham, NC: Duke
            University Press.

Farquhar, Mary Ann
1999   Children's Literature in China: From Lu Xun to Mao Zedong. Armonk, NY:
            M. E. Sharpe.

Fass, Paula S.
1977   The Damned and the Beautiful: American Youth in the 1920s. New York:
            Oxford University Press.
1989   Outside In: Minorities and the Transformation of American Education. New
            York: Oxford University Press.
1997   Kidnapped: Child Abduction in America. New York: Oxford University Press.

2003   Childhood and Globalization. Journal of Social History 36(4):963–977.
2007   Children of a New World: Society, Culture, and Globalization. New York:
            New York University Press.

Fass, Paula S., ed.
2004   Encyclopedia of Children and Childhood in History and Society. New York:
            Macmillan Reference.

Fass, Paula S., and Mary Ann Mason, eds.
2000   Childhood in America. New York: New York University Press.

Fee, Sarah
1997   Binding Ties, Visible Women: Cloth and Social Reproduction in Androy
            (Madagascar). Etudes Ocean Indien 23–24:253–280.
2002   Cloth in Motion. In Objects and Envoys: Cloth, Imagery and Diplomacy in
            Madagascar. Christine Mullen Kreamer and Sarah Fee, eds. Pp. 33–95.
            Seattle, WA, and London: Smithsonian Institution National Museum of
            African Art, Washington DC, in association with University of Washington
            Press.

Feeley-Harnik, Gillian
1989   Cloth and the Creation of Ancestors in Madagascar. In Cloth and Human
            Experience. Annette Weiner and Jane Schneider, eds. Pp. 75–116.
            Washington DC: Smithsonian Institution Press.
2003   Number One-Nambawani-Lambaoany: Clothing as an Historical Medium of
            Exchange in Northwestern Madagascar. In Lova/Inheritance: Past and
            Present in Madagascar. Zoe Crossland, Genese Sodikoff, and Will Griffin,
            eds. Pp. 63–103. Michigan Discussions in Anthropology 14. Ann Arbor:
            Department of Anthropology, University of Michigan.

Ferguson, James
2006   Global Shadows: Africa in the Neoliberal World Order. Durham, NC: Duke
            University Press.

Field, Norma
1995   The Child as Laborer and Consumer: The Disappearance of Childhood in
            Contemporary Japan. In Children and the Politics of Culture. Sharon
            Stephens, ed. Pp. 51–78. Princeton, NJ: Princeton University Press.

Fieser, James, and Bradley Harris Dowden
2006   Social Contract Theory. The Internet Encyclopedia of Philosophy.
            http://www.iep.utm.edu/s/soc-cont.htm, accessed June 2006.

Flanagan, Constance A.
1990   Change in Family Work Status: Effects on Parent–Adolescent Decision
            Making. Child Development 61(1):163–177.

**Flanagan, Constance A., and Bernadette Campbell, with Luba Botcheva, Jennifer
Bowes, Beno Csapo, Petr Macek, and Elena Sheblanova**
2003   Social Class and Adolescents' Beliefs about Justice in Different Social
            Orders. Journal of Social Issues 59(4):711–732.

Flanagan, Constance A., and J. S. Eccles
1993   Changes in Parental Work Status and Adolescents' Adjustment at School.
            Child Development 64(1):246–257.

Flanagan, Constance, Leslie S. Gallay, Sukhdeep Gill, Erin E. Gallay, and Naana Nti
2005   What Does Democracy Mean? Correlates of Adolescents' Views. Journal of
            Adolescent Research 20(2):193–218.

Flanagan, Constance, Patreese Ingram, Erika M. Gallay, and Erin E. Gallay
1997   Why Are People Poor? Social Conditions and Adolescents' Interpretation of
            the "Social Contract." *In* Social and Emotional Adjustment and Family
            Relations in Ethnic Minority Families. Ronald D. Taylor and Margaret C.
            Wang, eds. Pp. 53–62. Mahwah, NJ: Erlbaum.

Flanagan, Constance A., and Corinna J. Tucker
1999   Adolescents' Explanations for Political Issues: Concordance with Their Views
            of Self and Society. Developmental Psychology 35(5):1198–1209.

Fliegelman, Jay
1982   Prodigals and Pilgrims: The American Revolution against Patriarchal
            Authority, 1750–1800. Cambridge: Cambridge University Press.

Foner, Eric
1970   Free Soil, Free Labor, Free Men: The Ideology of the Republic Party before
            the Civil War. New York: Oxford University Press.

Fong, Vanessa
2007   Parent–Child Communication Problems and the Perceived Inadequacies of
            Chinese Only Children. Ethos 35(1):85–127.

Forman, Murray
2002   The 'Hood Comes First: Race, Space, and Place in Rap and Hip-Hop.
            Middletown, CT: Wesleyan University Press.

Forman, Murray, and Mark Anthony Neal
2004   That's the Joint! The Hip-Hop Studies Reader. New York: Routledge.

Fortes, Meyer
1984   Age, Generation, and Social Structure. *In* Age and Anthropological Theory.
            David I. Kertzer and Jennie Keith, eds. Pp. 99-122. Ithaca, NY: Cornell
            University Press.

Foucault, Michel
1979   Discipline and Punish: The Birth of the Prison. New York: Vintage Books.

Frank, Katherine
2006   Agency. Anthropological Theory 6(3):281–302.

Friedman, Jonathan
2000   Globalization, Class and Culture in Global Systems. Journal of World-Systems
            Research VI(3):636–656.

Fugelsang, Minou
1994   Veils and Videos: Female Youth Culture on the Kenya Coast. Stockholm:
            Coronet Books.

Fussell, Elizabeth, and Frank F. Furstenberg Jr.

2005   The Transition to Adulthood during the Twentieth Century: Race, Nativity, and Gender. *In* On the Frontier of Adulthood: Theory, Research, and Public Policy. Richard A. Settersten Jr., Frank F. Furstenberg Jr., and Rubén G. Rumbaut, eds. Pp. 29–59. Chicago: University of Chicago Press.

Galston, William A.

2001   Political Knowledge, Political Engagement, and Civic Education. Annual Review of Political Science 4:217–234.

Gammon, Robert, and Michele R. Marcucci

2002   Census: Racial Income Disparities Abound. Oakland Tribune, August 27: 1, 7.

Geschiere, Peter

1997   The Modernity of Witchcraft: Politics and the Occult in Postcolonial Africa. Charlottesville: University of Virginia Press.

Geschiere, Peter, and Frances Nyamnjoh

2000   Capitalism and Autochthony: The See-Saw of Mobility and Belonging. Public Culture 12(2):432–452.

Geurts, Kathryn Linn

2002   Culture and the Senses: Bodily Ways of Knowing in an African Community. Berkeley: University of California Press.

Giddens, Anthony

1990   The Consequences of Modernity. Stanford, CA: Stanford University Press.

2000   Runaway World: How Globalization Is Reshaping Our Lives. New York: Routledge.

Gillis, John R.

1996   A World of Their Own Making: Myth, Ritual, and the Quest for Family Values. New York: Basic Books.

Gilroy, Paul

1994   After the Love Has Gone: Bio-Politics and Ethno-Poetics in the Black Public Sphere. Public Culture 7(1):49–76.

Giroux, Henry A.

2003   The Abandoned Generation: Democracy beyond the Culture of Fear. New York: Palgrave.

Glickman, Lawrence B.

1997   A Living Wage: American Workers and the Making of Consumer Society. Ithaca, NY: Cornell University Press.

Goldscheider, Frances K., and Calvin Goldscheider

1999   The Changing Transition to Adulthood: Leaving and Returning Home. Thousand Oaks, CA: Sage Publications.

Good, Kenneth

1993   At the Ends of the Ladder: Radical Inequalities in Botswana. Journal of Modern African Studies 31(2):203–230.

1996   Towards Popular Participation in Botswana. Journal of Modern African Studies 34(1):53–77.

Gordon, Linda
1988   Heroes of Their Own Lives: The Politics and History of Family Violence, Boston, 1880–1960. New York: Penguin.
1996   Welfare Myths and Women's Lives—How We Got "Welfare": A History of the Mistakes of the Past. Social Justice 21(1):13–16.
1999   The Great Arizona Orphan Abduction. Cambridge, MA: Harvard University Press.

Green, Rebecca L.
2003   Lamba Hoany: Proverb Clothes from Madagascar. African Arts XXXVI(2):30–43.

Greven, Philip J.
1977   The Protestant Temperament: Patterns of Child-Rearing, Religious Experience, and the Self in Early America. New York: Alfred A. Knopf.

Grossberg, Lawrence
2005   Caught in the Crossfire: Kids, Politics, and America's Future. Boulder, CO, and London: Paradigm Publishers.

Gulbrandsen, Ornulf
2002   The Discourse of "Ritual Murder": Popular Reaction to Political Leaders in Botswana. In Beyond Rationalism: Rethinking Magic, Witchcraft, and Sorcery. Bruce Kapferer, ed. Pp. 215–233. New York: Berghahn Books.

Guy, Donna J.
1998   The Pan American Child Congresses, 1916–1942: Pan Americanism, Child Reform, and the Welfare State in Latin America. Journal of Family History 23(3):272–291.

Hacker, Jacob S.
2006   The Great Risk Shift: The Assault on American Jobs, Families, Health Care, and Retirement and How You Can Fight Back. New York: Oxford University Press.

Hakuhōdō Seikatsu Sōgō Kenkyūjo
1997   Kodomo no Seikatsu [The Lifestyle of Youth]. September 9, no. 260. Tokyo: Hakuhōdō Seikatsu Sōgō Kenkyūjo.
2004   Kodomo no Seikatsu. May 11, no. 397. Tokyo: Hakuhōdō Seikatsu Sōgō Kenkyūjo.

Halberstam, David
1998   The Children. New York: The Ballantine Publishing Group.

Halbfinger, David M.
1999   Suit Claims Pokémon Is Lottery, Not Just a Fad. New York Times, September 24: 5.

Hall, G. Stanley
1904   Adolescence: Its Psychology and Its Relationship to Physiology, Anthropology, Sociology, Sex, Crime, Religion, and Education, 2 vols. New York: D. Appleton.

REFERENCES

Hall, Jacqueline Dowd, James Leloudis, Robert Korstad, and Mary Murphy
1987   Like a Family: The Making of a Southern Cotton Mill World. Chapel Hill:
            University of North Carolina Press.

Hall, Stuart, and Tony Jefferson, eds.
1976   Resistance through Rituals: Youth Subcultures in Post-War Britain. London:
            HarperCollins Academic.
1991[1976] Resistance through Rituals: Youth Subcultures in Post-war Britain. London:
            Routledge.

Hanawalt, Barbara A.
1993   Growing Up in Medieval London: The Experience of Childhood in History.
            New York: Oxford University Press.

Hansen, Karen Tranberg
2005   Getting Stuck in the Compound: Some Odds against Social Adulthood in
            Lusaka, Zambia. Africa Today 51(4):3–16.

Hanson, Hal E.
1997   Caps and Gowns: Historical Reflections on the Institutions That Shaped
            Learning for and at Work in Germany and the United States, 1800–1945.
            Unpublished Ph.D. dissertation, University of Wisconsin.

Hardt, Michael, and Antonio Negri
2000   Empire. Cambridge, MA: Harvard University Press.

Hareven, Tamara K.
1995   Changing Images of Aging and the Social Construction of the Life Course.
            In Images of Aging: Cultural Representations of Later Life. Michael
            Featherstone and Andrew Wernick, eds. Pp. 119–134. London: Routledge.

Harvard Civil Rights Project
2005   http://www.civilrightsproject.harvard.edu, accessed July 2005.

Harvey, David
1989   The Condition of Postmodernity: An Enquiry into the Origins of Cultural
            Change. Oxford: Blackwell.

Hatakeyama Kenji and Kubo Masakazu
2000   Pokémon Suto-ri [Pokémon Story]. Tokyo: Nikei BP Shuppan Centā.

Healy, Melissa
1999   Pokémon Frenzy Disrupting US Schools. Daily Yomiuri, October 21: 27.

Hebdige, Dick
1979   Subculture: The Meaning of Style. London: Methuen.

Hecht, Tobias
1998   At Home in the Street: Street Children of Northeast Brazil. New York and
            Cambridge: Cambridge University Press.

Hecht, Tobais, ed.
2002   Minor Omissions: Children in Latin American History and Society.
            Madison: University of Wisconsin Press.

Hendrick, Harry
1997   Children, Childhood and English Society, 1880–1990. Cambridge: Cambridge University Press.

Herdt, Gilbert, and Stephen C. Leavitt, eds.
1998   Adolescence in Pacific Island Societies. Pittsburgh, PA: Pittsburgh University Press.

Herzfeld, Michael
1997   Portrait of a Greek Imagination: An Ethnographic Biography of Andreas Nenedakis. Chicago: University of Chicago Press.

Higham, John
1955   Strangers in the Land: Patterns of American Nativism. New York: Athenaeum.

Higonnet, Anne
1998   Pictures of Innocence: The History and Crisis of Ideal Childhood. London: Thames and Hudson.

Hiratsuka Akihito
1997   Tajiri Satoshi. Antore (July):168–171.

Hirson, Baruch
1979   Year of Fire, Year of Ash: The Soweto Revolt: Roots of a Revolution? London: Zed Books.

Hochschild, Jennifer
1995   Facing Up to the American Dream: Race, Class, and the Soul of the Nation. Princeton, NJ: Princeton University Press.

Hofstadter, Richard
1971   America at 1750: A Social Portrait. New York: Alfred A. Knopf.

Hoogvelt, Ankie
1997   Globalization and the Postcolonial World: The New Political Economy of Development. Baltimore, MD: Johns Hopkins University Press.

Hope, Ronald Kempe, Sr.
1996   Growth, Unemployment and Poverty in Botswana. Journal of Contemporary African Studies 14(1):53–67.

Hori Takahiro
1996   Nihon no omocha, anime wa kore de iinoka? [Are Japan's Toys and Animation a Good Thing?]. Tokyo: Chirekisha.

HoSang, Dan
2001   Youth Community Organizing Today. Occasional Papers Series on Youth Organizing 2. www.fcyo.org, accessed April 2007.

Hulbert, Anne
2003   Raising America: Experts, Parents, and a Century of Advice about Children. New York: Alfred A. Knopf.

REFERENCES

Human Rights Watch
1994   Final Justice: Police and Death Squad Homicides of Adolescents in Brazil.
            New York: Human Rights Watch/Americas.

Hung, Chang-tai
1985   Going to the People: Chinese Intellectuals and Folk Literature, 1918–1937.
            Cambridge, MA: Harvard University Press.

Hunter, Mark
2002   The Materiality of Everyday Sex: Thinking beyond Prostitution. African
            Studies 61(1):99–120.

Imig, Doug, and Sidney Tarrow
2000   Contentious Europeans: Protest and Politics in an Integrating Europe.
            Lanham, MD: Rowman & Littlefield.

Ivy, Marilyn
1995   Discourses of the Vanishing: Modernity, Phantasm, Japan. Chicago and
            London: University of Chicago Press.

Jackson, Stevi, and Sue Scott
1999   Risk Anxiety and the Social Construction of Childhood. In Risk and
            Sociocultural Theory: New Directions and Perspectives. Deborah Lupton,
            ed. Pp. 36–107. Cambridge: Cambridge University Press.

Jacobson, Lisa
2005   Raising Consumers: Children and the American Mass Market in the Early
            Twentieth Century. New York: Columbia University Press.

Jameson, Fredric
1993   Foreword. In Origins of Modern Japanese Literature, by Kojin Karatani.
            Durham, NC: Duke University Press.

Jefferson, Elana Ashanti, and Barbara Hey
2003   45 Is the New 30; Fortysomethings Are the New Babes. Miami Herald, July
            15. http://www.miami.com/mld/miamiherald/living/6302919.htm,
            accessed July 2003.

Jin Yiming
2000   Zhongguo shehui zhuyi jiaoyu de guiji [The Path of China's Socialist
            Education]. Shanghai: Huadong Normal University Press.

Jing, Jun
2000   Introduction: Food, Children, and Social Change in Contemporary China.
            In Feeding China's Little Emperors: Food, Children, and Social Change.
            Jun Jing, ed. Pp. 1–26. Palo Alto, CA: Stanford University Press.

Johnson, Walter
2003   On Agency. Journal of Social History 37(1):113–124.

Johnson-Hanks, Jennifer
2002   On the Limits of Life Stages in Ethnography: Toward a Vital Theory of
            Conjunctures. American Anthropologist 104(3):865–880.

Jones, Andrew
2002 The Child as History in Republican China: A Discourse on Development. Positions: East Asia Cultures Critique 10(3):695–728.

Jones, Jacqueline
1992 The Dispossessed: America's Underclasses from the Civil War to the Present. New York: Basic Books.

Jost, John T., Mazharan R. Banaji, and Brian A. Nosek
2004 A Decade of System Justification Theory: Accumulated Evidence of Conscious and Unconscious Bolstering of the Status Quo. Political Psychology 25(6):881–919.

Jost, John T., and Orsolya Hunyady
2005 Antecedents and Consequences of System-Justifying Ideologies. Current Directions in Psychological Science 14(5):260–265.

Juris, Jeffrey S.
2006 Global Justice Activism. *In* Youth Activism: An International Encyclopedia. Lonnie R. Sherrod, Constance A. Flanagan, Ron Kassimir, and Amy K. Syvertsen, eds. Pp. 289–295. Westport, CT: Greenwood Publishing Company.

Kaestle, Carl F.
1983 Pillars of the Republic: Common Schools and American Society, 1780–1860. New York: Hill and Wang.

Karatani, Kojin
1993 Origins of Modern Japanese Literature. Durham, NC: Duke University Press.

Katz, Cindi
2004 Growing Up Global: Economic Restructuring and Children's Everyday Lives. Minneapolis: University of Minnesota Press.

Katz, Michael. B.
1987 Reconstructing American Education. Cambridge, MA: Harvard University Press.

Keay, Douglas
1987 Aids, Education and the Year 2000! Woman's Own, September 23: 8–10.

Keeter, Scott, Cliff Zukin, Molly Andolina, and Krista Jenkins
2003 The Civic and Political Health of the Nation: A Generational Portrait. College Park, MD: CIRCLE (The Center for Information and Research on Civic Learning and Engagement) Report: How Young People Express Their Political Views. http://www.civicyouth.org, accessed April 2007.

Kelsall, Tim
N.d. Subjectivity, Collective Action and the Governance Agenda in Arumeru East. QEH Working Paper Series no. 42.

Kerber, Linda K.
1980 Women of the Republic: Intellect and Ideology in Revolutionary America. Chapel Hill: University of North Carolina Press.

Kerckhoff, Alan C.
1993 Diverging Pathways: Social Structure and Career Deflections. New York: Cambridge University Press.

Kett, Joseph
1977 Rites of Passage: Adolescence in America, 1790 to the Present. New York: Basic Books.

Kincaid, James
1998 Erotic Innocence: The Culture of Child Molesting. Raleigh, NC: Duke University Press.

Kirshner, Benjamin
In press Power in Numbers: Youth Organizing as a Context for Exploring Civic Identity. Journal of Research on Adolescence.

Klaits, Frederick
2005 The Widow in Blue: Blood and the Morality of Remembering in Botswana's Time of AIDS. Africa 75(1):46–63.
N.d. Death in a Church of Life: Moral Passion during Botswana's Time of AIDS. Unpublished MS, Duke University.

Koselleck, Reinhart
1985 Futures Past: On the Semantics of Historical Time. Keith Tribe, trans. Cambridge, MA: MIT Press.

Krims, Adam
2000 Rap Music and the Poetics of Identity. New York: Cambridge University Press.

Krugman, Paul
2005 The Big Squeeze. New York Times, October 17: A23.

Kubo Masakazu
1999 Sekai o haikai suru wasei monustā Pikachu [Pikachu, a Japanese Monster That Is Wandering the World]. Special issue, Bungei Shunjū 21:340–349.

Kulick, Don
1998 Travesti: Sex, Gender, and Culture among Brazilian Transgendered Prostitutes. Chicago: University of Chicago Press.

Lamb, Sarah
2007 Aging across Worlds: Modern Seniors in an Indian Diaspora. *In* Generations and Globalization: Youth, Age and Family in the New World Economy. Jennifer Cole and Deborah Durham, eds. Pp. 132–163. Bloomington: Indiana University Press.

Lambek, Michael, and Jacqueline Solway
2001 Just Anger: Scenarios of Indignation in Botswana and Madagascar. Ethnos 66(1):49–72.

Lareau, Annette
2003 Unequal Childhoods. Berkeley: University of California Press.

Larkin, Brian
1997   Indian Films and Nigerian Lovers: Media and the Creation of Parallel Modernities. Africa 67(3):406–440.

Larson, Reed, and David Hanson
2005   The Development of Strategic Thinking: Learning to Impact Human Systems in a Youth Activism Program. Human Development 48(6):327–349.

Lassonde, Stephen
1996   Learning and Earning: Schooling, Juvenile Employment, and the Early Life Course in Late Nineteenth Century New Haven. Journal of Social History 29(4):839–870.

1998   Should I Go, or Should I Stay? Adolescence, School Attainment, and Parent–Child Relations in Italian Families of New Haven. History of Education Quarterly 38(1):37–60.

2005   Learning to Forget: Schooling and Family Life in New Haven's Working Class, 1870–1940. New Haven, CT: Yale University Press.

Lave, Jean, Paul Duguid, Nadine Fernandez, and Erik Axel
1992   Coming of Age in Birmingham: Cultural Studies and Conceptions of Subjectivity. Annual Review of Anthropology 21:257–282.

Leahy, Robert
1983   Development of the Conception of Economic Inequality, vol. II: Explanations, Justifications, and Concepts of Social Mobility and Change. Developmental Psychology 19(1):111–125.

Ledoux, Marc Andre
1951   La jeunesse malgache. Cahiers Charles de Foucauld, numero special sur Madagascar, 1ere trimestre.

Levi, Giovanni, and Jean-Claude Schmitt, eds.
1997   A History of Young People in the West. Volumes 1 and 2. Cambridge, MA: Harvard University Press.

Levine, David
2004   Economics and Children in Western Societies: From Agriculture to Industry. In The Encyclopedia of Children and Childhood in History and Society, vol. 1. Paula S. Fass, ed. Pp. 295–299. New York: Macmillan Reference.

Levine, Robert
1997   Fiction and Reality in Brazilian Life: *Pixote. In* Based on a True Story: Latin American History at the Movies. Donald F. Stevens, ed. Pp. 203–216. Wilmingham, DE: SR Books.

Levy, Sheri R., Chi-yue Chiu, and Ying-yi Hong
2006   Lay Theories and Intergroup Relations. Group Processes and Intergroup Relations 9(1):5–24.

Lewellen, Ted C.
2002   The Anthropology of Globalization: Cultural Anthropology Enters the 21st Century. Westport, CT: Bergin and Garvey.

REFERENCES

Lewis, Amanda
2003   Race in the Schoolyard. New Brunswick, NJ: Rutgers University Press.

Lewis, Oscar
1961   The Children of Sánchez. London: Secker and Warburg.

**Lewis-Charp, Heather, Hanh Cao Yu, Sengsouvanh Soukamneuth,
and Johanna Lacoe**
2003   Extending the Reach of Youth Development through Civic Activism:
              Outcomes of the Youth Leadership Development Initiative. Social Policy
              Research Associates.

Liechty, Mark
2003   Suitably Modern: Making Middle-Class Culture in a New Consumer Society.
              Princeton, NJ: Princeton University Press.

Lin Ge
1999   Huangjin jiaojiao [Golden Guide to Family Education]. Beijing: Economic
              Daily Press.

Lindenmeyer, Kriste
1997   "A Right to Childhood": The U.S. Children's Bureau and Child Welfare,
              1912–1946. Champaign-Urbana: University of Illinois Press.

Liu, Lydia
1993   Translingual Practice: The Discourse of Individualism between China and
              the West. Positions: East Asia Cultures Critique 1(1):160–193.

Livingston, Julie
2005   Debility and the Moral Imagination in Botswana. Bloomington: Indiana
              University Press.

Lock, Margaret
1988   A Nation at Risk: Interpretations of School Refusal in Japan. *In* Biomedicine
              Examined. Margaret Lock and Deborah Gordon, eds. Pp. 377–414.
              Dordrecht: Kluwer Academic Publishers.
1991   Flawed Jewels and National Dis/Order: Narratives on Adolescent Dissent in
              Japan. Theme issue, "Japan: The Culture of Economics and the Economy of
              Culture," Journal of Psychohistory 18(4):507–531.

London, Jonathan
2006   Youth-Led Research, Evaluation, and Planning. *In* Youth Activism: An
              International Encyclopedia. Lonnie R. Sherrod, Constance A. Flanagan,
              Ron Kassimir, and Amy K. Syvertsen, eds. Pp. 698–703. Westport, CT:
              Greenwood Publishing Company.

Lummis, C. Douglas
1996   The Democratic Virtues. *In* Radical Democracy. C. Douglas Lummis, ed. Pp.
              143–157. Ithaca, NY: Cornell University Press.

Lutz, Catherine
1988   Unnatural Emotions: Everyday Sentiments on a Micronesian Atoll and
              Their Challenge to Western Theory. Chicago: University of Chicago Press.

Lutz, Catherine, and Lila Abu-Lughod, eds.
1990 Language and the Politics of Emotion. Cambridge: Cambridge University Press.

Mahmood, Saba
2001 Feminist Theory, Embodiment, and the Docile Agent: Some Reflections on the Egyptian Islamic Revival. Cultural Anthropology 16(2):202–236.

Maira, Sunaina, and Elisabeth Soep
2005 Introduction. In Youthscapes: The Popular, the National, the Global. Sunaina Maira and Elisabeth Soep, eds. Pp. xi–xxxv. Philadelphia: University of Pennsylvania Press.

Mannheim, Karl
1952[1928] The Problem of Generations. In Essays on the Sociology of Knowledge by Karl Mannheim. Paul Kecskemeti, ed. Pp. 276–322. London: Routledge and Kegan Paul.
1993 The Problem of Generations. In Essays on the Sociology of Knowledge. 2nd expanded edition, with an introduction by Volker Meja and David Kettler. Kurt H. Wolff, ed. Pp. 351–398. New Brunswick, NJ, and London: Transaction Publishers.

Markus, Hazel Rose, Patricia Mullally, and Shinobu Kitayama
1997 Selfways: Diversity in Modes of Cultural Participation. In The Conceptual Self in Context: Culture, Experience, Self-Understanding. Ulric Neisser and David A. Jopling, eds. Pp. 13–61. Cambridge: Cambridge University Press.

Márquez, Patricia C.
1998 The Street Is My Home: Youth and Violence in Caracas. Stanford, CA: Stanford University Press.

Marx, Karl
1978 The Marx-Engels Reader. Robert C. Tucker, ed. 2nd edition. New York: W. W. Norton.

Masquelier, Adeline
1999 Debating Muslims, Disputed Practices: Struggles for the Realization of an Alternative Moral Order in Niger. In Civil Society and the Political Imagination in Africa: Critical Perspectives. John L. and Jean Comaroff, eds. Pp. 219–250. Chicago: University of Chicago Press.
2001 "Prayer Has Spoiled Everything": Possession, Power, and Identity in an Islamic Town of Niger. Durham, NC: Duke University Press.
2005 The Scorpion's Sting: Youth, Marriage and the Struggle for Social Maturity in Niger. Journal of the Royal Anthropological Institute 11(1):59–83.

Massumi, Brian
2002 Parables for the Virtual: Movement, Affect, Sensation. Durham, NC: Duke University Press.

Mauss, Marcel
1967 The Gift: Forms and Functions of Exchange in Archaic Society. Ian Cunnison, trans. New York: W. W. Norton and Company, Inc.

McGray, Douglas
2002   Japan's Gross National Product of Coolness. Foreign Policy (May/June):44–54.

McMurtrie, John
2003   You Take Manhattan—Ishmael Reed Writes a Sweet, Bluesy Ode to His Town, Gritty, Misunderstood, Lovable Oakland. San Francisco Chronicle, October 20: 1, 6.

McNeal, James
1999   The Kids Market: Myths and Realities. New York: Paramount Publishing.

Mead, Margaret
1964[1928] Coming of Age in Samoa: A Psychological Study of Primitive Youth for Western Civilization. New York: William Morrow.

Meyer, Birgit
1998   Commodities and the Power of Prayer: Pentecostalist Attitudes toward Consumption in Contemporary Ghana. Development and Change 29(4):751–776.

Mickelson, Roslyn Arlin
1990   The "Attitude-Achievement" Paradox among Black Adolescents. Sociology of Education 63(1):44–61.

Mills, C. Wright
1959   The Sociological Imagination. New York: Oxford University Press.

Mintz, Sidney
1960   Worker in the Cane: A Puerto Rican Life History. New Haven, CT: Yale University Press.

Mishel, Lawrence, Jared Bernstein, and Sylvia Allegretto
2007   The State of Working America 2006/2007. An Economic Policy Institute Book. Ithaca, NY: ILR Press.

Mitchell, J. Clyde
1956   The Kalela Dance: Aspects of Social Relationships among Urban Africans in Northern Rhodesia. Manchester: Manchester University Press.

Mitchell, Timothy
2002   Rule of Experts: Egypt, Techno-Politics, Modernity. Berkeley: University of California Press.

Mitchell, Tony, ed.
2001   Global Noise: Rap and Hip-Hop outside the USA. Middletown, CT: Wesleyan University Press.

Miyazaki, Hirokazu
2004   The Method of Hope: Anthropology, Philosophy, and Fijian Knowledge. Stanford, CA: Stanford University Press.
2006   Economy of Dreams: Hope in Global Capitalism and Its Critiques. Cultural Anthropology 21(2):147–172.

Moody, Harry
1993   Overview: What Is Critical Gerontology and Why Is It Important? *In* Voices and Visions of Aging: Toward a Critical Gerontology. Thomas Cole, Andrew

Achenbaum, Patricia Jakobi, and Robert Kastenbaum, eds. Pp. xv–xli. New York: Springer Publishing Company.

Morgan, Edmund
1975   American Slavery/American Freedom: The Ordeal of Colonial Virginia. New York: W. W. Norton.

Moscovici, Serge
1988   Notes toward a Description of Social Representations. European Journal of Social Psychology 18(2):211–250.

Munn, Nancy
1992   The Cultural Anthropology of Time: A Critical Essay. Annual Review of Anthropology 21:93–123.

Nakanishi Shintar
1998   Pokémon būmu to Pokémon shōku [The Pokémon Boom and the Pokémon Shock]. In Kodomo hakusho [Children's Encyclopedia]. Pp. 273–279. Tokyo: Nihon Kodomo o Mamorukaihen, Sōdobunka.

Nakazawa Shin'ichi
1997   Poketto no naka no yasei [Wildness in the Pocket]. Tokyo: Iwanami Shoten.

Nakkula, Michael
2003   Identity and Possibility. In Adolescents at School: Perspectives on Youth, Identity, and Education. Michael Sadowski, ed. Pp. 7–18. Cambridge, MA: Harvard University Press.

Nasaw, David
1985   Children of the City: At Work and at Play. New York: Oxford University Press.

Nayak, Anoop
2003   Race, Place and Globalization: Youth Cultures in a Changing World. New York: Berg.

Neilson, Brett
2003   Globalization and the Biopolitics of Aging. CR:The New Centennial Review 3(2):161–186.

Neyzi, Leyla
2001   Object or Subject? The Paradox of "Youth" in Turkey. International Journal of Middle Eastern Studies 33(3):411–432.

Ngomane, Tsakani, and Constance Flanagan
2003   The Road to Democracy in South Africa. Peace Review 15(3):267–271.

Nieuwenhuys, Olga
1996   The Paradox of Child Labor and Anthropology. Annual Review of Anthropology 25:237–251.

Nihon Keizai Shinbun
1999   Nihon anime kaigai ni eikyōryoku [The Influence of Japanese Animation Overseas]. Nihon Keizai Shinbun, December 1: 3.

Nikkei Entertainment
1998   Shin hitto no Shingenchi Pokekuro Sedai [The Pokémon Generation from the Epicenter of the New Hit]. Nikkei Entertainment (January):48–50.

Nintendo
1999   Nintendo jiseidaiki happyō [Announcement about the Next-Generation Machines at Nintendo]. May 12. Kyoto: Nintendo.

Nkwame, Valentine
2002   School Girls Collapse in Fits of Hysteria. Arusha Times, March 16–22. http://www.arushatimes.co.tz, accessed January 2004.

Norris, Pippa, ed.
1999   Political Citizens: Global Support for Democratic Governance. New York: Oxford University Press.

Nteta, Doreen, Janet Hermans, and Pavla Jeskova, eds.
1997   Poverty and Plenty: The Botswana Experience. Gaborone: The Botswana Society.

Nyamjoh, Francis
2005   Fishing in Troubled Waters: Disquettes and Thiofs in Dakar. Africa 75(3):295–324.

Oberschall, Anthony
1989   The 1960 Sit-Ins: Protest Diffusion and Movement Take-Off. Research in Social Movements, Conflict and Change 11(1):31–53.

Odem, Mary E.
1995   Delinquent Daughters: Protecting and Policing Adolescent Female Sexuality in the United States, 1885–1920. Chapel Hill: University of North Carolina Press.

Ogbu, John, and Signithia Fordham
1986   Black Students' School Success: Coping with the Burden of "Acting White." Urban Review 18(3):176–206.

Ōhira Ken
1990   Yutakasa no seishinbyōri [Pathology of Abundance]. Tokyo: Iwanami Shoten.

Olsen, Laurie
1997   Made in America: Immigrant Students in Our Public Schools. New York: The New Press.

Ong, Aihwa
1999   Flexible Citizenship: The Cultural Logics of Transnationality. Durham, NC: Duke University Press.
2006   Neoliberalism as Exception: Mutations in Citizenship and Sovereignty. Durham, NC: Duke University Press.

Orellana, Marjorie Faulstich, Barrie Thorne, Anna Chee, and Wan Shun Eva Lam
2001   Transnational Childhoods: The Participation of Children in Processes of Family Migration. Social Problems 48(4):572–591.

Ortner, Sherry B.
1996   Making Gender: The Politics and Erotics of Culture. Boston: Beacon Press.
2003   New Jersey Dreaming: Capital, Culture, and the Class of '58. Durham, NC: Duke University Press.

Osgood, D. Wayne, E. Michael Foster, Constance A. Flanagan,
and Gretchen R. Ruth, eds.
2005   On Your Own without a Net: The Transition to Adulthood for Vulnerable
          Populations. Chicago: University of Chicago Press.

Palladino, Grace
1996   Teenagers: An American History. New York: Basic Books.

Palmer, Julian S., Song Younghwan, and Hsien-Hen Lu
2002   The Changing Face of Child Poverty in California. New York: National
          Center for Children in Poverty, Millman School of Public Health, Columbia
          University.

Parker, Richard G.
1991   Bodies, Pleasures, and Passions: Sexual Culture in Contemporary Brazil.
          Boston: Beacon.

Pazderic, Nickola
2004   Recovering True Selves in the Electro-Spiritual Field of Universal Love.
          Cultural Anthropology 19(2):196–226.

Pearce, Nickki J., and Reed W. Larson
2006   How Teens Become Engaged in Youth Development Programs: The Process
          of Motivational Change in a Civic Activism Organization. Applied
          Developmental Science 10(3):121–131.

Peligal, Rona
1999   Locating an Urban African Community in the History of Arusha, Tanzania,
          1920–1967. Unpublished Ph.D. dissertation, Columbia University.

Perullo, Alex
2005   Hooligans and Heroes: Youth Identity and Hip-Hop in Dar es Salaam,
          Tanzania. Africa Today 51(4):75–101.

Piot, Charles
1999   Remotely Global: Village Modernity in West Africa. Chicago: University of
          Chicago Press.

Pollack, Linda
1984   Forgotten Children: Parent–Child Relations from 1500 to 1900. Cambridge:
          Cambridge University Press.

Ponniah, Thomas
2004   The World Social Forum: The Revolution of Our Time. April Biccum, inter-
          viewer. Situation Analysis: A Forum for Critical Thought and International
          Current Affairs 4(1):7–15.

Porter, Karen
1996   The Agency of Children, Work, and Social Change in the South Pare
          Mountains, Tanzania. Anthropology of Work Review 17(1-2):8–19.

Potter, Russell A.
1995   Spectacular Vernaculars: Hip-Hop and the Politics of Postmodernism.
          Albany: State University of New York Press.

REFERENCES

Pratt, Mary Louise
1992   Imperial Eyes: Travel Writing and Transculturation. New York: Routledge.

Pugh, Allison
2006   The Economy of Dignity: Children, Consumption, and Inequality.
        Unpublished Ph.D. dissertation, University of California, Berkeley.

Pusey, James
1983   China and Charles Darwin. Cambridge, MA: Harvard University Press.

Qin Yan
1999   Zhongguo zhongchan jieji: Welai shehui jiegou de zhuliu [China's Middle
        Class: The Central Tendencies of a Social Structure That Has Not Yet
        Arrived]. Beijing: Zhongguo jihua chubanshe.

Radin, Paul, ed.
1926   Crashing Thunder: The Autobiography of an American Indian. New York:
        D. Appleton.

Raison-Jourde, Françoise
1991   Bible et Pouvoir à Madagascar au XIX Siècle: Invention d'une identitè
        Chrétienne et construction de l'état. Paris: Karthala.

Ranger, Terence O.
1975   Dance and Society in Eastern Africa: 1890–1970: The Beni Ngoma.
        Berkeley: University of California Press.

Ratsiraka, Didier
1975   Ny Boky Mena: Charte de la Revolution socialiste malgache tous azimuts.
        Antananarivo: Imprimerie d'ouvrages educatifs.

Raum, Otto Friedrich
1996[1940] Chaga Childhood: A Description of Indigenous Education in an East
        African Tribe. New introduction by Sally Falk Moore. Hamburg: LIT.

Remes, Peter
1999   Global Popular Music and Changing Awareness of Urban Tanzanian Youth.
        Yearbook for Traditional Music 31:1–26.

Richardson, Rev. J.
1885   A New Malagasy-English Dictionary. Antananarivo: The London Missionary
        Society.

Rifkin, Jeremy
1995   The End of Work: The Decline of the Global Labor Force and the Dawn of
        the Post-market Era. New York: G. P. Putnam's Sons.

Roberts, Ken
2003   Change and Continuity in Youth Transitions in Eastern Europe: Lessons for
        Western Sociology. Sociological Review 51(4):484–500.

Rodgers, Daniel T.
1998   Atlantic Crossings: Social Politics in a Progressive Age. Cambridge, MA:
        Harvard University Press.

Rofel, Lisa
1999   Other Modernities: Gendered Yearnings in China after Socialism. Berkeley: University of California Press.

Röggenbuck, Stefan
1996   Historia social de la infancia callejera limeña. Apuntes 39:89–112.

Rose, Frank
2001   Pocket Monster: How DoCoMo's Wireless Internet Service Went from Fad to Phenom and Turned Japan into the First Post-PC Nation. Wired (May):126–135.

Ross, Andrew
2006   Fast Boat to China. High-Tech Outsourcing and the Consequences of Free Trade: Lessons from Shanghai. New York: Random House.

Ross, Dorothy
1969   G. Stanley Hall: The Psychologist as Prophet. Chicago: University of Chicago Press.

Rothman, David J.
1971   The Discovery of the Asylum: Social Order and Social Disorder in the New Republic. Boston: Little, Brown, and Company.

Rothman, Sheila M.
1978   Woman's Proper Place: A History of Changing Ideals and Practices, 1870 to the Present. New York: Basic Books.

Ruddick, Sue
2003   The Politics of Aging: Globalization and the Restructuring of Youth and Childhood. Antipode 35(2):334–362.

Rutherford, Danilyn
2002   Raiding the Land of Foreigners: The Limits of Nation on an Indonesian Frontier. Princeton, NJ: Princeton University Press.

Scheper-Hughes, Nancy, and Carolyn Sargent
1998   The Cultural Politics of Childhood. *In* Small Wars: The Cultural Politics of Childhood. Nancy Scheper-Hughes and Carolyn Sargent, eds. Pp. 1–33. Berkeley: University of California Press.

Scheve, Julia, and Amy K. Syvertsen
2006   Anti-Tobacco Youth Activism. *In* Youth Activism: An International Encyclopedia. Lonnie R. Sherrod, Constance A. Flanagan, Ron Kassimir, and Amy K. Syvertsen, eds. Pp. 77–81. Westport, CT: Greenwood Publishing Company.

Schlegel, Alice, and Herbert Barry III
1991   Adolescence: An Anthropological Inquiry. New York: The Free Press.

Schloss, Marc
1988   The Hatchet's Blood: Separation, Power, and Gender in Ehing Social Life. Tuscon: University of Arizona Press.

Schoeni, Robert F., and Karen E. Ross
2005   Material Assistance Received from Families during the Transition to
            Adulthood. *In* On the Frontier of Adulthood: Theory, Research, and Public
            Policy. R. A. Settersten, Frank F. Furstenburg Jr., and R. G. Rumbaut, eds.
            Pp. 396–416. Chicago: University of Chicago Press.

Schor, Juliet B.
2004   Born to Buy: The Commercialized Child and the New Consumer Culture.
            New York: Scribner.

Schrag, Peter
2006   California: America's High-Stakes Experiment. Berkeley: University of
            California Press.

Schrum, Kelly
2004   Some Wore Bobby Sox: The Emergence of Teenage Girls' Culture,
            1920–1945. New York: Palgrave Macmillan.

Scott, James
1985   Weapons of the Weak: Everyday Forms of Peasant Resistance. New Haven,
            CT: Yale University Press.

Seiter, Ellen
1993   Sold Separately. New Brunswick, NJ: Rutgers University Press.

Selzer, Mark
1992   Bodies and Machines. New York: Routledge.

Sennett, Richard
1998   The Corrosion of Character: The Personal Consequences of Work in the
            New Capitalism. New York: W. W. Norton and Company.

Seremetakis, Nadia, ed.
1994   The Senses Still: Perception and Memory as Material Culture in Modernity.
            Chicago: University of Chicago Press.

Settersten, Richard A., Jr., Frank F. Furstenberg Jr., and Ruben G. Rumbaut, eds.
2005   On the Frontier of Adulthood: Theory, Research, and Public Policy.
            Chicago: University of Chicago Press.

Shanahan, Michael J.
2000   Pathways to Adulthood in Changing Societies: Variability and Mechanisms
            in Life Course Perspective. Annual Review of Sociology 26:667–692.

Sharp, Lesley
2002   The Sacrificed Generation: Youth, History and the Colonized Mind in
            Madagascar. Berkeley: University of California Press.

**Sherrod, Lonnie R., Constance A. Flanagan, Ron Kassimir,
and Amy K. Syvertsen, eds.**
2006   Youth Activism: An International Encyclopedia. Westport, CT: Greenwood
            Publishing Company.

Si Xia
1999   Aixin jiaoren [Teaching with a Loving Heart]. Nanjing: Nanjing University
            Press.

Simmel, Georg
1971[1904]   Fashion. *In* Georg Simmel on Individuality and Social Forms. Donald N.
Levine, ed. Pp. 294–323. Chicago: University of Chicago Press.

Skocpol, Theda
1992   Protecting Soldiers and Mothers: The Political Origins of Social Policy in the
United States. Cambridge, MA: Harvard University Press.

Smeeding, Timothy M., Lee Rainwater, and Gary Burtless
2001   Poverty in a Cross-National Context. *In* Understanding Poverty. Sheldon H.
Danziger and Robert H. Haveman, eds. Pp. 162–192. New York: Russell Sage.

Smith, Jackie
2004   Exploring Connections between Global Integration and Political
Mobilization. Journal of World Systems Research 10 (Winter):255–285.

Smith, James
2001   Of Spirit Possession and Structural Adjustment Programs: Education,
Government Downsizing, and Their Enchantments in Neo-liberal Kenya.
Journal of Religion in Africa 31(4):427–456.

Smith, Michael P., and Luis E. Guarnizo, eds.
1998   Transnationalism from Below. New Brunswick, NJ: Transaction Publishers.

Song, Miri
2003   Choosing Ethnic Identity. Cambridge: Polity Press.

Stambach, Amy
2000   Evangelism and Consumer Culture in Northern Tanzania. Anthropological
Quarterly 73:171–179.

Steedman, Carolyn
1995   Strange Dislocations: Childhood and the Idea of Human Interiority. London:
Virago Press.
1998   Strange Dislocations: Childhood and the Idea of Human Interiority.
Cambridge, MA: Harvard University Press.

Stephens, Sharon
1995   Introduction: Children and the Politics of Culture in "Late Capitalism." *In*
Children and the Politics of Culture. Sharon Stephens, ed. Pp. 3–48.
Princeton, NJ: Princeton University Press.

Stolle, Dietland, and Michele Micheletti
2006   Political Consumerism. *In* Youth Activism: An International Encyclopedia.
Lonnie R. Sherrod, Constance A. Flanagan, Ron Kassimir, and Amy K.
Syvertsen, eds. Pp. 470–476. Westport, CT: Greenwood Publishing Company.

Stoller, Paul
1989   The Taste of Ethnographic Things: The Senses in Anthropology.
Philadelphia: University of Pennsylvania Press.

Strathern, Marilyn
1988   The Gender of the Gift. Berkeley: University of California Press.

REFERENCES

Stroeken, Koen
2005   This Is Not a Haircut. Neoliberalism and Revolt in Kiswahili Rap. Image and
            Narrative, http://www.imageandnarrative.be/worldmusicb_advertising/
            koenstroeken.htm, accessed December 2007.

Strom, Stephanie
1999   Japanese Family Values: I Choose You, Pikachu! New York Times, November
            7: 4.

Sun Yunshao
1999[1993] Xia lingying de jiaoliang [The Test of Summer Camp]. In Jiaoyu: Women
            you hua yao shuo [Education: We Have Something to Say]. Yang Dongping,
            ed. Pp. 54–58. Beijing: Shehui kexue chubanshe.

Swedenburg, Ted
2001   Islamic Hip-Hop vs. Islamophobia: Aki Nawaz, Natacha Atlas, Akhenaton in
            2001. In Global Noise: Rap and Hip-Hop outside the USA. Tony Mitchell,
            ed. Pp. 57–85. Middletown, CT: Wesleyan University Press.

Takeda Yoshi
1998   Mienai kazoku, part 3: Ko to shūdan o yuragugeru infura o [The Family
            That Can't Be Seen, part 3: Shaking Up the Space between the Individual
            and the Group]. Nikkei Dezain (February):38–44.

Tanaka, Stefan
1997   Childhood: Naturalization of Development into a Japanese Space. In
            Cultures of Scholarship. Sally Humphreys, ed. Pp. 21–56. Ann Arbor:
            University of Michigan Press.

Tardieu, Ambroise
1858   Etude Medico-Legale sur les Attentats Aux Moeurs. Annales d'Hygiene
            Publique et de Medicien Legale, sess. 2, 9:137–198.

Tarlo, Emma
1996   Clothing Matters: Dress and Identity in India. Chicago and London:
            University of Chicago Press.

Terrio, Susan
In press   Judging Muhammad: Juvenile Delinquency, Immigration, and Exclusion at
            the Paris Palace of Justice. Stanford, CA: Stanford University Press.

Thorne, Barrie
1993   Gender Play: Girls and Boys in School. New Brunswick, NJ: Rutgers
            University Press.
2003   The Crisis of Care. In Work-Family Challenges for Low-Income Parents and
            Their Children. Ann C. Crouter and Alan Booth, eds. Pp. 165–178.
            Mahwah, NJ: Lawrence Erlbaum Publishers.
2005   Unpacking School Lunchtime: Structure, Practice, and the Negotiation of
            Differences. In Developmental Pathways through Middle Childhood:
            Rethinking Contexts and Diversity as Resources. Catherine R. Cooper,
            Cynthia Garcia Coll, Todd Bartko, Helen Davis, and Célina Chapman, eds.
            Pp. 63–87. Mahwah, NJ: Lawrence Erlbarum Publishers.

Thorne, Barrie, Marjorie Faulstich Orellana, Wan Shun Eva Lam, and Anna Chee
2003   Raising Children, and Growing Up, Across National Borders: Comparative Perspectives on Age, Gender, and Migration. *In* Gender and U.S. Immigration. Pierrette Hondagneu-Sotelo, ed. Pp. 241–262. Berkeley: University of California Press.

Torre, Maria Elena, and Michelle Fine
2006   Participatory Action Research (PAR) by Youth. *In* Youth Activism: An International Encyclopedia. Lonnie R. Sherrod, Constance A. Flanagan, Ron Kassimir, and Amy K. Syvertsen, eds. Pp. 456–462. Westport, CT: Greenwood Publishing Company.

Townsend, Nicholas
1997   Men, Migration and Households: An Exploration of Connections over Time and Space. Journal of Southern African Studies 23(3):405–420.

Troyna, Barry, and Richard Hatcher
1992   Racism in Children's Lives. New York: Routledge.

Tsing, Anna
2000   The Global Situation. Cultural Anthropology 15(3):327–360.

Tucker, Jill, and Alex Katz
2002   Whites Shun Public Schools: Census Shows Nearly 50% of Caucasians Don't Use City Education System. Oakland Tribune, August 27: 1, 7.

Turner, Victor
1967   The Forest of Symbols. Ithaca, NY: Cornell University Press.
1969   The Ritual Process. Ithaca, NY: Cornell University Press.
1974   Drama, Fields, and Metaphors: Symbolic Action in Human Society. Ithaca, NY: Cornell University Press.

Tyack, David B.
1974   The One Best System: A History of American Urban Education. Cambridge, MA: Harvard University Press.

Ueda, Reed
1994   Postwar Immigrant America: A Social History. Boston: Bedford Books of St. Martin's Press.

Urla, Jacqueline
2001   "We Are All Malcolm X!" Negu Gorriak, Hip-Hop, and the Basque Political Imaginary. *In* Global Noise: Rap and Hip-Hop outside the USA. Tony Mitchell, ed. Pp. 171–193. Middletown, CT: Wesleyan University Press.

Utas, Mats
2005   Victimcy, Girlfriending, Soldiering: Tactic Agency in a Young Woman's Social Navigation of the Liberian War Zone. Anthropological Quarterly 78(2):403–430.

Valladares, Lícia, and Flávia Impelizieri
1991   Ação invisível: O atendimento a crianças carentes e a meninos de rua no Rio de Janeiro. Rio de Janeiro: Instituto Universitário de Pesquisas do Rio de Janeiro.

REFERENCES

Van Ausdale, Debra, and Joe R. Feagin
2001   The First R: Children Learning Race and Racism. New York: Rowman & Littlefield.

Veblen, Thornstein
1992[1899] The Theory of the Leisure Class. London: Transaction Publishers.

Walkowitz, Judith R.
1992   City of Dreadful Delight: Narratives of Sexual Danger in Late-Victorian London. Chicago: University of Chicago.

Walley, Christine J.
2004   Rough Waters: Nature and Development in an East African Marine Park. Princeton, NJ: Princeton University Press.

Wall Street Journal
1994   Study This, Baby: Chinese Fetuses Bear Heavy Course Loads. Wall Street Journal, February 8.

Walters, Ronald G.
1978   American Reformers: 1815–1860. New York: Hill and Wang.

Walton, Christopher R.
1991   Surviving the Ultimate Crisis: What Happened behind the Scenes at Covenant House That Led to Its Rapid Growth and How It Survived the Wrenching Departure of Its Founder. Fund Raising Management 22:24–28.

Wang Donghua
1999   Faxian muqin [Discovering Mother]. Chengdu: Sichuan renmin chubanshe.

Watson, James, ed.
1997   Golden Arches East: McDonald's in East Asia. Palo Alto, CA: Stanford University Press.

Watts, Roderick J., and Constance Flanagan
2007   Pushing the Envelope on Youth Civic Engagement: A Developmental and Liberation Psychology Perspective. Journal of Community Psychology 35(6):779–792.

Watts, Roderick J., Derek M. Griffith, and Jaleel Abdul-Adil
1999   Sociopolitical Development as an Antidote for Oppression: Theory and Action. American Journal of Community Psychology 27(2):255–272.

Weber, Max
1946   Max Weber: Essays in Sociology. H. H. Gerth and C. Wright Mills, trans. and eds. New York: Oxford University Press.
1987   The Protestant Ethic and the Spirit of Capitalism. Talcott Parsons, trans.
[1930]   London and Sydney: Unwin Paperbacks.

Weiner, Annette B., and Jane Schneider, eds.
1989   Cloth and Human Experience. Washington DC: Smithsonian Institution Press.

Weisner, Thomas S., and Lucinda P. Bernheimer
1998   Children of the 1960s at Midlife: Generational Identity and the Family Adaptive Project. *In* Welcome to Middle Age! (And Other Cultural

Fictions). Richard Shweder, ed. Pp. 211–257. Chicago: University of Chicago Press.

Weiss, Brad

1996　The Making and Unmaking of the Haya Lived World: Consumption, Commoditization and Everyday Practice. Durham, NC, and London: Duke University Press.

2004a　Contentious Futures: Past and Present. *In* Producing African Futures: Ritual and Reproduction in a Neoliberal Age. Brad Weiss, ed. Pp. 1–20. Leiden and Boston: Brill.

In press　Street Dreams and Hip-Hop Barbershops: Popular Cultural Practices in Urban Tanzania. Bloomington: Indiana University Press.

Weiss, Brad, ed.

2004b　Producing African Futures: Ritual and Reproduction in a Neoliberal Age. Leiden: Brill.

Wellman, Barry

2001　Physical Place and Cyberspace: The Rise of Personalized Networking. International Journal of Urban and Regional Research 25(2):227–252.

Williamson, Judith

1986　Woman Is an Island: Femininity and Colonization. *In* Studies in Entertainment. Tania Modleski, ed. Pp. 99–118. Bloomington: Indiana University Press.

Willis, Paul

1977　Learning to Labor: How Working Class Kids Get Working Class Jobs. New York: Columbia University Press.

Wolff, Larry

1998　When I Imagine a Child: The Idea of Childhood and the Philosophy of Memory in the Enlightenment. Eighteenth-Century Studies 31(4):377–401.

Wray, Laura, and Constance A. Flanagan

2006　An Inconvenient Truth about Youth. Op Ed. Washington Post, September 11: A17.

Wulff, Helena

1995　Introducing Youth Culture in Its Own Right: The State of the Art and New Possibilities. *In* Youth Cultures: A Cross-cultural Perspective. Vered Amit-Talai and Helena Wulff, eds. Pp. 1–18. London: Routledge.

Yamada Masahiro

2004　Kibōkakusa shakai [The Society with Different Desires]. Tokyo: Chikuma Shobō.

Yamato Michikazu

1998　Kūzen no hakai genshō "Pokémon" chō hitto no nazo [The Riddle of the Super Hit Pokémon That Is an Unprecedented Social Phenomenon]. Gendai (January):242–249.

Yang, Zhao

2000　State, Children, and the Wahaha Group of Hangzhou. *In* Feeding China's

REFERENCES

    Little Emperors: Food, Children, and Social Change. Jun Jing, ed. Pp.
    185–198. Palo Alto, CA: Stanford University Press.

Ye Shengtao (Ye Shaojun)
1958[1929] Schoolmaster Ni Huan-chih. A. C. Barnes, trans. Peking: Foreign Languages
    Press.

Youniss, James, and Miranda Yates
1997   Community Service and Social Responsibility in Youth. Chicago: University
    of Chicago Press.

Zaloom, Caitlin
2004   The Productive Life of Risk. Cultural Anthropology 19(3):365–391.

Zeldin, Shepherd, Annette Kugsen McDaniel, Domitri Topitzes, and Matt Calvert
2000   Youth in Decision Making: A Study on the Impacts of Youth on Adults and
    Organizations. Chevy Chase, MD: National 4-H Council.

Zelizer, Viviana A.
1985   Pricing the Priceless Child: The Changing Social Value of Children. New
    York: Basic Books.

2000   The Purchase of Intimacy. Law and Social Inquiry 25(3):817–848.

Zhao, Bin
1997   Consumerism, Confucianism, Communism: Making Sense of China Today.
    New Left Review 222:43–59.

Zhengming
1993   Beijing guizu xuexiao de jueqi [The Rise of Beijing's Aristocrat Schools].
    Zhengming 9(9):38–39.

Zhou Zuoren
1920   Ertong de wenxue [Children's Literature]. Xin qingnian [New Youth]
    4(8):1–7.

Index

School for Advanced Research Advanced Seminar Series

PUBLISHED BY SAR PRESS

Participants in the School for Advanced Research advanced seminar "Global Comings of Age: Childhood, Youth and Social Re-Generation in a Time of Global Flows," Santa Fe, New Mexico, April 18–22, 2004. From left: Deborah Durham, Anne Allison, Tobias Hecht, Constance Flanagan, Barrie Thorne, Ann Anagnost, Paula Fass, Brad Weiss, and Jennifer Cole.